POWER TO THE PEOPLE

LAURA INGRAHAM

POWER TO THE PEOPLE

Since 1947
REGNERY
PUBLISHING, INC.
An Eagle Publishing Company • Washington, DC

Library of Congress Cataloging-in-Publication Data

Ingraham, Laura.
 Power to the people / Laura Ingraham.
   p. cm.
 Includes bibliographical references and index.
 ISBN 978-1-59698-516-2
 1. Social problems—United States. 2. Social values—United States.
 3. Elite (social sciences)—United States. 4. United States—Social
 conditions—1980–5. United States—Politics and government—
 2001–6. United States—Moral conditions. 7. Liberalism—United
 States. 8. Conservatism—United States. I. Title.
  HN65.I64 2007
  306.0973'09045—dc22

                              2007026719

Published in the United States by

Regnery Publishing, Inc.
One Massachusetts Avenue, NW
Washington, DC 20001
www.regnery.com

Manufactured in the United States of America

10 9 8 7 6 5 4 3 2 1

Books are available in quantity for promotional or premium use. Write to Director of Special Sales, Regnery Publishing, Inc., One Massachusetts Avenue NW, Washington, DC 20001, for information on discounts and terms or call (202) 216-0600.

For
Chuck and Ina
Lorraine and Joe
and the
troops who keep us free

CONTENTS

Introduction 1

》》》 CHAPTER ONE

Power to the Family 13

》》》 CHAPTER TWO

Don't Fence Me In . . . But Please Fence Them Out! 41

》》》 CHAPTER THREE

Protecting the People 71

》》》 CHAPTER FOUR

Judging the Judges 101

》》》 CHAPTER FIVE

Keeping It Local 133

》》》 CHAPTER SIX

Saving our Pornified Culture 157

》》》 CHAPTER SEVEN

School's Out . . . of Control 195

》》》 CHAPTER EIGHT

The Revenge of the "Loud Folks"...................... 231

》》》 CHAPTER NINE

Blinding Us with Science............................ 257

》》》 CHAPTER TEN

Taking the Real Power Trip......................... 285

Acknowledgments 319

Notes 323

Index... 349

INTRODUCTION

It's **nighttime** in America.

Or at least it feels that way.

Frustration. Anger. Confusion. These emotions ambush us whenever we stop to consider how estranged we have become from politics and the culture. We are like strangers in a foreign land. We feel there is nowhere to turn for help, no safe harbor where our values are protected. We have few leaders willing to represent and fight for those values. We see our country veering so off course in so many areas that we feel powerless to turn it around. It can all seem overwhelming and demoralizing. Kind of like a Nancy Pelosi speech.

Whether you know it or not, many of the most important decisions in your life are being made for you. They are being made by out-of-touch politicians, agenda-driven educrats, haughty life-tenured judges, and executives in a polluted entertainment industry—all of whom believe they know better than you. Responsibility and accountability are principles that they preach but do not practice. They have their agendas—and when little people get in the way, watch out. They are perpetrating a massive power grab. Watch your wallet. Hide your children. Lock up the livestock. They're coming for you.

How do we reclaim the power that is rightfully ours?

If you've ever listened to my radio show, you'll remember that at the end of the introductory sound-bite montage, a scratchy, shrill-sounding woman screeches: "Power to the Peeeople!" Those mellifluous tones belong to a self-styled urban "human rights activist" (translation: leftist with a bullhorn) named Efia Nwangaza. For her, "Power to the People" really means power to the Marxists, socialists, antiwar activists, international bureaucracies, non-governmental organizations, and illegal alien umbrella groups. Power *over* the people who are too busy working and taking care of their families to join the protest culture.

Real Power to the People

During the 1960s, Vietnam protestors and John "Imagine No Religion" Lennon used the phrase as a battle cry of rebellion against their elders, "The Establishment." Forty years later, they have *become* "The Establishment"—and just look at what their rebellion hath wrought. Years ago, I made an executive decision to take the phrase "Power to the People" away from those who never really meant it. For decades, the American Left tried to convince us that their agenda was all about empowerment. There was "Women Power!" and "Black Power!" and "Gray Power!" and "Rainbow Power!" and now there's even "Green Power!" We were encouraged to revel in "free love" and to take a free ride courtesy of all the fools who did the 9 to 5 thing.

For all their empowerment and anti-establishment blather, what they really meant was they were more than happy to help themselves to positions of power and influence. In the meantime, they made the nation a slave to fringe groups, political correctness, expanding bureaucracies, and our own consumerism. They worked feverishly to move more decision-making to Washington—taking power from the people and giving it to bureaucrats and politicians who want to spend our money, make our decisions, and tie us up with red tape. So much for "empowerment."

They have us right where they want us.

Now someone out there will inevitably say, "Wait a minute, Laura. Liberalism has been in decline for most of our recent political history! Isn't there some Republican blame to go around?" To some extent, yes. We are all to blame. Yet it is undeniable that the American Left has been at the controls of our culture for most of our lives—dominating academia, the courts, the media, and Hollywood.

Most Americans were too busy earning an honest living, raising their children, and going to church to notice what was slowly happening around them. Or they thought there was nothing they could do to stop it. With liberalism rejected at the ballot box, they assumed that elected representatives would live up to their pledges to protect and defend the country and our way of life. But too often, the same politicians who claimed to be "for the people" turned against us, our principles, and our dreams.

Their "Power to the People" movement was a scam.

It's time to take our power back.

Rights? What Rights?

Our Declaration of Independence reminds us of the "unalienable rights" that are ours to enjoy: "life, liberty, and the pursuit of happiness." These rights are dependent upon one another for survival.

We often forget that we have been "endowed" with these rights by our "Creator." How seldom we think of Him and our duty to Him as we exercise these precious rights.

In this age of widespread human embryo destruction, abortion, euthanasia, and cloning, how can we credibly protect the right to *life*? What is *liberty*? How do we exercise it without encroaching on the rights of others? And what does it mean to *pursue happiness*? Is that just a permission slip to indulge our every appetite? Is it a free pass to super-size our meals, wallow in porn, and swell our coffers, regardless of the impact on others?

Too often we have believed that "freedom" means that we have no duties or responsibilities to others. That "anything goes" mentality may appear to be empowering, but it is not. Instead, it creates a sense of anarchy that makes most Americans very unhappy.

The Founding Fathers did not risk their lives, their fortunes, and their sacred honor so we could become spoiled, pampered, narcissistic, and focused solely on our own pleasure. An ordered society was the Founders' goal—a place where we could live our lives in limitless possibility—but only if we fulfilled our obligations. They wanted us to have the liberty to tap into our creative powers, for our own good and for the good of our countrymen. This is the pathway to true happiness. But that society is only possible if we, the people, have a shared set of values, a common set of beliefs that bind us together. The Founders did not view liberty as a license, but as a sacred responsibility to be used for the good. They understood that liberty cannot be separated from virtue.

When we act irresponsibly, when we act selfishly, when we are lazy, or weak—that's when we are most likely to give away our power. And "experts" are ever-ready to impose their own brand of order, set their own course for the future, and make sure you march in lockstep. The more power we give to the elites, the more they become the rulers and we become the ruled.

The good news is it's never too late. Although we have been pushed to the edge of the ravine, we can still save ourselves. But only if we face reality and acknowledge that our cultural and political leaders have failed us—and that we allowed this to happen. Here's where things stand:

⟫⟫⟫ Family Matters

The American family is besieged by a hostile culture, destructive government policies, and by our own selfishness. Under attack from all sides, the traditional family is now regarded as just another social arrangement, no better than any other. Despite every statistic showing that traditional family life is the healthiest for us and for the future of the society, the dominant culture continues to degrade its significance. Individualism is wonderful, but individuals without families are lost. Families are a true source of power.

⟫⟫⟫ "Where's the Fence?"

Facilitated by a well-funded alliance of Latino and business lobbies, and by elites in both parties, illegals have crashed our borders in unprecedented numbers. Six years after September 11, this is a national disgrace. By now illegal aliens have received the message loud and clear: crime does pay—especially when it involves our immigration laws. Americans and legal residents are fed up with politicians who want to write new laws to "fix" the problem when the government doesn't enforce the immigration laws already on the books. Our national power and identity comes in part from our shared American culture and language. This power will continue to be eaten away if we don't stop the double-talk and defend our borders.

⟩ ⟩ ⟩ Falling Off the Learning Curve

It has been said many times that learning is power. Shaping the minds of future generations is one of the most important responsibilities that parents and teachers have. Unfortunately we have been bullied into relinquishing our children to bloated bureaucracies, second-rate Marxist intellectuals, and legions of "education experts." The old emphasis on excellence and merit has been swallowed up by ideologically biased curricula and politically correct teaching methods that are shortchanging our students—and our country. In many of our universities things are even bleaker. There is a total lack of ideological diversity on most college faculties—or, at best, the diversity ranges from Howard Dean liberals to spittle-flecked Marxists. If a professor is criticized for abusing his tax-payer-funded classroom by propagandizing against America (rather than teaching his presumed subject), he hides behind the tattered old veil of academic freedom. Why don't these faculties just get it over with, and start offering majors in Anti-Americanism? What a great way to spend $45,000 a year.

⟩ ⟩ ⟩ America First

America must be defended, and vigorously. While it may be impossible to prevent every future attack, Americans must have confidence that our government is doing all it can to protect the homeland. That means that we should not squander our military power on what are largely humanitarian (a.k.a. nation-building) missions. The interests of America and our own security must always come first and guide our foreign policy. Our military is overstretched, underfunded, and approaching the breaking point. And not to ruin your day, but China is well on its way to being the next global superpower.

❱❱❱ Take Back That Gavel

Any time the elites can take decisions away from the people and entrust them to unelected judges, they will. When judges wade into controversial social issues that are best left to the voters, we all lose. On issues from abortion to profanity on television, we are being disenfranchised from our own political system. It's reasonable to ask why we should even bother writing to our congressman or voting for elected representatives when, on any critical issue, all it takes is five life-tenured justices on the Supreme Court to overturn the will of the people. In just the last few years the justices have eroded our property rights, banished the Ten Commandments from courthouses, and begun micromanaging the War on Terror. But what do they care? They answer to no one. They have lifetime job security, summers off, and a never-ending supply of boondoggle speaking gigs. Who would want to retire with those perks? As we go about our busy lives, the courts are busy siphoning power away from us and our elected representatives. The Supremes often seem more worried about offending the feelings of the *New York Times* editorial board than they are about offending the intent of the Framers or the will of the people.

❱❱❱ Your New-Media Lifeline

The Internet, talk radio, and cable television busted the monopoly of the left-wing elites who had been our self-appointed information gatekeepers for decades. They knew the stories they reported, or chose not to report, could profoundly affect the views of Americans. "All the news that's fit to print." "That's the way it is." They were telling us, the "little people" what *they* thought we should know. Conservatives, meanwhile, had only *National Review* and a few other journals to turn to for intellectual nourishment. So it was a relief when the media elite's stranglehold was broken by one man. Twenty years ago, radio host Rush Limbaugh hit the airwaves and connected with Americans who were sick of Dan Rather, fed up with the *New York Times,* and bored to death by Bill Moyers. The first time I heard *The Rush Limbaugh Show,* I thought, "Finally!" His informative and entertaining approach to the news and political fights of the day spawned an entire industry (including *The Laura Ingraham Show*) that now reaches tens of millions of Americans every day. But don't take any of our shows for granted. At this very moment, ambitious and embittered Democrats—frustrated by the flame-out of Air America—are plotting ways to silence conservative talk radio. And you know if they could figure out a way to shut down conservative blogs, they'd do that too. Stay tuned for more details.

❯❯❯ Keeping It Local

Our ability to influence is greatest when decisions are made closest to home. Think about it: your assemblyman votes to increase the state sales tax. In protest, you can picket outside his office, heck, you can walk into his office and give him a piece of your mind. But when Congress passes a tax hike, your complaints are handled by twenty-three-year-old Hill staffers who would rather be hitting the bars and surfing YouTube. And letters to the editor only go so far. Trying to reach Washington from Duluth is like trying to reach around Rosie O'Donnell at an all-you-can-eat buffet. It is no wonder, then, that so many local and state decisions have been hijacked by the feds. And it's only getting worse.

❯❯❯ Blinding Us with Science

Scientists and medical researchers have added immeasurably to the length and quality of our lives. The vast majority have dedicated themselves to the development of innovative treatments and technologies to eradicate deadly diseases and generally advance the cause of human life. These are noble goals. Nevertheless, it is up to us to establish moral and ethical boundaries to ensure that we are not throwing our humanity out with the petri dish. Are we really so fearful of being branded "anti-progress" and "heartless" that we won't speak up against runaway science when we know we should?

Let's be honest, a lot of what our culture is doing in the name of science is really being done out of vanity. We don't want to die. Not today. Not tomorrow. Not ever. And even if we do live to a ripe old age, we don't want to look like it. Whatever happened to the entire concept of aging gracefully? Meg Ryan went from cute to scary. Some pols' faces have been pulled so tight it's a wonder they can close their eyes at night. Exactly what is empowering about giving ourselves butt lifts and pec implants, and our sixteen-year-old daughters boob jobs? And let's not forget about the "designer baby" craze sweeping Europe and growing ever-more popular here, which promises families the "perfect child." Aldous Huxley, call your office.

》》》 The Culture Clash

You know it, and I know it. Boys *and* girls have gone wild. It's both the fault of the sex-saturated media circus and permissive parenting. Even hands-on parents are having trouble stemming the tide of cultural sewage seeping into their homes on a daily basis. They feel as though they can no longer shape their children's values. Parents find the messages pushed on television, in films, in music, and even in school antagonistic to traditional notions of right and wrong. Pornography is a multi-billion dollar industry in America and is making multi-millionaires of sicko producers, twisted directors, and pathetic "actors"—who have now made inroads into the mainstream culture. Their influence can now be seen in the streetwalker antics of Paris Hilton, Britney Spears, and all their various imitators. (What *is* Nicole Richie's talent?!) Even television "news" shows dip into the porn pond in their coverage of such pressing questions as whether Anna Nicole Smith's artificial breasts would decompose at the same rate as the rest of her natural body. This is absolute madness. So why are we watching this trash? And how is it reshaping America?

⟩⟩⟩ Reaching Higher Ground

In the end, we need to face the most important truth: there is no chance that we will prevail in any of these battles if we don't retain our belief in God. God is the engine that drives all we do. And faith in God is the foundation of the Republic—and any healthy society. Every decision, from how we treat the grocery store clerk to how we treat the government of Iran will be greatly influenced by our beliefs. What good is returning "power" to the people if it is not the power to do good? And what better way is there to foster this spirit than through faith? It is faith, which calls us to be self-sacrificial and to love others, that has made us a great nation.

Every now and again we have to ask ourselves, what's the point of this thing called America, anyway? Is the point to make as much money as possible in our lifetimes? Is this nation called to some higher purpose? Are we living the way God wants us to live? And if not, why not? What is life about?

There are plenty of people in our country who think these questions absurd. These are usually the same people who cheer every time the ACLU files a lawsuit to remove a cross on public land. Whether it is evicting Baby Jesus statues from manger scenes at Christmas, or forbidding the Menorah from being lit at a public park during Hanukah, there exists a pronounced anti-religious fervor in the left-liberal culture that has been imposed upon a predominantly religious America. The media elites savor and stoke this animosity. Every other week, a magazine, a book, or a television documentary asserts some "new discovery" that attempts to prove that Jesus Christ and His followers either didn't exist or were actually quite happy with sexual promiscuity and summered at Lake Como. On television and in film, faithful people, traditional Christians, are portrayed as wild-eyed zealots or members of dangerous secret cults. When was the last time you saw a member of NOW or PETA depicted that way? The goal of the elites is to drive religious voices from the public square. They want to erode traditional religious faith, and make you feel goofy, or backward, or out of line when you offer a religious perspective on public policy or cultural issues. They want you to shut up about God so the secularists can monopolize the public discourse and public policy. We can't let that happen. Our Judeo-Christian tradition has done more good for American and the rest of the world than left-wing secularism ever will.

* * * * *

We have a lot of work to do. We must shake off our lethargy and reconnect with our American heritage.

What follows is a call to arms. We need to fight for our culture, for our country. We need to revive our understanding of traditional, conservative principles—the true empowerment agenda. As we focus much of our attention on the Islamic terrorists and enemy states, we cannot lose sight of what is happening here at home. I will expose the threats we face from an emboldened cultural L eft, from the global liberal elite, from science worshippers, and from politicians who spend more time on their hair than serving their constituents. I will offer solutions for how we can use our power—individually and together—to pursue life, liberty, and true happiness. The purpose of this book is not just to rile you up (I do that every day on the radio). The goal is to incite you to do your part to protect the country that we love. It is ours to lose. And there are many here and abroad who are more than willing to take it from us. Let's get to work. Time is of the essence. We are up to the task, and we will be stronger for having fought the good fight. And if we remember what our Founding Fathers knew—that God is with us, and that with Him, everything is possible—we will never lose heart. We *will* prevail.

Power to the People!

1

POWER TO THE FAMILY

"I **hope all those kids aren't hers!"** a woman standing a few peo-ple behind me in line whispered to her friend. They both looked to be in their forties, each with a small child in tow. They were well dressed in that preppy, quilted-jacket-wearing, weekend sort of way. "No way... they can't *all* be hers," the friend gasped, oblivious to the fact that I could hear everything. "Can you imagine having that many? Forget it!"

I was in line with six children ages five to thirteen to see *Shrek 2*, having volunteered to take them to the movie to give their parents a break one Sunday. The six—three boys and three girls—hailed from a family of eight. They were eager to get their popcorn and Twizzlers and get into their seats, but were otherwise well behaved.

After the "forget it!" line I couldn't stop myself from turning around to confront these women. "Anything I can help you with, ladies?" I asked. These suburban housewives were caught off guard and pretended they didn't understand what I was saying. I repeated myself. Finally, the brunette meekly said, "You have such a lovely family." I answered that they were not mine but that my friend Becky, their mother, was pregnant with her ninth child. The two women just stood there, uncomfortably, with frozen half-smiles, slightly nodding their heads. They were stunned.

Until that moment, I didn't realize the extent to which the dominant culture frowns on big families. Maybe this is because I don't have any children myself. But in talking to my friends with large families, I've learned that the reaction in many quarters to parents with five, seven, or nine children today falls somewhere between shock and revulsion. The comments run the gamut: "How does that mother have the time?" "She must never sleep." And my personal favorite: "That's so selfish."

The popular culture generally portrays people with large families as freaks, relics of a bygone age to be studied by sociologists in a laboratory somewhere. In case you're wondering, the Waltons (and their seven kids) are no longer part of the cultural "in crowd." If *Eight Is Enough* were produced today it would have to be called *Two Is Enough*, just so everyone could feel comfortable.

In an April 2007 episode of the ABC television drama *Brothers & Sisters*, forty-something Kitty Walker (Calista Flockhart) and her mother (Sally Field) run into old family rivals, the Joneses (also mother and daughter) at lunch. Kitty's contemporary Lizzie (Jenna

Elfman) is pregnant, and her mom beams that it's her fifth child. A look of total shock comes over Kitty's face. "Five...five?! Are you kidding me? Five?! Really?" she remarks nervously to Lizzie, and then adds: "Well, it's just that five seemed so normal when we were growing up, but now it just seems so...surreal." The Joneses are portrayed as the annoying, cookie-cutter perfect, Stepford Family types. Lizzie comes off as a ditzy young mother while Kitty is a single, professional brainiac. This reinforces what the culture has told us all along: smart women would never be so stupid as to be tied down with five kids today! So...surreal.

The Hand That Rocks the Cradle

It didn't happen overnight, but when it comes to family issues, the fringe has become the mainstream and the mainstream has become the fringe. A few generations ago, it was not that uncommon for married couples to have as many as ten children. In fact, in the 1960s Rose Kennedy and her daughter-in-law, Ethel (wife of Bobby), were getting style points for having nine and eleven children, respectively. From *Time* magazine, October 21, 1966: "'I just love big families,' Ethel Kennedy, thirty-eight, is fond of saying. That is fortunate. She and Bobby are expecting their tenth child in the spring."

These days, having such a large family earns you strange glances, shocked reactions, and castigations from environmentalists and anti-population growth wackos. Somehow "be[ing] fruitful and multiply[ing]" is considered self-indulgent by those who put a high value on attaining a certain lifestyle. (These people consider it *selfish* for adults to devote themselves to supporting a large family, but it is apparently *unselfish* to spend your money on a lifestyle made up of frequent and exotic vacations, state-of-the-art gadgets, spa treatments, golf lessons, club memberships, boarding schools, and fancy summer camps. If you can follow that logic, please explain it to me.)

Wait a minute, you may be asking yourself, I thought this was a book about politics—about empowering the people. What does the debate about large versus small families have to do with power?

Everything. Families are where it all starts for us, and the way we treat families tells us where we are headed as a society. Whether we are open to children and welcome them joyfully says a lot about our priorities and our future.

What I heard in the theater, and what we see in the culture every day, is a lack of respect for families and parental authority. True, we hear a lot from the political and cultural Left about "the children." They endlessly lecture the rest of America about what "the children" want and need. Higher taxes are for "the children." Greenhouse gas limits are for "the children." Government-controlled healthcare is for "the children." Public acceptance of all types of social behavior (an excuse for boorishness), manner of dress (slovenly and slutty), and language (foul) helps "the children" keep an open mind. Relaxed immigration laws are for "the children of Mexico."

Whether parents know it or not, there is a cultural battle raging right now for the hearts and minds of their children. The cultural and political Left in America understands that whoever controls our children controls the future. The Left talks about children as a collective class: "*the* children" (like "the workers"). Often times, beautiful little children are used as mere political props (by both parties). Who can forget how San Francisco congresswoman Nancy Pelosi used dozens of children as her backdrop when she was sworn in as the first female Speaker of the House? Yeah, she was taking the gavel "for the children" all right.

Families don't view their offspring in this way—as political tools or as a future voting bloc. For parents and for siblings there is no "the children." There are only *specific* children—very real individual children who smile and cry in their own way, experience heart-break and joy in their own way, and who have their own personal strengths and weaknesses. Each child is unique, and each must be loved and nurtured according to his or her own needs.

But bureaucracy, and politicians with big government plans "for the children," can't see individual children. Like the character in the great Russian novel *The Brothers Karamazov* who realizes, "The more I love humanity in general, the less I love man in particular," the more our politicians love "the children," the less they seem to want and care for actual children. The worst (but logical) expression of this cultural failing is the claim that it is wrong to bring children into this "horrible world" we have created. Wrong again. You don't make the world better by eliminating the most precious ingredient—children.

Families not only reflect who we are, they show us who we will be. Perhaps the greatest power any of us has is the power to pass along our beliefs, values, and traditions to a child. This is not a new thought. While you may not have heard of the nineteenth-century American poet William Ross Wallace, I'll bet you've heard the last two lines of this excerpt from his most famous poem:

> Infancy's the tender fountain,
> Power may with beauty flow,
> Mother's first to guide the streamlets,
> From them souls unresting grow—
> Grow on for the good or evil,
> Sunshine streamed or evil hurled
> For the hand that rocks the cradle
> Is the hand that rules the world.

This is poetry that speaks a truism: Those people who pass along their values to the next generation have a disproportionate effect on the future.

In 2005 *Foreign Policy* magazine published a striking article that discussed these themes in some detail. The news was not promising for the secular Left. It noted that in the United States, the percentage of women born in the late 1930s who remained childless was near 10 percent.[1] On the other hand, nearly *20 percent* of women born in the late 1950s have not had children.[2] The author pointed out that "(t)he greatly expanded segment of contemporary society, *whose members are drawn disproportionately from the feminist and countercultural movements of the 1960s and '70s, will leave no genetic legacy.* Nor will their emotional or psychological influence on the next generation compare with that of their parents."[3] (Thank God for small miracles!) According to the article, 17.4 percent of baby boomer women had only one child.[4] But these children account for only 7.8 percent of the next generation. By contrast, only 11 percent of baby boomer women had four or more children.[5] Those children account for almost 25 percent of the next generation.[6] The article concludes that these trends are pushing American society to the right:

> This dynamic helps explain, for example, the gradual drift of American culture away from secular individualism and toward religious fundamentalism. Among states that voted for President George W. Bush in 2004, fertility rates are 12 percent higher than in states that voted for Sen. John Kerry. It may also help to explain the increasing popular resistance among rank-and-file Europeans to such crown jewels of secular liberalism as the European Union. It turns out that Europeans who are most likely to identify themselves as "world citizens" are also those least likely to have children.[7]

It doesn't take Stephen Hawking to understand that the more children you have to whom you can pass on your cultural, religious, and political values, the more likely your values will survive into the future. So far, conservatives have done an admirable job of resisting the pressure that discourage many young Americans from creating families. And as a result, our influence—and our power—has grown.

Contrary to what so many feminists told a generation of women, families are actually quite liberating. The stronger your family is, the more independent you can be. A family that sticks together and helps each other is more likely to survive economic downturns, less likely to need government-provided health care, and less likely to need day care. Its children will be better prepared for school, and its grandparents will be better prepared for retirement. At every stage of life, its members will have more freedom—and be less dependent on government or other large institutions—than people who lack family support. So if we really want to empower the average person, the best thing we can do is to strengthen families.

Unfortunately, there are formidable forces at work trying to undermine families in America today. In particular, there are cultural forces attacking the very concept of the family and government policies placing families at a disadvantage.

Behind the Anti-Child Bias

Back to those carping women at the theater. Their comments reflect a view in our society today that is all too common—that there is something wrong, or even slightly wicked, about large families.

Given how unusual such families are these days, what difference does it make whether the elites approve of them or not?

The reason is simple. Large families are a test of how you feel about families in general. If you believe something is good, you want it to grow. Businessmen want their companies to be as big as possible. Bureaucrats want their bureaucracies to be as big as possible. And Ted Kennedy wants his tumbler to be as big as possible.

So why does the "bigger is better" ethos only apply to less important things like hamburgers or house size?

Doubts about big families really represent doubts about all families. Some people argue that small clans are better because they enable parents to give more attention to each child. But this argument often reflects doubts about the willingness of parents to raise and love more than a few children, and it ignores how much children learn from their siblings. Others may say that small families are better because they are more stable financially. But only the most hard-hearted skeptic could really believe that another SUV or an annual cruise to Bermuda is worth more than a child. Yes, families, like most good things in life, require sacrifice. But even the headache of a second mortgage, the indignity of hand-me-downs, and the blandness of store brand cereal for breakfast every morning are fair prices to pay for parents and children of large families. Others say that we need fewer children to avoid harming the environment. Once again, however, this argument criticizes *all* parents, not just the ones with large families. It also betrays a view that humans are simply consumers. The fact is, people are producers too; and it is human creativity, not barrenness, that drives progress, including improving the environment.

Let me be clear. I'm not saying large families are *better* than small families. My point is simply that the *real* reason that large families make so many people uncomfortable is that *families* make people uncomfortable.

Families Are Bad for You

The modern mind does not view families as the fundamental building block of a free society but rather a threat to individual liberty. That's because service to others is viewed as enslaving, while service to self is the highest ideal. We know the opposite is true.

The family, as an institution, has been under attack for a very long time. Over a hundred years ago, Henrik Ibsen's play *A Doll's House* argued that intelligent women were oppressed by traditional family roles. George Bernard Shaw in his play *Mrs. Warren's Profession* tried to make the point that a woman engaged in prostitution was freer than a married woman, and that both use sex to get what they need from men. Over fifty years ago, playwrights like Tennessee Williams, Arthur Miller, and Eugene O'Neill were packing Broadway theaters with dramas about dysfunctional families and the tormented children they produced. This family=slavery storyline went from being avant-garde in Ibsen's day to being cliché today. Yet the entertainment industry is still spewing out anti-family drivel. Recent movies and TV shows, from *Imaginary Heroes* to *Weeds*, have portrayed the so-called "typical" suburban family as a cesspool of every conceivable vice, from avarice, to envy, to lust.

This flood of suspicion and criticism directed at the family, promoted by the elites for generation after generation, has certainly had a major effect on how we view families. The emotionally abusive father, the cold and distant mother, the hapless aunts and uncles—these stock characters in subtle but powerful ways have affected not only how we think about families, but how we operate within them.

Though there were a smattering of positive depictions of family life on television in the '70s, '80s, and '90s (*The Waltons*, *Family Ties*, and *Life Goes On*), other nastier fare eventually swept in. The venal antics of *Married with Children* (complete with a lecherous father, a tarted-up mother, and foul-mouthed kids) became a mega hit for FOX. Now we are awash in the randy doings of the *Desperate Housewives* of Wisteria Lane. And if you look closely at today's glut of forensic shows and crime dramas, dysfunctional parents and crazy relatives are everywhere.

A friend of mine recently suggested that I check out the cable channel Lifetime for even more disturbing depictions of family life in

America. I regret having followed his tip. If you are a woman who believes that every man is either two-timing you, three-timing you, or is a homicidal lunatic just itching to cut you into pieces, Lifetime is your network. In between reruns of *The Golden Girls* and *Will and Grace*, Lifetime runs wall-to-wall movies with plots that follow an all-too-familiar pattern. The first movie I caught was titled *Lethal Vows*. This 1999 movie starring John Ritter tells the tale of a seemingly good doctor whose second wife dies mysteriously. It is up to the first wife to expose him as a murderer. Proving, I guess, that three is more than company—it can be downright deadly!

As part of Lifetime's "men are bastards" theme week, it featured the film *Black and Blue* based on the hit novel by Anna Quindlen. In this winner, a woman named Fran is physically and verbally abused by her detective husband. (The abusers are always in law enforcement or the military—now why would that be?) The deranged sleuth eventually tracks down his runaway bride. (I don't want to ruin the ending!) Total garbage. Lifetime doesn't only showcase bad old movies, but makes original stinkers, too, like *The Staircase Murders*. This one, starring Treat Williams as a best-selling author, concerns yet another "loving husband and father" who pushes his wife down the stairs for fun. Per usual, this film is based on a true story. Much of the waste on Lifetime is *based* on a true story, while being only marginally true.

One of the newest original offerings on Lifetime is called *Army Wives*—a *Desperate Housewives* during wartime. How inspiring!

Look, I have nothing against escapist thrillers or over the top domestic dramas, but how many times can you watch a woman marry Prince Charming only to wake up next to Ted Bundy? The overarching theme of this type of "entertainment" is that men (especially husbands) are out to get you. They lie, they cheat, they steal, they abuse you—and if you don't cap the guy during breakfast, he may well push you down the stairs. So, the best answer: swear off marriage and family!

If any other group was consistently defamed in this way, there would be protests and calls for executives to resign. But fathers are maligned and it's no big deal. It is worth asking whether the cumulative effect of these depictions undermines confidence in stable, loving marriages—or heck, even encourages men to be abusive bums. After taking in a day's worth of this garbage I was ready throw myself down the stairs!

Parenting 101— It's Not About *You* Anymore

From everything I have observed in my friend's families, being a good parent is not a life on the red carpet, marked by "champagne wishes and caviar dreams." It's more about sippy cup spills and leaky Huggies. Mothers I know today are juggling so much. Many of my friends decided that work and young children were just too much to handle. Although there are plenty of moms who don't have a choice about whether to work or not, I do not know a single mom who regrets her decision to stay home during her children's formative years. Debbie, Melinda, and Sue (my mom meters)—all tell me that there is no substitute for "being there" for their kids.

A large federally funded study lends support to this view.[8] Its findings indicate that children younger than kindergarten age who spend more time in childcare are more likely to have behavioral problems through the sixth grade. The National Institute of Child Health and Human Development has tracked 1,300 children and linked aggressive, anti-social conduct to the amount of time they spent in non-maternal child care. Feminists who decades ago told women they could "have it all"—work, family, left-wing volunteer work—were not thinking about their children. As Wendy always tells me of her children ages five and seven, children don't want to "have it all," they want their mom and dad.

Unfortunately, today we have an explosion of "PlayStation parenting." Instead of focusing on our children, too many modern parents focus on themselves. They outsource their parenting responsibilities to nannies, the television, computers, and, yes, videogames—anything to keep their kids occupied while they focus on their own goals. Other couples are limiting the size of their families or not having families at all because children are so "expensive." Somehow, prior generations managed to maintain larger families with much less money and much smaller closets. How did they do it?

The statistics tell the story. According to the Rutgers National Marriage Project, in 1970, 73.6 percent of women, ages twenty-five to twenty-nine, had already begun childbearing and had at least one minor child of their own. By 2000, the share of such women was only 48.7 percent. "Life with children is receding as a defining experience of adult life," author of the Rutgers report, Barbara Dafoe Whitehead, wrote. "Parents today feel out of synch with the larger adult world."[9]

Equally as disturbing, we are now seeing the rise of so-called "hipster parents." These moms and dads, in the words of columnist David Brooks, "turn their babies into fashion-forward, anti-corporate indie-infants in order to stay one step ahead of the cool police."[10] In some of the trendier parts of the country, certain parents are trying very hard—too hard—to show that even if you're a parent, you can still be hip. They even have their own online magazine, Babble.com, for the "new urban parent." Brooks' description nails it:

> Babble is a normal parental advice magazine submerged under geological layers of attitudinizing. There are articles about products from the alternative industrial complex (early '60s retro baby food organizers). There's a blog from a rock star mom (it's lonely on the road). There's a column by L.A.'s Rebecca Woolf, a sort of Silver Lake Erma

Bombeck. ("Who says becoming a mom means succumbing to laser tattoo removal and moving to the suburbs?")[11]

Yeah, nothing's cooler than a mom with a tattoo.

Again, the sad thing here is that this is all self-focused. It has nothing to do with what's good for the child and has everything to do with a bizarre obsession with an immature self-image that is often harmful to the child.

These "new urban parents" are spending so much time trying to be cool that they are ignorant of the fact that one of the biggest problems facing families these days is what the American Psychological Association (APA) calls the "sexualization" of girls.[12] A recent APA report criticizes the sexed-up content of the music and images that are marketed to young girls, and finds a connection between turning young girls into "eye candy" and eating disorders, low self-esteem, and depression in girls and women.[13] As I discuss in more detail in Chapter 6, the glut of pornography in this culture is a big problem.

HEY MOMMY AND DADDY! MONEY CAN'T BUY THEM LOVE!

You've heard of the parents who spend $300 on their child's Halloween costume? $1,000 on a designer prom dress? Even $10,000 for their daughter's boob job? Well, it turns out there is an entire industry that has popped up around parents' desires to turn Olivia and Max into mini-epicureans. "[W]hy not introduce children to the best at a time when they are so completely open-minded?" asks Daniel Kron, owner of Miami-based Genius Jones, a high-end furniture store for kids. The *Financial Times* reported that sales of his pint-sized take-off of Mies van der Rohe's leather Barcelona chair were up 80 percent in 2006. Price tag? A measly $4,000. And for whom are parents buying this stuff again?

Source: Jenny Dalton, "Design for the Little Darlings," *Financial Times*, February 25, 2007.

But a recent article by Judith Warner in the *New York Times* also pointed out that too many mothers are so worried about their own sexiness that they are setting a bad example for their daughters. Their focus is on the self—as in *themselves*, and specifically, on their sexuality. Warner contends that these women feel sexually under-appreciated, so they jump at the chance to take "pole dancing" classes and strip-aerobics sessions at their health club—which supposedly bestows upon them "a new kind of erotic identity":

> These new evening antics of the erstwhile book club set are supposed to be fabulous because they give sexless moms a new kind of erotic identity. But what a disaster they really are: an admission that we've failed utterly, as adult women, to figure out what it means to look and feel sexy with dignity. We've created an aesthetic void. Should we be surprised that stores like Limited Too are rushing in to fill it? (Now on sale: a T-shirt with two luscious cherries and the slogan "double trouble.")[14]

If you've seen *The Graduate*, you know that sexed-up moms are hardly a new thing. But it's difficult to imagine even Mrs. Robinson taking a pole-dancing class in the name of fitness. By raising these points, I do not intend to be too hard on parents. Parents have a more difficult job today than they did thirty-plus years ago when the culture itself didn't work so hard against them. I am not a parent, and believe me, I think parenting is the most important challenge anyone can undertake. I marvel at those who do it well against tough odds. We should support a culture that reinforces that notion. My friend Stephen, who has four young children with his wife Beth, said to me once, "When you become a parent, the hard thing for a lot of us men is that we really have to come to terms with the fact that the days of being 'cool' are behind us." Of course, now I understand what most fathers and mothers understand: raising healthy, productive, moral children is beyond *cool*. When I am sitting in the back of the church on Sundays, I love watching moms and dads tending to their fidgety, goofy, sleepy children. These are beautiful moments. When I was twenty-five, loud, squirming children in these settings bothered me. Not anymore. Today, I see it all as life-affirming.

A priest friend of mine once told me about the sorts of things that drive couples with children to the brink, and at the top of the list was a failure to sacrifice for the children. He told me about one thirty-something father who was feeling "cheated" that he was "losing his own identity" with all the demands of family life. The response to him from my priest friend was blunt:

> The time you spend with your children may prevent you from having the promotion you've always wanted, may force you to sacrifice friendships and hobbies that you wanted to pursue, and may even place a strain on your marriage. But this is what you must do. You are their father and the relationship you have with these children will affect them for the rest of their lives.

Everybody Is a Family!

Does it really matter what a family looks like? Are two parents—a mom and dad—better than one? Today it's not politically correct to answer "yes" to that question. The old cultural critics, from Henrik Ibsen to Eugene O'Neill, could at least agree on a common definition of family: a mother, a father, and their children. Grandparents, aunts, uncles, and cousins are all basic relationships that were known to the ancients. For the most part, the definition of a family has been unchanged since at least the rise of Christianity almost two thousand years ago.

In recent years the traditional definition of the family has given way to more of an "anything goes" way of thinking. There are a whole raft of after-school specials and made-for-TV movies pushing the idea that any group of people who love each other should be considered a "family." True to form, HBO is on the cutting edge here. In 2005 it launched a new series called *Big Love* about a polygamist man, his three wives, and seven children. HBO's Web site describes the characters in *Big Love* as "just another suburban family trying to live the American dream."[15] Critics love it.

Economic arrangements are, and should be, distinct from marriages ordained by God and recognized by the government. Marriage exists, for many of us, as a sacrament. That some married people have civil ceremonies does not alter the fact that the word "marriage" is a lifelong commitment before God between one man and one woman. This question is not ultimately about straight, gay, polygamist, or single people—it is about advancing an agreed upon, societal norm that furthers the interests of *children* and therefore society. What is in the best interest of couples is all well and good—but our societal focus must be upon the welfare of children: the future of our country. As David Blankenhorn, author of the book *The Future of Marriage*, has written:

> Marriage is fundamentally about the needs of children....
> [And] what children need most are mothers and fathers. Not
> caregivers. Not parent-like adults. Not even "parents."
> What a child wants and needs more than anything else are
> the mother and the father who together made the child, who
> love the child, and who love each other.[16]

The whole point of marriage is to bind a woman and a man together for the purpose—or at least the possibility—of begetting and nurturing children. This intimate institution is also quite public, because it is a public pronouncement of what matters most—creating more healthy, loved, well-formed citizens. Your wedding vows are not just promises to one another, they are oaths to God, to your extended families, and to the community. Most important on a practical level, they are a promise to your children.

The traditional family is the best incubator of our future. All of us come from families. And the most ideal family for a child is one that consists of a married mother and father. Study after study demonstrates that the traditional family is healthy for children. Kids reared in traditional families are:

> More likely to enjoy warm relationships with both parents.
> Less likely to divorce or become unwed parents themselves.
> More likely to be successful in school and graduate from college.
> More likely to be healthy.
> Less likely to abuse substances.
> Less likely to experience child abuse.
> Less likely to commit crimes.[17]

There exists between a man and a woman a complementarity that benefits children. Studies demonstrate that "mothers devote special attention to their children's physical and emotional needs, whereas fathers devote their primary efforts to character traits.... [This creates an] efficient, balanced, human child-rearing regime."[18] Now I realize that not everyone, due to circumstances beyond their control, can have both mom and dad in the house. Children can be raised successfully without either mother or father, but the *exception* to the rule should not displace the rule— the *rule* is by necessity, like all general rules of society, based on the wisdom of centuries.

There are heroic examples of single mothers and fathers struggling to give their children all they have—and succeeding. They need our support and prayers. But the ideal (and I think many of those single parents would agree) is to have two parents at home—preferably the two people who brought the child into the world. Despite the fact that half of all marriages end in divorce and that some people fail to reach the ideal—that ideal must be defended and promoted. We can't risk our children on anything less.

The words of the most vocal activists for alternative family arrangements reveal their true disdain for the institution of marriage. Judith Stacy, a professor of sociology at New York University, believes redefining marriage is long overdue. In her journal article, "Good Riddance to the Family," she argues: "[I]f we begin to value the meaning and quality of intimate bonds over the customary forms, there are few limits to the kinds of marriage and kinship patterns people might wish to devise." (Give Professor Stacy her way and we might all be seeing "Much Bigger Love" at a Justice of the Peace near you.)

NYU seems to be an incubator of this sort of mushy headed thinking. Ellen Willis, the head of NYU's Center for Cultural Reporting and Criticism wrote of her hope that the debate over marriage would result in "an implicit revolt against the institution [of marriage] into the very heart, further promoting the democratization and secularization of personal and sexual life."[19] This is what our society needs? What seems to motivate many of these academic activists is not the welfare of children or the good of society, but their own selfish political goals and personal cravings.

If we accept these innovative "family arrangements" as twenty-first-century marriage, it will have long-term destructive effects on children, and on our future. Liberals want us to abide by nature's laws when it comes to whales, the ice caps, and guppies, but when it comes to the family, we are supposed to accept all sorts of rank innovations and radical revisions. I think this is folly. Stable marriages strengthen the foundation of our society, and it is in our public interest to protect their vitality. Even for those who reject the idea that God ordained the family in its traditional form, our decades of experimenting with the alternatives should be pretty good evidence that humans, by their unchanging nature, are most happy in the setting of a traditional family. If the family deconstructionists don't understand this, kids do. A study conducted by New America Media and the University of California Office of the President asked more than six hundred young people, ages sixteen to twenty-two, what they considered "the most pressing issue facing [their] generation" today. Their greatest concern: family breakdown by 24 percent—topping the list. Sandy Close, the executive director overseeing the project said, rightly, that there is a "deep yearning for traditional structures and values."[21]

> # A NATURAL VISION
>
> 》 》 》 "Today the family is often threatened by social and cultural pressures that tend to undermine its stability; but in some countries the family is also threatened by legislation which at times directly challenge its natural structure, which is and must necessarily be that of a union between a man and a woman founded on marriage. Family must never be undermined by laws based on a narrow and unnatural vision of man."[20]
>
> **—John Paul II**

With the central importance of family in mind, governments have been endorsing marriage and families for centuries. Unfortunately, today, too often government policies don't support families. Indeed, more often than not, government is the enemy.

From a political perspective, Hillary Clinton's mantra that "it takes a village to raise a child" has been a masterstroke. The genius behind this phrase lies in its ambiguity. All of us recognize that rearing children is very difficult, and that parents need help and support from the larger community. In fact, we want and expect community organizations, including the government, to help parents.

Unfortunately, that's *not* what Hillary and her comrades have in mind when *they* talk about the village. Remember, cultural elites are not friendly to the traditional family. They think that instead of government *helping* families, government should, in many ways, *replace* families when it comes to dealing with children. (Maybe Hillary meant to title her book *It Takes a Village Government.*) As a result, the proper relationship between families and government has been turned upside down: government tries too hard to act *as* a parent, while not doing enough to *help* parents. Let's consider each of these points in turn.

The Government Makes a Bad Parent

Since the dawn of time, elites have sought to replace parents. Hundreds of years before Christ, Plato put forth the argument that children should be reared and educated by society as a whole, with no particular connection to their biological parents. In recent years, the United Nations Children's Fund ("UNICEF") has promoted its "Convention on the Rights of the Child,"[22] which would give children countless rights vis-à-vis their parents, including the right to receive "information and ideas of all kinds, regardless of frontiers, either orally, in writing or in print, in the form of art, or through any other media of the child's choice."[23] (Take that, you mothers trying to keep your kids off the Internet!) For the most part, we Americans have been fortunate to avoid any huge problems in this area, and most American parents still have the freedom to *be* parents. (In fact, we haven't even approved UNICEF's silly convention.) Nevertheless, the history of the U.S. welfare system provides a good example of why the government makes a bad parent.

By the 1960s, one of the nation's most perceptive observers had noticed that government welfare programs had a dangerous side effect of weakening traditional families. In 1965, Daniel Patrick Moynihan, at the time working for the Department of Labor, issued a report critical of the effects of government programs on African American families. In particular, he observed that African American families in the inner city were "crumbling" in part because the government was taking the place of fathers as the main breadwinner. He also pointed out that the lack of committed fathers contributed to a host of difficulties for these families.

Despite Moynihan's unassailable report, the federal government would not rethink its approach to welfare for thirty years. The Moynihan Report was roundly dismissed and the matter closed, except for one problem: Moynihan's predictions came true. A recent article on the subject noted that even after efforts to reform welfare in the 1990s, the problems facing African American families are, in many ways, even more severe than they were in 1965: Almost 70 percent of African American children are born to single mothers. Those mothers are far more likely than married mothers to be poor, even after a post-welfare-reform decline in child poverty. They are also more likely to pass that poverty on to their children.[24]

In other words, we are still suffering from the problems identified by the Moynihan report more than forty years ago. And the problems are nationwide. Illegitimacy rates among Caucasians and Hispanics are also disturbingly high.

The Moynihan Report was written by a liberal—in the true sense of the word—who warned very clearly of the dangers of expecting government money to replace the many benefits that children receive from a strong, two-parent family.

We can argue—and we will continue to argue—about how much the government can and should do to help poor families. We should all agree, however, that in the future, government efforts will be designed to *strengthen* families, not to pretend that they don't matter. If we want "the village" to help "the children," then we should insist that "the village" do everything it can to ensure that children are brought up in loving, and ideally two-parent families.

Other Government Screw-Ups— Taxes and No-Fault Divorce

Given that strong families are so important to our country, you might assume that the tax code would be designed to benefit traditional families. Wrong. More often than not, the code actually undermines them. Consider the sad story of the Alternative Minimum Tax (AMT), which was originally designed to target wealthy households that had used deductions to avoid paying income tax. Unfortunately, because the AMT has not been indexed to inflation, it now affects many middle-class families. Indeed, a recent report argued that the AMT effectively penalizes families:

> AMT imposes penalties on marriage and having children. Couples will be more than twenty times as likely as singles to face the AMT in 2010. Because the AMT prohibits deductions for dependents, 85 percent of married couples with two or more children will face the AMT, 97 percent among such couples with income between $75,000 and $100,000. About 6 million taxpayers will face the AMT in 2010 simply because they have children.[25]

The "village" idiots continue to tax children. And though there are congressional proposals to exempt those making less than $250,000 a year from the AMT,[26] with the Democrats running the show, expect to feel the tax bite elsewhere. The AMT is a travesty and it should be scrapped for everyone, but especially for families.

And what about increasing the child tax credit, eliminating income level restrictions on it, and making it permanent? We should encourage what is good. If the government needs to make up the difference, slap some additional taxes onto pornography. Use the code to discourage what is truly destructive and demeaning. But give parents a break.

As painful as the AMT is, the estate tax is even more anti-family, both in theory and in application. Here's how it works: when you die, the IRS totals up your estate and taxes everything over a certain amount. If your estate is worth more than that amount, your heirs cannot have their full inheritance—they only get what is left *after* the government takes its cut. Forget the fact that the estate was already taxed once—when the money in it was earned! In 2001, Congress passed a law phasing out the estate tax, which will vanish completely in 2010. But if Congress doesn't act to extend the law, the estate tax will reappear, in its pre-2001 form, in 2011! It's like Freddy Krueger showing up at your memorial dinner. So if you were planning on passing *all* your hard earned wealth onto your relatives, 2010 would be an ideal year to die. (More morbid pundits have predicted an outbreak of patricide that year.)

Ever since our country's founding, American fathers and mothers have hoped that their children could enjoy a higher standard of living than they did. But today's tax code penalizes generosity to family and discourages the transfer of (already taxed) monies to children. This is criminal. The estate tax is like the long chute near the end of "Chutes and Ladders"; just when a family appears to be making real economic progress, the tax sends you sliding back.

Then there are those government policies that overturn the game, entirely. Every other day some Hollywood star or politician calls their marriage quits. It's practically epidemic. That serial divorcé Charlie Sheen once said of his breakups, "You buy a car, it breaks down, what are you going to do?"[27] I guess treat your wife like an old Buick, Charlie: We sometimes forget that until 1969, it was actually quite difficult to obtain a divorce in America. That all began to change after California passed its Family Law Act of 1969. Before that act, Californians could only be divorced for the following reasons: adultery, extreme cruelty, willful desertion, willful neglect, habitual intemperance, conviction of a felony, and incurable insanity.[28] In other words, someone came out of the divorce looking *really* bad. But after the new act went into effect on January 1, 1970, couples seeking a divorce were required only to show that their marriage suffered from "irreconcilable differences."[29] This "no-fault" divorce law represented a radical change in American attitudes toward marriage.[30] Within five years, forty-four states had followed California's lead and approved some type of no-fault divorce reform.[31] Not surprisingly, the U.S. divorce rate surged from 2.9 per 1000 people in 1968 to 5.3 per 1000 people in 1979.[32] While it has declined slightly since then, it has never returned to pre-1970 levels.[33]

No-fault divorce has degraded the sanctity of marriage—transforming it into little more than state sanctioned dating. It has also put an enormous burden on the legal system and endangered the welfare of children. Georgia chief Supreme Court justice Leah Ward Sears has reported that in her state alone, 65 percent of the cases at the Superior Court level involve domestic relations cases. As a result of this breakdown of the family, some 14,000 children were in the care of the Georgia Division of Family and Children Services in 2006. One out of every four children in that state, under eighteen had a case with the Office of Child Support Enforcement.[34] And this is in conservative *Georgia*! Imagine what is happening in other states.

Thankfully there are some common sense solutions being advanced to curb the rampant divorce rate and to protect children. Louisiana was one of the first states to pass a one-year waiting period for no-fault divorces for couples with children younger than eighteen. And many scholars and family rights activists are encouraging states to mandate classes preparing couples for marriage before granting their licenses. Seems sensible, even for an older-model Sheen.

Returning *POWER TO THE PEOPLE*: Where Do We Go from Here?

If we really want to give power to the people, we have to empower families. Strong and successful families are our future, they ensure that our values and traditions live on into the next generation, and they are much less likely to yield power to the elites who think that government, rather than family, knows best.

So what should we do? First, let's all take responsibility for what is happening in our own families and the culture that surrounds us. We have to be unafraid to speak up and defend the traditional family whenever and wherever it is defamed. We cannot be cowed by elites into sitting by and letting others gut the very future of our country. We all have a stake in this fight. We all have an obligation to reverse the trend. We all need to have the courage to tell the smut peddlers of popular culture, "Back away from my child!"

And it's not just forces in the popular culture that are trying to push parents out of the way, "health care" professionals can also step way over the line. When doctors speak, most of us listen and trust them. Then there are people like Rebecca Hagelin, author of the great book *Home Invasion*. A few years ago, Rebecca took her thirteen-year-old daughter Kristin to her female pediatrician (we'll call her "Dr. Smith") for a routine sports physical for her junior high track team. The doctor told Rebecca that part of the physical included a "private chat" with Kristin.

"Excuse me?" Rebecca asked. "What do you mean by private chat?"

"Oh, there are some things I need to talk to Kristin about and you can't be in the room," she said matter-of-factly.

Incredulous, Rebecca shot back, "I need to be here for any conversation you have with Kristin."

"But you can't," the doctor insisted. "We're going to be talking about private things and you have to leave."

Rebecca bristled, "She's a minor. I'm her mother. And I *will* be in the room for everything."

Dr. Smith was stunned but proceeded anyway. "Okay, Kristin, now I'm going to have that talk with you just like I would if your mom were not here."

She reminded Kristin that drinking was illegal until she is twenty-one and that smoking is really, really bad. Then came the money comments: "Sex is a little trickier," Dr. Smith said. "You're getting to the age where girls are having boyfriends, and some of them will be kissing and touching and doing other things. You have to do what is right for *you*."

At this point, Rebecca blew a gasket. "Excuse me, but my daughter knows that sex is only for marriage."

The good doctor looked at Rebecca in disbelief then turned to the thirteen-year-old, "Well, that's what some people think, but you have to do what is comfortable for you."

That was the end of the exam. Rebecca walked out with her daughter.

Parents would be disturbed to know that it is common practice among pediatricians these days to tell the moms and dads to leave the room so the "professional" can have private chats with children—chats that involve controversial topics like abortion, premarital sex, masturbation, and birth control. Doctors think they can—and should—talk to children in a way that parents can't. It's a trend that extends from doctors' offices, to schools, to government. The "experts" know best. Parents are too ignorant, too "traditional," and too incompetent to be left "unsupervised" to direct the lives of their own children.

Good for Rebecca for saying "back away from my child!" It's difficult to stand up to experts, doctors, and supposed authority figures. And too many parents just take it. Think about what *that* approach communicates to your child.

Parents need plenty of support in their struggles, especially with the cultural odds stacked against them. Luckily there are plenty of groups that—coming from a traditional perspective——can help parents. One is Family Life Today, a thirty-year-old organization that hosts conferences and radio shows, and offers tips and plans for aiding parents, husbands, and wives in their newsletter and on their Web site (FamilyLife.com). Many similar groups exist including the Catholic group for fathers, St. Joseph's Covenant Keepers (Dads.org).

Simply believing in traditional marriage, wanting it to work, and loving your husband or wife doesn't guarantee a marriage that is all roses. Thankfully, there are groups like Covenant Keepers (CovenantKeepers.org) and Retrovaille (Retrovaille.org) exist, to help those couples who have the will to find the way to save struggling marriages. These are groups that *really* do what they do "for the children."

The Selfless Among Us

What happens when the family fails a child? When a child loses his or her way and has nowhere to turn? The consequences can be disastrous—unless someone decides that a child's life is worth saving. One of the most selfless and most admirable people I've ever interviewed on my radio show is John Croyle. He founded the Big Oak Boys' Ranch and Big Oak Girls' Ranch in Northeastern

Alabama which are both dedicated to providing loving, safe, nurturing environments to neglected or abused children. Croyle was a top prospect for the NFL in the early 1970s when he played for the legendary Crimson Tide coach Bear Bryant. When he graduated he had to make a decision about whether to become a pro-athlete or to follow a dream he had to open a Christian boys' home. Croyle said in the end the choice was simple. As much as he loved football, God made it clear to him that there was only one path he could take—helping children in need. "In the end it wasn't even a close call—I have zero regrets," he told me. Since 1974 when he opened Big Oak Ranch, he and his wife Tee have markedly impoved the lives of hundreds of children.

* * * * *

Despite what the dominant culture tells you, remember that parents are still the most important influence on their children. The time we have on this earth is flying by, so spend your family time wisely. Arm your children with your life experiences, the lessons you learned the hard way. A lot of these will sink in, even as your teens roll their eyes. (And ignore those forty-five-year-olds who dress like they're eighteen, the ones who are in the front row at the John Mayer concert, who'll also roll their eyes at you when you discipline your kids.)

As you will see in Chapter 6, there is a lot you can do to protect your family and hold back the tide of cultural waste that masquerades as entertainment or wisdom today. Entertainment companies, the fashion industry and social networking Web sites will do their best to burrow under your children's skin. Don't let them. Every day you have countless opportunities to influence your family by your own example. Use the time you have to exercise power that will show results long after you are gone. You have the power to leave a mark on future generations. Use it wisely.

2

DON'T FENCE ME IN . . . BUT PLEASE FENCE THEM OUT!

What I remember most about the new double border fence along the San Diego-Tijuana divide was the trash. I stood atop a nearby hillside with a U.S. Border Patrol agent surveying the mounds of discarded paper, bottles, diapers, and cans piled high against the first section of the barrier. Bags of rotting garbage had been thrown over the walls into U.S. territory. Rows of tin-roofed shacks were built so close to the border that the fence wall and the rear of the shacks were one and the same.

ETL WORKS—DUH!

▶ ▶ ▶ Stop the presses! Enforcing the laws and beefing up border security works. Border patrol agents made more than 200,000 fewer apprehensions at the border between October 2006 and June 2007 than during the same period the previous year. (Still, 682,468 crossings is an obscene number!) Also, 43,135 OTMs (Other than Mexicans) were stopped crossing the southern border during that same period—which is down 48 percent. That's good news but we still have a long way to go. Hundreds of thousands of illegal aliens still manage to get through every year. This is unacceptable.

Source: Jerry Seper, "Fewer Illegals Arrested at Border," *Washington Times*, July 9, 2007.

The first time I thought much about illegal immigration was in 1997, when I was working as a political analyst for *CBS Evening News*. Each weekend I contributed taped pieces about people or issues that I thought weren't getting the coverage they deserved. A friend tipped me off to what was happening along the border area south of San Diego, so I checked it out. Residents and border agents told me stories about how before the double fence was built in 1994, the town of Imperial Beach had been overrun with illegal aliens who had simply walked across the border from Mexico. Stories of dozens of illegal aliens simultaneously wandering on the beach—hungry and in need of shelter—were common. Imperial Beach had also become a favorite drop-off and pick-up point for smugglers of humans and drugs. Property values in the area were either stagnant or dropping, as tourism declined.

The Border Patrol agent showed me video of what the surveillance cameras had captured just a few years earlier. In broad daylight, hundreds of people at one time overwhelmed the immigration border crossing station and streamed into the U.S. without permission and without inspection. I could not believe what I was seeing. Our border had become totally meaningless. I was stunned. After years of complaints about life in this border area, the federal government launched "Operation Gatekeeper." It was an effort to stem the flow of illegals across this fourteen-mile stretch, where 45 percent of all illegal crossings into the U.S. had taken place. The number of border patrol agents doubled, special high-tech lighting was installed, and new barriers with sophisticated monitoring devices were built.

It should have surprised no one that enforcement actually worked. More than ten years later the economy of Imperial Beach is booming. Fewer illegals are found on a nightly basis sleeping under cars, trashing the environment, damaging property, and frightening residents. Most of the garbage is now confined to the area immediately surrounding the border barriers themselves.

I recall at the time asking my border patrol agent escort whether he worried that this new enforcement effort was merely pushing the problem eastward. Looking across the border, he paused and said, "I hope not....I wouldn't have wished what we've been through on anyone."

* * * * *

There can be no divided allegiance here. Any man who says he is an American, but something else also, isn't an American at all. We have room for but one flag, the American flag.... We have room for but one language here, and that is the English language, for we intend to see that the crucible turns our people out as Americans, of American nationality, and not as dwellers in a polyglot boarding house; and we have room for but one sole loyalty, and that is loyalty to the American people.[1]

Who said that?

If you guessed Pat Buchanan or Tom Tancredo—nice try.

Actually those were the words of Theodore Roosevelt. Shortly before he died in 1919, he wrote of the country's need for "Americanization," a theme he had stressed for years. Our twenty-sixth president lamented that we were becoming "hyphenated Americans," with divided allegiances that prevented true assimilation. Still, Roosevelt had an enormous compassion and admiration for immigrants who played by the rules.

> [W]e should insist that if the immigrant who comes here in good faith becomes an American and assimilates himself to us, he shall be treated on an exact equality with everyone else, for it is an outrage to discriminate against any such man because of creed, or birthplace, or origin. But this is predicated upon the man's becoming in very fact an American, and nothing but an American. If he tries to keep segregated with men of his own origin and separated from the rest of America, then he isn't doing his part as an American.... [2]

How simple—yet how profound.

There is little doubt that if Roosevelt were alive today, he would be floored by the magnitude of our illegal immigration problem—not to mention the attitude of those who think enforcing our borders is optional. As someone who believed that every immigrant should learn English within five years or be deported, "TR" would today be considered by elites on the Right and the Left as "restrictionist," "anti-Hispanic," or "xenophobic." Heck, he would make Tancredo look like an immigration squish. Roosevelt believed in English-only public schools—meaning no foreign languages spoken or taught. Such a statement today would constitute a hate crime at the politically correct cocktail parties in Malibu and Manhattan.

Despite how reviled these views would be today in certain political, academic, entertainment, and business circles, I would bet that most of the rest of us are closer to Roosevelt on immigration than we are to La Raza.

No issue better demonstrates the huge divide between the people and the "elites" than illegal immigration. And at no time in our history was this split more apparent than during the recent debate over "comprehensive immigration reform." Business lobbyists, Latino activists, President Bush, and senators in both parties pitted themselves against the American people who wanted border enforcement first. This "B.E.F." coalition included traditional conservatives, working class Democrats, African Americans, and recent legal immigrants. They forced the administration and Republican champions of this amnesty to defend the three-hundred-plus-page bill. They flooded Capitol Hill with calls, e-mails, and faxes. The more people learned about the "bipartisan" legislation, the less they liked the whole idea. "Z visas" for criminal aliens? In-state tuition for children of illegals? Legal status for gang members who merely pledge to renounce their gang affiliation? Border enforcement "certified" simply when monies are allocated? No wonder this bill won the nickname "shamnesty."

The more infuriated and involved we the people became, the more personally insulting the bill's advocates became. Conservative columnist Linda Chavez wrote a piece comparing the B.E.F. coalition's views to the Nazi's genetic purification campaign. The *Wall Street Journal* editorial writers joked that B.E.F. types only liked immigrants from Europe. And the crowning glory came from President Bush, who accused the bill's opponents of "fear mongering."

WHO'S "TOMMY"?

In a pathetic last-minute emotional appeal for amnesty, Senate Majority Leader Harry Reid claimed that someone named "Tommy" phoned his office fearful of what would happen to his "friend from Mexico" if the bill didn't pass. Now only if Senator Reid could get one of his imaginary friends to write better floor statements for him!

My personal favorite was Republican senator Lindsey Graham, an ardent supporter of a "pathway to legalization," who warned that "the loud folks" were getting out of hand. What he really meant was that the people were becoming a nuisance. The nerve of the voters actually reading this bill! The audacity of them for listening to talk radio and tying up the Senate switchboard! Lindsey Graham is a prime example of how someone can be a Republican Southerner with a military background and still side with the elites against the people. In my entire life I have never witnessed our political leaders acting in such a blatant disregard of their constituents. Ultimately, the common sense of Americans won out over the arrogance of leaders in both parties. Amnesty was defeated—at least for now.

The vast majority of Americans desperately want our borders protected—and we want it done *now*. We are weary of the excuses and empty promises put forward by the Republican National Committee, the White House, and the Democratic leadership on this vital issue of national, economic, and cultural security. We do not understand why, even after the devastating attacks on September 11, our government still allows hundreds of thousands of illegal aliens to cross our borders every year. We do not want our public schools burdened with a massive influx of non-English speaking children of parents who broke our laws. We are livid that our

THE BIG RIP-OFF REVEALED

》》》 Households headed by unskilled workers cost federal, state, and local governments $22,449 on average, according to a 2007 study by the Heritage Foundation. Considering that two-thirds of all illegal immigrants are unskilled workers, and estimating 12 million illegals currently living here in the country, the undocumented population could be costing $180 billion more than they are contributing. The Heritage Foundation study concludes with a reference to President Bush's guest-worker plan: "Policies which would substantially increase the inflow of low-skill immigrant workers receiving services would dramatically increase the fiscal deficits described in this paper and impose substantial costs on U.S. taxpayers."

Source: Robert E. Rector, et al., "The Fiscal Cost of Low-Skill
Households to the U.S. Taxpayer," Heritage Foundation, April 4, 2007.

health care costs skyrocket year after year as illegal immigrants take advantage of free health care at emergency rooms across the country. We are astounded to see the resurgence of diseases we thought we had long since conquered, such as tuberculosis, carried by illegal aliens who enter the country without any medical screening. We are horrified to learn how the illegal alien invasion feeds crime and gang activity in our country. We are fed up with a government that has ignored our wishes on an issue that will transform every major aspect of our lives—imperiling America's future.

It is true that we have recently made some progress in cross-border apprehensions and workplace enforcement. There has also been a small increase in the number of illegal aliens deported annually. The Bush administration will invariably answer any border enforcement complaint by pointing to high-tech advances in border monitoring, the increase in the number of U.S. Border Patrol agents, and the elimination of the "Catch and Release" treatment for illegal aliens found in the United States. My response is: *Of course you should be doing all those things! And what took you so long?* A country that cannot or will not defend its borders ceases to be a country.

This Land Is *My* Land

With the "immigration protests" of 2006, we saw hundreds of thousands of illegal aliens emboldened by the political and business culture that perpetuated the immigration disaster. They took to the streets, waving Mexican flags (until organizers realized it was a bad PR move), as speakers demanded full citizenship rights. Posters photographed at some of the rallies featured slogans such as: "You Stole Our Homeland!" and "If you think I'm 'illegal' because I'm a Mexican, learn the true history because I'm in *my* homeland!"[3]

We watch this madness unfold on a daily basis and we wonder how things spiraled so far out of control.

Our president and his party's leadership are oblivious to what this issue means to us. In March 2007, Bush traveled to Mexico, stood alongside Mexican president Felipe Calderon (who once likened our border fence to the Berlin Wall), and made this touching promise: "Mr. President, my pledge to you and your government, but more importantly, the people of Mexico, is I will work as hard as I possibly can to pass comprehensive immigration reform." It's outrageous that a U.S. president promised citizens of another country that he'll do better for *them* on immigration.

Despite the claims from the open border crowd that "of course, we're all for border enforcement," these people basically view the enforcement of current immigration laws as a waste of time and resources. They use euphemisms to disguise what they really want, which is amnesty—basically erasing the distinction between illegal and legal immigration. Terms such as "path to citizenship" or "earned citizenship" amount to amnesty wrapped in a pretty serape. Their answer to every objection raised by border enforcement advocates is "we can't deport 12 million people!" (This is a favorite line of George W. Bush.) When we point out that massive deportations are not necessary if our immigration laws are vigorously enforced,[4] they immediately resort to Plan B—dismissing us as racists or xenophobes.

Something called "Latino Lobby Day" is convened annually in Richmond, Virginia, where a variety of Latino rights groups descend on the state capital to assert the "rights" of

"GUEST WORKERS" SOUND GOOD, BUT...

"Never under any condition should this Nation look at an immigrant as primarily a labor unit. He should always be looked at primarily as a future citizen and the father of other citizens who are to live in this land as fellows with our children and our children's children. Our immigration laws, permanent or temporary, should always be constructed with this fact in view."[5]

—Theodore Roosevelt

illegals. "We're here to express our outrage at a very mean-spirited set of bills that have been introduced in the legislature in Virginia," one Latino lobbyist told the *Washington Post.*[6] He added that a number of the proposed laws "are based on myth and hate." This type of bumper sticker rhetoric led Virginia's Democratic governor Tim Kaine to assure the crowd that his state was a "welcoming place" for everyone.[7] Central American gang members, drug pushers, and the human smugglers must have been happy to hear that.

People who think they are a lot more politically and culturally enlightened than you believe that globalization and international trade have made traditional concerns about border enforcement moot. They favor "solutions" such as a temporary worker card or a "path to citizenship," both of which would ensure that the pool of low-skilled workers continues to increase in the United States. (Of course advocates of the temporary workers plan have never explained why "temporary" workers wouldn't just choose to stay here permanently.)

Let's face it—businesses want to drive down wages whenever possible. The cheaper the labor costs, the bigger the bottom line for shareholders and executives. This seems fine and dandy until we consider what this scenario ultimately means for the American family—lower wages. And of course both illegal aliens and temporary workers (most fleeing desperate economic conditions in their home countries) end up being exploited in the process. Certainly we should all have empathy for people trying to feed their families, but that doesn't mean we should sit by idly while our borders are being overrun.

Politicians without Borders

Why is there such a split between elite and popular opinion on immigration and border enforcement? One big reason is that

TOP 5 ILLEGAL IMMIGRATION SOB STORY HEADLINES

))) "California Latinos fearful after immigration raids," Reuters, January 25, 2007.

))) "Border Crackdown Spawns Violence: More Deaths Occurring as Smugglers Fight Over Valuable Human Cargo," *Washington Post*, February 19, 2007.

))) "Immigrants advised about their rights: community groups prepare the undocumented to deal with more law enforcement sweeps," *Los Angeles Times*, March 5, 2007.

))) "Battling Deportation Often a Solitary Journey," *Washington Post*, January 8, 2007.

))) "Immigration Raids Can Divide Families," Associated Press, March 11, 2007.

regular people pride themselves on being Americans, while the elites pride themselves on being cosmopolitan (from Greek words basically meaning *citizen of the world*).

Additionally, the specific costs of open borders do not hit the elites as hard as they hit the working class.

Case in point: illegal immigrant crime. To listen to the open border advocates and the dinosaur media, one would think that every illegal immigrant living here is like celebrity dog-trainer Cesar Millan (a.k.a. "The Dog Whisperer").[8] Illegally in this country—yes, but also entrepreneurial, ambitious, and law-abiding. The "local illegal does good" sob stories have gotten old fast (see box at left). You'd think establishment politicians and the *New York Times* would be embarrassed to keep pouring it on, but they aren't.

In the fall of 2006, at a dinner for Hillsdale College, White House political sage Karl Rove gave the dinner speech to a restless conservative audience. Just weeks before what President Bush would call a midterm election "thumping," Rove was beating the drum for "comprehensive immigration reform."

You know, I've started to keep a file. A file about the kid who graduates from Princeton and can't go study at Oxford because he's an illegal alien. The valedictorian and the salutatorian of a high school class who's an illegal alien. The guy who saves the people from the burning apartment who's an illegal alien. We've got to find a way to deal with these people in a compassionate way, to say there's a difference between somebody who came here yesterday and somebody who came here five years ago.[9]

Conservative writers John O'Sullivan and Mark Steyn, sitting at the table with me, were visibly annoyed.

I felt like leaping up and saying, "I keep a file, too! In my file are the cases of Raul Gomez, who murdered Colorado police detective Donald Young;[10] and Diego Pillco, who allegedly killed a Manhattan actress by hanging her from her shower rod;[11] and Alfredo Rodriguez Gonzalez, an illegal immigrant roofer accused of aggravated rape of a newlywed in Louisiana."[12]

And Karl, why no mention of the Americans killed each year by illegal aliens driving drunk? Let's not forget that illegal immigration is a crime itself, and unfortunately many illegals continue their lawbreaking ways once here. Of course, if you live in a Manhattan co-op with a doorman or in a neighborhood with private security, then you are more insulated from the common criminals and these everyday questions of law

LET THEM EAT BOLOGNA!

❱❱❱ Maricopa County sheriff Joseph Arpaio in Arizona has taken it upon himself to change immigration enforcement in one of the states hardest hit by the problem of illegals. He puts his local deputies through border patrol training. His department checks the immigration status of all its prisoners.

In April 2007, he arrested 500 illegal immigrants, and has had to set up tent cities to house all of these border scofflaws. Sounds expensive, right? Not when prisoners only get two meals a day—"brunch" and dinner. A bologna sandwich and an apple don't cost much.

and order. The simple fact is that illegal immigration has ravaged entire communities with increases in violent and drug-related crime, and in these areas the system is on the verge of being totally overwhelmed. Yet you would never know this by watching the evening news or reading most of the newspapers. When is the last time CBS or the *New York Times*, reported on violent crime committed by illegal immigrants? Perhaps they are too busy doing stories on how difficult life is for the illegal immigrant—or the rare case when deportation separates a parent from a child born in the U.S. (I always wondered why such parents do not take their children back to their home country with them.) FOX News Channel's Geraldo Rivera loves these stories.

Getting good numbers on the criminal illegal alien prison population is not easy. Justice Department statistics separate out only *citizens* and *non-citizens*, and the latter group includes legal permanent residents and green card holders. Some have estimated that more than a quarter of our prison population is made up of criminal illegal aliens.[13] In 2005, the GAO studied a sample of illegal alien criminals (again, shouldn't *all* illegal aliens be considered criminals?) and found an average of eight arrests and thirteen offenses per criminal alien. The audit examined one hundred criminal cases involving illegal immigrants, and found that seventy-three illegals accounted for 429 arrests, 878 charges, and 241 convictions. The most popular crimes were burglary, robbery, theft, and drug-related crimes.[14]

The recidivism among criminal illegal aliens is undoubtedly related to the obscene "sanctuary" policies that jurisdictions across the United States have in place. These policies prevent various state

LEFT COAST PAYS BIG-TIME

》》》 California spent $635 million to imprison illegal immigrants in 2003, according to the GAO. Nevertheless, knuckleheads in state and local government keep supporting "sanctuary" policies that shield illegals from inquiries about their immigration status. Go figure.

officials from inquiring about a person's immigration status or assisting federal immigration officials.

Gangs comprised of illegals, such as the deadly Salvadoran MS-13, have been terrorizing communities from Northern Virginia to Long Island since the 1980s. Their crimes range from human and drug trafficking, murder (often by machete), rape, extortion, and armed robbery. MS-13 is now the most powerful gang in America and operates in more than thirty states.

No speeches about *this* by Karl Rove.

When Enforcing the Law Is Illegal

It would be one thing if our immigration laws went unenforced because we lacked the resources or the manpower. Instead, our immigration laws go unenforced due to the willful disdain and inaction of local and federal officials. An appalling by-product of this is that at times, illegal aliens are treated with more deference than our border patrol agents. The most famous recent example of Uncle Sam's war on border enforcement is the case of Ignacio Ramos and Jose Compean.

On February 17, 2005, border guards Ramos and Compean saw Mexican Osbaldo Aldrete-Davila abandon his van (later found to contain eight hundred pounds of marijuana) and begin to flee. Ramos and Compean say Aldrete-Davila had a gun. The two border agents shot at Aldrete-Davila, but he escaped. They then filed falsified reports about the incident, and appeared to try to cover up the shooting.

STATES OF DENIAL

》》》 A federal audit conducted in 2005 slammed the state of Oregon and the city of San Francisco for taking millions in federal funds to combat illegal immigration, *while preventing police or state government officials from enforcing immigration laws.* San Francisco's administrative code actually prohibits the release of information about the immigration status of its inmate population.

The drug-smuggling thug was given a "humanitarian visa," flown to the U.S. and granted immunity to testify against Ramos and Compean. The two agents are now serving eleven- and twelve-year sentences in federal prison. And as an added bonus, Aldrete-Davila is now suing the U.S. government for $5 million. Ramos and Compean may not be saints. They were probably guilty of administrative misconduct for their actions after the shooting. But how can anyone not conclude that our government has perverse priorities when our border agents have more to fear from prosecutors than do drug runners?

Too bad Ramos and Compean could not take advantage of "sanctuary policies" that some of our major cities have put in place to shield illegals. Los Angeles, for example, stacks the deck in favor of immigration law breakers, despite the fact that the city has been slammed by an illegal alien crime wave. The Manhattan Institute's Heather Mac Donald found that in 2004, 95 percent of all outstanding murder warrants involved illegal alien suspects.[15] She blasted the LAPD rule called Special Order 40, adopted almost three decades ago, which effectively erected a wall between state and federal immigration enforcement:

> In Los Angeles, for example, dozens of members of a ruthless Salvadoran prison gang have sneaked back into town after having been deported for such crimes as murder, assault with a deadly weapon, and drug trafficking. Police officers know who they are and know that their mere presence in the country is a felony. Yet should a cop arrest an illegal gang-banger for felonious reentry, it is he who will be treated as a criminal, for violating the LAPD's rule against enforcing immigration law.

The law prohibits officers from "initiating police action where the objective is to discover the alien status of a person":[16]

[T]he police may not even ask someone they have arrested about his immigration status until after they have filed criminal charges, nor may they arrest someone for immigration violations. They may not notify immigration authorities about an illegal alien picked up for minor violations. Only if they have already booked an illegal alien for a felony or for multiple misdemeanors may they inquire into his status or report him.[17]

Big city mayors with high populations of illegals are so intent on ignoring the problem that they will vilify any politician calling for enforcement. In 2003, New York's billionaire mayor Michael Bloomberg asked all his supporters to refuse to give money to the campaigns of Republican congressmen Charlie Norwood and Tom Tancredo. Tancredo, of course, is the most infamous border hawk of all, and Norwood had proposed the

MUCHO DINERO PARA MEXICO

In 2006, Mexican "immigrants" (legal and illegal) sent a whopping $23 billion home. That constitutes a 15 percent increase in what was sent the year before. Nice deal for Mexico. Raw deal for America.

CLEAR Act, which would make it clear that the NYPD, LAPD, and other local police forces could enforce immigration laws. Enough to make a billionaire's blood boil.

"Jobs Americans Won't Do," and Other Insults

When President Bush parrots the line "jobs Americans won't do," you get the feeling he's really talking about "jobs Yale alumni won't do." If you're a politician, a journalist, or a college professor, your job probably isn't threatened by the illegal alien workforce. However, if you work construction, cook at a restaurant, or work at a landscaping company, an unlimited flow of cheap, unskilled labor will drive down your wages.

It is also true that lower wages often means lower costs for consumers—until you factor in the massive cost for social services and incarceration. For the elites, the impact is simpler: home additions are cheaper, yard work is cheaper, and restaurant tabs are cheaper.

From coast to coast, the parking lots of 7-Elevens and Wal-Marts overflow with Mexicans or Central Americans, mostly illegal, looking for work. Contractors and homeowners swing by in cars and pickup trucks and grab a few to do painting, yard work, window cleaning, or other home repairs. The crowds at a parking lot in Herndon, Virginia, spurred local politicians to use tax dollars to build a "day-laborer" center, despite the public's outrage about the project.

In January 2007, the *Washington Post* told the story of a Home Depot parking lot in the African American Brentwood neighborhood of D.C. On weekdays, more than one hundred young Hispanic men, mostly Salvadorans, wait there for jobs. The *Post* described the scene: "Three grocery carts overflowed with garbage bags nearby. The ground was littered with Styrofoam cups, beer bottles and paper plates, a point of contention with the neighbors.... [There were] workers sleeping on the shopping center property, goods stashed in the alley near [one neighbor's] house, and people urinating on the retaining wall."[18]

FLASHBACK

》》》 In August 2001, at a 7-Eleven parking lot in suburban Falls Church, Virginia, September 11 hijackers Hani Hanjour and Khalid Almihdhar hired an illegal immigrant who helped them obtain fake drivers' licenses. Having this phony identification helped them move about the area more smoothly in the month before they committed mass murder.

Charlotte Blair, who has lived in Brentwood for thirty-six years, was fed up:

"'It's kind of a scary situation...Women walking up through there with a whole group of men. I just don't feel comfortable. I would like to see the place cleared.'"

Local politician Tommy Ward felt none of her pain, according to the *Post*: "He wants to see a multicultural center, with educational programs and a one-stop workforce station to ensure all workers are treated fairly by their employers." All paid for by the taxpayers of the District of Columbia, of course. Why not sponsor a softball league for illegals, too?

If politicians like the idea of these day-laborer centers so much, then why don't they put them in the neighborhoods where *they* live? Try to build such facilities in the upscale neighborhoods of upper northwest Washington, D.C., or McLean, Virginia, and see how far you get. When a day-laborer center was proposed in the village of Southampton on Long Island, people there pitched a fit. A *New York Post* article quoted an anonymous "high-profile restaurant owner" as complaining, "[W]ho wants to look at portable toilets while they are eating?"[19] Keep the illegals washing the dishes in the back of the kitchen where nobody can see them—that's the idea.

It's about Security, Stupid!

While illegal immigration's effect on crime and jobs may hit the working class the hardest, *everyone* ought to worry about its impact on national security. Thankfully, our government *is* starting to pay attention to this, but it remains an area of grave concern.

Although it is estimated that more than 85 percent of those crossing our border illegally every year are Mexican,[20] our government is most worried about OTMs (Other Than Mexicans) from Special Interest Countries (SICs). Reports from Texas sheriffs paint a

BORDER THUGS & DRUGS

》》》 Along our southwest border, from October 2006 through June 2007, Border Patrol agents seized 1.47 million pounds of marijuana (up 27 percent) and 9,514 pounds of cocaine (up 22 percent) compared with the same period in the previous fiscal year.

Source: Jerry Seper, "Fewer illegals arrested at border," *Washington Times*, July 9, 2007.

frightening picture of the potential national security problem we have along the border. Sheriff Sigifredo Gonzalez of Zapata County told a House subcommittee in July 2006: "To avoid apprehension, we feel many of these terrorists attempt to blend in with persons of Hispanic origin when entering the country.... We feel that terrorists are already here and continue to enter our country on a daily basis."

Are terrorists already here? These statements are a wake-up call:

❯ "Several al Qaeda leaders believe operatives can pay their way into the country through Mexico and also believe illegal entry is more advantageous than legal entry for operational security reasons."

> —Admiral James Loy, Deputy Secretary, Department of Homeland Security, Testimony before the Senate Select Committee on Intelligence, February 2005.

❯ "The U.S. continues to experience a rising influx of other than Mexican nationals (OTMs) illegally entering the country."

> —David Aguilar, Chief Officer, U.S. Border Patrol, U.S. Customs and Border Protection, Testimony before the U.S. Senate Subcommittee on Terrorism, June 7, 2005.

Let's not forget the would-be New York subway bomber Gazi Ibrahim Abu Mezer, an illegal alien and criminal in Canada who skipped parole and was caught twice crossing into the U.S. illegally.

He was released into Canada both times. He then slipped back through our northern border and was only caught when a neighbor informed the police that Mezer had turned his apartment into a bomb factory.

In the Mezer case, New York's subway riders were either very blessed or very lucky or both. We cannot afford to roll the dice when it comes to stopping terrorists from killing Americans—perhaps thousands of us.

Run of the Roost

Just as we don't keep out illegals, we don't keep track of them once we know they're here. First, we don't enforce our visa restrictions. At least three September 11 hijackers had expired visas on the day they committed their mass murder. Better immigration enforcement might have foiled the plot. As noted above, Hani Hanjour and Khalid Almihdar used the illegal immigrant network—operating in broad daylight just yards away from the well-traveled Columbia Pike.

Second, our government looks the other way while businesses court illegals, either as customers or employees. Most states tacitly allow illegal immigrants to attend state colleges and pay in-state tuition. Nine states have recently passed laws making that policy explicit.[21]

Bank of America and Citibank have both made it public that you can get a bank account or credit card with a "Matricula Consular" identification—a card available at any Mexican consulate in the United States. These are the ID cards of choice for illegals living in the United States. A Citibank branch one block from the White House had a big poster in the window in 2004 declaring in Spanish that if you have a Matricula Consular, you can get a credit card.

These big banks also profit by taking their slice from the $23 billion in "remittances" Latin American and Caribbean immigrants

(legal and illegal) send home from the United States each year. A
2007 *Financial Times* article worried that the recent surge in immigration enforcement might harm this industry. "A recent clamp-
down by U.S. migration officials on illegal immigrants could be
contributing to a sharp slowdown in growth" of the remittance
industry, the *FT* reported. (Remittances to Mexico grew by only *5
percent* in the fourth quarter of 2006, just eight times the rate of
the U.S. economic growth. The horror!)[22]

It is sad, but perhaps predictable, that for some businessmen,
making money is more important than making us safer. Pro-busi-
ness elites resist almost any efforts to ramp up enforcement at the
border, tighten visa requirements, or enforce immigration laws at
the workplace. Such initiatives elicit scorn from staff at libertarian
think-tanks such as the Washington, D.C.-based Cato Institute.
One of Cato's recent beefs involves the U.S. government's "failure"
since September 11 to expand the list of countries exempt from our
visa requirements. At present, the citizens of twenty-eight countries
can visit the U.S. without a visa.

Cato's Daniel Griswold calls the government's concern about
preventing another attack by radical Muslims "legitimate but mis-
directed," because our visa policy is "discouraging hundreds of
thousands of peaceful and well-meaning people from visiting the
United States for business and pleasure—costing our country lost
economic opportunities totaling millions of dollars and the good-
will of millions of people."

What Griswold refuses to acknowledge, though, is the fact that
it was our mismanaged visa system that allowed the September 11
terrorists access to the U.S. in the first place. While we do not
want to burden nations unnecessarily that have proven their loyalty and friendship to us, we also must not be bullied by business
interests to loosen visa requirements while security concerns
remain unaddressed.

Just weeks after the September 11 attacks, between late October
and December 1, 2001, we welcomed to our shores 7,000 men

from countries where al Qaeda is active. Men from Saudi Arabia—the home of fifteen of the nineteen hijackers—were still eligible for "Visa Express," an expedited process for entry into the U.S.[23]

Returning *POWER TO THE PEOPLE*

〉〉〉 Is the Genie Out of the Bottle?

It is easy for us to get discouraged about stopping this lunacy when leaders in both political parties, the White House, the media, our universities, think tanks, and most in the business world basically want unlimited immigration. The more we learn about illegal immigration's devastating consequences for our country—our schools, our health care system, our prison population—the more many of us feel abandoned and cheated by the people who were supposed to represent us in Washington. Why did President Bush lobby so passionately for "comprehensive immigration reform" when an overwhelming majority in his own party and even a majority of Democrats didn't want it? And why didn't he work so hard on issues conservatives cared about—cutting government spending and defeating McCain–Feingold, to name a few? We have written letters, e-mailed, telephoned Congressional offices, and stopped our contributions to politicians who don't listen. Yet our political leadership just seemed to blow it all off. They knew what was best and we were going to learn to like it.

As we saw with the defeat of the Bush amnesty plan, we all have the power to influence the system. All of us have an obligation to become more involved. The political elites and Latino rights groups want you to be apathetic. They want you to think that all hope is lost, that America is becoming, as author Victor Davis Hanson called it, "Mexifornia." Get used to it. Learn Spanish.

The good news is that millions of Americans are responding with a defiant "no way." As one iteration of amnesty was being debated on Capitol Hill in the Spring of 2006, a full-time mom in Virginia and a college senior in Texas launched a campaign to make the Senate understand what the people wanted. Through a Web site, Send-A-Brick.com, a grassroots effort burgeoned. Americans mailed about 10,000 bricks to members of the U.S. Senate, giving new meaning to "comprehensive immigration reform." Some of the bricks were painted with messages, including "No Amnesty." All of the bricks sent the message: build a wall.

By the fall, the amnesty and "amnesty lite" bills had faded away. Before Election Day 2006, the Senate passed and the president signed a bill authorizing the construction of seven hundred miles of triple-layer border fence. While voters have been asking, "Where's the fence?!" ever since, the fact is they forced the government to take a baby step.

The brick story should stand as an inspiration to Americans concerned about returning power to the people. If you annoy Congress enough, you might get some attention and results.

When amnesty reared its ugly head again a year later, many of us wanted to do more than send bricks to Congress. We wanted to throw some. (Only Styrofoam ones, of course.) Patriotic Americans rose up against the elites in both parties. We made a huge difference. Senators Trent Lott, Lindsey Graham, John McCain, and John Kyl were flabbergasted by the outpouring of rage that followed their lame effort to fast-track amnesty. After hundreds of thousands of calls, e-mails, and letters rained down on Capitol Hill, they started to pay attention.

))) States of Recognition

Despite feverish opposition from left-wing activist groups, many states and localities are doing what the federal government hasn't done—they are enacting laws and pushing policies aimed at reducing the flow of illegals into their communities. Local law enforcement agencies in Virginia and California have already begun undergoing federal immigration enforcement training that would allow cops to arrest illegal immigrants for being "undocumented."

In early 2007, Virginia's House of Delegates passed a measure barring charities from using state funding to help illegal immigrants over the age of eighteen. A Democratic politician opposed to the measure said this of her opposition: "I think they have put together an agenda that says we are going to *beat up* on illegal aliens." (Italics added.) Denying some illegal immigrants access to taxpayer money now is *beating them up*?

Northern Virginia has seen a number of citizen activist groups sprout up in response to the influx of illegals into their communities. One such group called Help Save Manassas drew an accusatory response from the usual suspects because of its concern about overcrowding and the use by illegals of

WHEN ANNOYING IS GOOD

》》》 Congressional offices receive bags of mail and thousands of e-mails every day from constituents, and it's easy to assume these letters and e-mails have no impact. But if it didn't bother them, why did Democrats, upon gaining control of Congress in 2007, immediately propose a measure to force grassroots groups to comply with "lobbying" laws—laws that wouldn't even apply to labor unions or some corporations?

public services. "Whether or not these policies flow from bias against Latinos, it is Latinos who are going to feel the brunt of it—and not just illegal Latinos but all Latinos," Kent Willis, the Virginia director of the ACLU, told the *Washington Times*. "The result of these policies is profiling at its worst."

The ACLU does everything in its power to intimidate Americans and lawful residents from preserving their way of life and helping law enforcement. Start a pro-enforcement group and risk being called a racist. That's what it's come to. But don't be silenced—remember, it is your country, your state, your town, your neighborhood.

CHEAP LETTUCE AT A PRICE

>>> Illegal immigration costs American taxpayers an estimated $30 to $50 billion annually, according to the Federation for American Immigration Reform.

Various common-sense proposals are being drafted and considered by state legislatures across the country. Measures such as denying in-state college tuition to illegal immigrants, punishing employers who hire illegal workers, authorizing police to work with federal immigration officials trying to identify and apprehend illegal aliens, and limiting the number of unrelated people who can live in one apartment at the same time. Invariably these initiatives are highly popular among the voters, but are seen as nativist or worse by those who really have no use for borders at all.

And those credit cards for illegals? Representative Marsha Blackburn of Tennessee sponsored a bill on Capitol Hill that would disallow the use of the Matricula Consular for opening bank accounts and getting credit cards. Excellent idea.

As we saw with the impressive grassroots opposition when the Senate tried to ram through "comprehensive immigration reform" before Memorial Day 2007, we do have the power to make Washington listen to us. They can call us names, call us "loud," call us "fear-mongers," but that should deter none of us from having our say about one of the most important issues of our time.

>>> Support Politicians Who Will Enforce the Law

This should be a no-brainer, shouldn't it? Should Senators Lindsey Graham and Chuck Hagel be reelected after their abominable support of amnesty? Conventional wisdom has been that border enforcement is a losing issue politically. In 2006, the open-borders media relished the loss of Arizona congressman J. D. Hayworth.

He had increasingly made immigration enforcement his number one campaign issue.

The *Wall Street Journal*'s lead editorial on November 10, 2006, titled "Immigration Losers," came close to blaming Democratic takeovers of the House and Senate on Republicans' tough stances on illegal immigration. The *Journal*'s prime examples of "Immigration Losers" were Hayworth and his fellow Arizonan, Randy Graf, who ran for an open seat.

Regarding Hayworth, the analysis failed to give adequate weight to the fact that his campaign had been dragged down by his connections to disgraced lobbyist Jack Abramoff, or that his opponent, Democrat Harry Mitchell, ran to Hayworth's *right* on border enforcement. (Not to mention the negative ripple effect of a wildly unpopular war in Iraq.) Oh, and then there was the insignificant fact that Arizona voters overwhelmingly passed four tough immigration measures—including one that would prevent illegal aliens from receiving non-emergency benefits such as in-state college tuition and child care assistance.[24] As for Graf, he lost to Democrat Gabby Giffords, who tried to match Graf on immigration toughness. The *National Journal* wrote of Giffords: "By stressing her commitment to border security in a district bordering Mexico and heavily affected by illegal immigration, she's undercutting the appeal of her Republican opponent." And when she came to Washington, Giffords declared, "Believe me, I'm all immigration all the time."

The elite media refuse to admit the obvious—lax immigration enforcement had a terribly demoralizing effect on the GOP base. Also, the *Journal* didn't use much space to cover elections that didn't fit with their open borders bias. Congressman Brian Bilbray, for instance, a Republican from the San Diego area, won his special election by focusing his campaign on tough border enforcement. But the media left *that* trend virtually unreported. Typical.

In Herndon, Virginia, where the politicians voted to build a taxpayer-funded hangout for the illegal immigrants and one-stop shopping for scofflaw contractors, voters made their voices heard. In the May 2006 election, they ousted Mayor Michael O'Reilly and two town councilmen who supported the day laborer center. At least one other candidate, running for the Council on a pro-illegal immigrant plank lost in 2005. The *Washington Post* reported that the groups favoring the day laborer center "called it a small election in a small town, carrying no larger message."

Got that? If pro-enforcement candidates win, it's a fluke. If they lose, it's a referendum.

More states and localities across the country are coming to realize that illegal immigration is a freight train coming straight at them. From crime rates, to educational burdens, to health care expenditures, to environmental concerns, to housing, illegal immigration has taken a costly toll. Beyond the nation's "sanctuary city" mayors and Washington politicians who cynically vote for a border fence with no intention of funding it, there are federal, state, and local officials who do get it. They need your support—monetary and moral. If there are no B.E.F. politicians in your district, then recruit some. Heck, run yourself. I'm sure you've done crazier things.

❱❱❱ Immigration Enforcement Begins at Home

Americans across the country have begun to mobilize against the open borders crowd in big ways and small. Moms send bricks to Congress and new "Minutemen" patrol the Southern border where the feds have fallen down. Writing letters and placing calls to our elected officials is a good thing, but at the same time we also must take more responsibility for our own communities. Let's face it, many of us are part of the problem. We must stop rewarding illegal behavior in our own homes.

If you need your gutters cleaned, or a house cleaner once a week, you might find that hiring an illegal immigrant from the 7-Eleven parking lot is cheaper than hiring a citizen or a legal resident. You might even believe that it's impossible to hire someone legally in this country for some menial tasks—after all, the president tells us that these are "jobs Americans won't do."

This mantra is repeated so often that sometimes I even start buying it. But in January 2007, Chuck from Rockville, Maryland, called into my show when we were discussing this issue and clarified things for me. He runs a kitchen and bath remodeling business in the D.C. suburb. His crew is comprised of four men, all foreign born. "I have two Iranians, one Bolivian, and I got one Salvadoran," he told my audience.

Is kitchen and bathroom remodeling a "job Americans won't do?" Hardly. Chuck's four-man crew speaks three different languages, but all of them are Americans. "They all took the citizen test and they became citizens," he proudly noted.

Chuck described himself as just "a regular person" trying to run a business and play by the rules. He believes politicians have dropped the ball on immigration, and he seemed to anticipate the criticisms that the elites would level against his views.

> **Chuck:** I'm not uncompassionate. I don't have ice water in my veins. I feel for people. Humans are humans. But I abide by the law and so do the gentlemen who work for me. And if you want to keep your society intact, I believe you have to enforce the rules of the land and abide by the laws, and that goes all the way through paying taxes, etc., and being a good citizen....
>
> **Laura:** But how do you compete with companies paying their illegal workers a fraction of what you pay your legal ones?

Chuck: If you do quality work and you're punctual, you do a professional job for the customer, people don't mind spending the money.

Isn't it worth a few extra bucks to hire citizens and legal immigrants to retile your bathroom? Or if you are really ambitious and have the time, turn it into a fun house project. News flash: most of America still does its own gardening! Be part of the solution and ask your contractor about his workers' status. If you don't get a satisfactory answer, ask more questions.

> # NAILS ON A CHALKBOARD!
>
>))) "Family values don't stop at the Rio Grande."[25]
>
> **—George W. Bush**

We retain our cultural identity as a nation and our integrity on a personal level when we take proactive steps to ensure that those who work for us are living here legally. Yes, for some, this may mean giving up some conveniences. Getting your lawn mowed legally might become more expensive. You might pay more for dinner at a restaurant if the owners no longer hired illegals at absurdly low wages to fill your water glasses and mop the floor. But regular Americans can start to make a dent in the problem of illegal immigration by reducing the incentives for illegal immigration. I'm for reducing our dependence on foreign oil *and* foreign illegal workers.

))) A Fight Worth Fighting

We must continue to press our elected officials to carry out their duty to protect and defend the United States of America. Our recent victory against elites pushing amnesty is only temporary. The opposition will regroup and we must be ready. Without our borders we become just one North American union of people without a core language or tradition. Eliminating the incentives we have dangled in front of illegals for decades is a key element of the battle to securing our own future. Each one of us must use every lawful means at our disposal to defend this country from becoming just a figure on the global balance sheet.

We need to remind our children—and ourselves—that America is a unique and wonderful country that we are blessed to call home. Civic duty demands we question and challenge our government, charity demands we treat foreigners with care and respect, and tolerance demands we be respectful to other nations. But patriotism, too, is a virtue.

It's too easy to take America for granted. It's also harmful. What's wrong with being unapologetically in love with being an American? Nothing at all. In fact, often it takes a new (and legal) immigrant to remind us of this. On one particularly cold and rainy day in New York City recently, I hailed a cab driven by an Ethiopian man in his fifties. He was beaming with a friendly demeanor. "Why are you in such a good mood?" I asked. "Why shouldn't I be?" he laughed.

> # POWER TO AMERICAN VOICES
>
>))) Laura,
>
> I suggest that we replace every elected official in Congress with an illegal alien because I've heard it said that they will do the work that American citizens won't do.
>
> Damon S.
>
> Lincoln, NE

"I just got my green card and live in the best country in the world!" He played by the rules and was thrilled to be here. That made me smile.

» » » CHAPTER **3**

PROTECTING THE PEOPLE

It was just past nine o'clock in the morning. I had finished up my usual routine on the stationary bike and was heading toward the weight room, when my cell phone rang. It was my brother Curtis calling from California.

"Are you watching the news?" He sounded panicked.

"I was just watching the *Today* show—if you can call that news."

"Go look at the television. A plane crashed into the World Trade Center."

Five seconds later I stood there covered in sweat, transfixed by the images that had stunned the nation. Before hanging up, I muttered, "Curtis, they're going to hit here (D.C.) next."

I remember standing there in disbelief as so many of my fellow gym members just kept on exercising.

"Do you realize what this is? This is huge," I said to a few of the twenty-somethings on the elliptical trainers. One young woman rolled her eyes. The other motioned to her headphones. She was watching MTV. How could the billowing smoke, the red flames, and the chaos being reported on the ground not cause every American to stop what he was doing and take notice?

By the time I arrived home, the second tower had been hit along with the Pentagon. Local news stations were reporting that all major roads into and out of Washington had been shut down, so I hopped on my mountain bike for the twenty-minute ride to the Pentagon. It was one of those beautiful end-of-summer mornings, tinged with the crispness of fall. It felt eerie to be pedaling in the middle of Rock Creek Parkway, normally a busy commuter roadway, and then onto Route 110, an interstate that was totally empty except for me and a few pedestrians.

About twenty of us, on foot and on bikes stopped at an exit ramp off the freeway. The firefighters were nowhere near getting the flames under control and thick, black smoke rose into the air. Federal employees who had walked all the way from their offices downtown, a family of tourists from Kansas City (who were totally freaking), and a punked-out bike messenger all stood watching in silence. A few of us tried to get closer but police had already set up a barrier. We all wanted to do something but there was nothing we could do. I don't think I have ever felt more helpless in my life.

I tried to reach my radio show producer on the cell phone, when suddenly two huge military helicopters appeared out of nowhere. The sound was deafening. The powerful blade rotation caused a tornado of dirt and debris to swirl up in the air around me. At that moment, there was no doubt in my mind: we were at war.

Recall how you felt on September 11. Amid grief for victims and anger at the murderers, most Americans wondered where and when the next plane would hit. Were hidden bombs set to go off in cities across America? Would this happen again tomorrow? The following Tuesday?

The first aftershock came only a week later, when the first of the anthrax attacks happened. Five people were killed, seventeen were left seriously ill, and post offices, mail rooms, and government buildings had to be fumigated. Everyday Americans were left wondering if opening the mail could be a fatal event.

A year later, everyone within commuting distance of Washington, D.C., was gripped with fear and anger during the three-week killing spree of snipers John Allen Muhammad and Lee Boyd Malvo. While police lacked even a suspect and chased an imaginary white van, the snipers killed ten people, wounded five more, and left taunting messages reading: "Your children are not safe anywhere at any time." Public schools in D.C. and the surrounding counties cancelled their outdoor athletic events, nearly erasing the 2002 high school football season in the area. People were afraid to pump their own gas or go shopping.

We felt powerless.

Imagine if jihadist suicide bombers hit dozens of multiplex movie theaters next week and killed hundreds or thousands of Americans from Manchester, New Hampshire, to Medford, Oregon? Would you be itching to go out on the town with your friends? What if "individual jihadists" penetrated security at public schools across the nation? Would parents want to send their children to school?

The single most important, and most legitimate, role of government is to defend its people and its soil. A people without security cannot ever be truly free.

When terrorists strike, they kill dozens or hundreds or thousands, but they also disrupt the lives of millions. Let's face it, if we suffer another massive attack on U.S. soil, the last thing that the American people will want is to waste time with some protracted debate about "protecting civil liberties."

While border enforcement is the front-line in the war against the Islamic radicals, we will not be secure if we only focus on the homefront. Our government also needs to pursue a foreign policy that is relentlessly and solely directed at keeping America safe.

Unfortunately, many of our politicians and scribblers have other uses in mind for our soldiers, sailors, Marines, and airmen. Most on the Left cringe at the idea of an American foreign policy dedicated to protecting American lives by whatever means necessary. Many people, ranging from Hollywood moguls to conservative columnists, want our military to use its might to spread democracy around the planet or keep oppressive governments in line the world over. Some corporate leaders believe our foreign policy should be subject to their economic interests rather than the interests of American security.

It will take hard work to ensure that in the future our foreign policy is grounded in a simple principle: protecting Americans.

When to Fight?

Seven years ago, then presidential candidate Governor George W. Bush had it right. After eight years of President Clinton's slashing the defense and intelligence budget (the so-called "peace dividend"), and deploying American troops on humanitarian missions around the world, it was time to redefine America's defense and foreign policy.

In his second debate with Al Gore in 2000, Bush stated clearly what his guiding light would be: "First question is what's in the best interests of the United States? What's in the best interests of our people? When it comes to foreign policy that will be my guiding question. Is it in our nation's interests?"

On the Clintonian brand of feel-good foreign policy, Bush didn't mince words: "I don't think our troops ought to be used for what's called nation-building. I think our troops ought to be used to fight and win war. I think our troops ought to be used to help overthrow the dictator when it's in our best interests." Although recognizing the "horrible situation" in Rwanda, Bush reminded us that it is unwise to deploy our military when regional powers are better equipped to address the problem:

> We need to use our influence to have countries in Africa come together and help deal with the situation. The administration...made the right decision on training Nigerian troops for situations just such as this in Rwanda, and so I thought they made the right decision not to send U.S. troops into Rwanda.[1]

Then governor Bush articulated the proper (and conservative) approach to foreign policy, although I would have preferred even more bluntness. Our president ought to use our military for the sole purpose of fighting and winning battles that will make Americans safer from terrorists or enemy nations. We should unleash our military wherever such force can reduce a threat to American safety, but we ought to use our military *only* in the service of American safety.

A few months earlier, the journal *Foreign Affairs* ran an article by a former Bush "41" National Security Council staffer named Condoleezza Rice. The piece argued that our government ought to unabashedly pursue a foreign policy dedicated to serving "the national interest," even if this earns us labels of "isolationist."[2]

Rice, who was also candidate Bush's foreign policy advisor, criticized the Clinton administration for "a loss of focus on the mission of the armed forces." Rice's words in this article are an excellent articulation of a sound foreign policy:

> The president must remember that the military is a special instrument. It is lethal, and it is meant to be. It is not a civilian police force. It is not a political referee. And it is most certainly not designed to build a civilian society. Military force is best used to support clear political goals, whether limited, such as expelling Saddam from Kuwait, or comprehensive, such as demanding the unconditional surrender of Japan and Germany during World War II.... U.S. intervention in... "humanitarian" crises should be, at best, exceedingly rare.
>
> This does not mean that the United States must ignore humanitarian and civil conflicts around the world. But the military cannot be involved everywhere. Often, these tasks might be better carried out by regional actors, as modeled by the Australian-led intervention in East Timor. The U.S. might be able to lend financial, logistical, and intelligence support. Sometimes tough, competent diplomacy in the beginning can prevent the need for military force later. Using the American armed forces as the world's "9-1-1" will degrade capabilities, bog soldiers down in peacekeeping roles, and fuel concern among other great powers that the United States has decided to enforce notions of "limited sovereignty" worldwide in the name of humanitarianism. This overly broad definition of America's national interest is bound to backfire as others arrogate the same authority to themselves. Or we will find ourselves looking to the United Nations to sanction the use of American military power in these cases, implying that we will do so even when our vital interests are involved, which would also be a mistake.[3]

Makes you want to stand up and cheer, right? The Bush White House in 2007 sounds very different from the Bush campaign in 2000. His administration often speaks as if the U.S. military's role is chiefly to make life better for the Iraqis or the Afghans, rather than for American citizens. Mostly, he speaks of our war efforts in high and lofty tones, detached from the simple idea of protecting American lives. A favorite line of his is: "Freedom is the Almighty God's gift to every person, every man and woman who lives in this world."[4]

That is a beautiful sentiment, but if we see our role as its enforcer, then every repressive dictatorship is fair game for U.S. military involvement. When Saddam Hussein was captured, President Bush told America that "Justice was being delivered to a man who denied that gift from the Almighty to the people of Iraq."[5] It sounded like we were carrying out a global justice campaign.

And while it is obviously true that Saddam had violated sixteen UN Security Council resolutions,[6] that particular justification for going to war is also problematic in hindsight. I myself am guilty of repeating the obligatory "he violated UN Resolution 1441 and many other resolutions, too" line. Yet many of us don't trust the UN or respect its mandates. The point was that we Americans thought our nation's security was at risk with Saddam in power. The fact that the UN passed resolutions it never intended to enforce is beside the point.

Americans are the most compassionate, most generous people on earth. Through private giving and foreign aid, America gives more to global humanitarian efforts than any other nation.[7] We are the opposite of the stingy stereotype that America trash-talkers love to perpetuate. We believe that it is no coincidence that our free enterprise system, Judeo-Christian values, dedication to liberty, and representative democracy have yielded the most prosperous and powerful nation in the world. We agree that with this power comes some responsibility. But most of us are very uneasy about sending our soldiers, sailors, airmen, and Marines to fight wars for purely humanitarian reasons. And we certainly do not want to wage such "feel good" wars just because the UN wants us to or in order to spread democracy and build up other nations.

Our military is filled with talented and dedicated people with wide-ranging skills, but what it does best is protect and defend America. That sometimes requires killing a lot of bad guys. In Iraq, we have asked our military to be all things to all people. When I was in Baghdad in February 2006 with the army's 4th Infantry Division, I witnessed a twenty-three-year-old female West Point graduate in a meeting with a local mayor where she was part soldier, part diplomat, and part reconstruction project coordinator. The young lieutenant was the consummate professional, but I wondered whether this was too much to expect from our fine soldiers.

My concern grew worse a year later when top military officials reported complaints from the field to the president and the defense secretary. According to the *New York Times*: "Among particular complaints, the officers cited a request from the office of Secretary of State Condoleezza Rice that military personnel temporarily fill more than one-third of 350 new State Department jobs in Iraq that are to be created under the new strategy."[8] In other words, Rice would turn full-time soldiers into full-time diplomats.

Most Americans supported the Iraq war at the outset, because they thought it would harm the ability of our enemies to kill Americans. If Saddam Hussein *was* in possession of stockpiles of weapons of mass destruction, we wanted our military to prevent the possibility of their being used against us. After September 11 most of us believed that we had to deal with serious threats to America's security before they dealt with us. Yet very early on, the Bush administration drifted away from the rationale that this was a war of preemptive self-defense to a discussion of more abstract ideals. We saw this new rhetoric on full display in President Bush's second inaugural address, where he said that the goal of his foreign policy would be "to seek and support the growth of democratic movements and institutions in every nation and culture." Other high-minded but nebulous declarations included, "America's belief in human dignity will guide our policies."

In his second term, we heard more of the same "freedom is on the march" descriptions of what was happening in Iraq, yet the public began turning away from the war. In the eyes of many Americans, the only thing marching was the Mahdi Army. While the media broadcast images of death and destruction in Iraq, the White House wasn't making the case that would justify the sacrifices of our troops and tax dollars. We needed to hear exactly how this war was making us safer.

Instead, we got talk of "staying the course" in order to secure a stable Iraqi democracy. We were told that the war was working because Iraqi girls are going to school for the first time and because purple-thumbed Iraqis were voting in huge numbers. These were noble successes, but the rhetoric often made Iraq sound like a humanitarian campaign. When we needed a concrete understanding of the threat posed by a failed effort in Iraq, we too often heard abstractions.

And when we don't get abstractions from the Republican leadership, we get shameful publicity stunts from the Democrats. A low point in the debate about Iraq came in late July 2007 when Majority

YOUNG BRITS IN LOVE... WITH JIHAD

》》》 A 2007 poll of Muslims in Britain revealed that younger Muslims are more radical and hard-core than their parents. The U.K.'s *Guardian* reported that 37 percent of sixteen- to twenty-four-year-olds said they would prefer living under Sharia law, while only 17 percent of their elders over the age of fifty-five agreed with them. About one-third of the young Muslims polled supported the death penalty for Muslims who convert to other religions.

Source: Stephen Bates and agencies, "More Young Muslims Back Sharia, Says Poll," *The Guardian*, Monday, January 29, 2007.

Leader Harry Reid presided over an all-night "Defeat-a-thon," in an attempt to force a troop withdrawal from Iraq in by the following Spring. One after another, Democrats and a few wobbly Republicans, stood up and waved the white flag for the world to see. From Senators Barbara Boxer and Ted Kennedy we heard that the best way to protect America is to retreat from Iraq—the place that bin Laden himself described as the "central front" of al Qaeda's war against the infidels. The high drama came when Senate staffers rolled cots into a Senate conference room for the tired lawmakers. Well, the good news is that American voters seem to have grown tired of *them*. Their approval ratings hovered in the low 20s.

So while Republicans need to better define our national security interests in Iraq and around the world, the Democrats have shown they haven't a clue what the phrase "national security" even means!

The Enemies List

It seems obvious, but it's a point often lost in the political ether: we need to know our enemies in order to defeat them.

❱❱❱ Number One: The Islamic Jihadists

Our chief enemies are the Islamic jihadists who have been attacking America for nearly thirty years, ever since Iranian "students" seized our embassy in Tehran in 1979, and held Americans hostage for 444 days. They attacked our Marine barracks in Lebanon in 1983 (killing 241);[9] they blew up our embassies in Kenya and Tanzania in 1998 (killing 257);[10] they drove a boat filled with explosives into the hull of the USS *Cole* in 2001 (killing seventeen);[11] and of course, they tried to take down the World Trade Center in 1993 (killing six)—all this happened before the September 11 attacks that killed more than 3,000 people.[12] And since September 11, they have conducted terrorist attacks in Bali, Jakarta, Istanbul, Madrid, London, Delhi, Amman, and Somalia, not to mention Iraq, Afghanistan, and elsewhere, spreading death and suffering around the world.

The jihadists fight for nothing less than Islamic conquest of the world—a global caliphate. In August of 1996, Osama bin Laden issued a "Declaration of War Against the Americans Who Occupy [Saudi Arabia]."[13] A few months later, he said the following:

> We declared jihad against the U.S. government, because the U.S. government is unjust, criminal, and tyrannical. It has committed acts that are extremely unjust, hideous, and criminal whether directly or through its support of the Israeli occupation.
>
> For this and other acts of aggression and injustice, we have declared jihad against the U.S., because in our religion it is our duty to make jihad so that God's word is the one exalted to the heights and so that we drive the Americans away from all Muslim countries.[14]

While bin Laden, a Sunni, does not speak for the entire Muslim world, his sectarian rivals seem to be reading from the same chapter. In August 2006, thousands of Shiites, inspired by cleric Moqtada al-Sadr, marched through Baghdad chanting, "Death to America! Death to Israel!"[15] In February 2006, when I visited the Karrada neighborhood of Baghdad, there were murals galore honoring the corpulent, America-hating al-Sadr. I could almost smell him.

Anti-Western propaganda has been a staple of the Islamic world long before the rise of al-Sadr. Sadly, many young Muslims were raised to hate all things American or related to America. On the fifth anniversary of September 11, al Jazeera conducted an unscientific online poll that asked viewers "Do you support Osama bin Laden?"

Again, it was just an online poll, but it's still disturbing that 49.9 percent of respondents answered "yes."[16]

Similarly, a year after the July 7, 2005, subway bombing in London, Britain's Channel 4 news asked British Muslims what they thought of the bombings.[17] Nearly a quarter of those surveyed said that the British government's support of the wars in Iraq and Afghanistan justified the July 7 subway attacks. Meanwhile, 45 percent believe that an American-Israeli conspiracy brought about the September 11 attacks.

Things seem to be getting worse, not better. Even among Muslims who were born and raised in Europe, we see a disturbing surge of radicalism. The Pew Global Attitudes Survey in mid-2006 found "roughly one-in-seven Muslims in France, Spain and Great Britain feel that suicide bombings against civilian targets can at least sometimes be justified to defend Islam."[18]

In the same Pew Global Attitudes survey, we see that these radical attitudes are not confined to any one country or region, but are a major force in the Islamic world:

> ❯ 44 percent of Nigerian Muslims believe suicide attacks are "often" or "sometimes" justified (only 28 percent said they were never justified). Bin Laden is more popular than ever there—61 percent of Muslims expressed some confidence in him, up 17 percent from three years earlier.
> ❯ Fewer than half of Jordan's Muslims believe terror attacks are never justified.
> ❯ Only 45 percent of Egyptian Muslims say terror is never justified.
> ❯ Although confidence in Osama bin Laden is decreasing throughout most of the Muslim world, still 25 percent of Jordanians, a third of Indonesians, and 38 percent of Pakistanis all expressed some degree of confidence in him.

If these surveys are accurate, then we have a major problem on our hands: potentially more than 100 million Muslims worldwide support jihad against the West.

While American Muslims are far more assimilated and comfortable living in a Western culture, there is even reason to be concerned here. According to another Pew survey, approximately one-quarter of all young American Muslims believe that suicide bombing is sometimes justified.[19] This adds up to hundreds of thousands living here who approve of this horrific tactic where innocents are usually killed in the name of Allah. Disturbing? You bet it is.

❱ ❱ ❱ Number Two: The States of Terror

Of course most terror organizations would be nowhere were it not for the funding and support they receive from their state sponsors. Hezbollah and Hamas—two of the world's most deadly terrorist groups—are financed by Iran and Syria. The diminutive Mahmoud Ahmadinejad, the Iranian president who delights in defying American, European, and UN demands that he stop his nuclear pursuits, predicts a future without the United States or Israel. In 2006, he traveled to the Grand Mosque in Jakarta, Indonesia, and after praying declared, "my brothers, Islam will be the victor and tyranny will be defeated," inspiring some in the crowd to chant "Fight America! Fight Israel!"[20] Ahmadinejad's proclaimed longing for the "Twelfth Imam," is interpreted by many as a wish to induce Armageddon.

The Syrian government, in turn, serves as a lackey to Iran. In March 2005, CIA director Porter Goss testified to the Senate Armed Services Committee that the Syrian government had not been cooperative with American efforts to find al Qaeda terrorists hiding in Syria.[21] More to the point, it is beyond dispute that both Syria and Iran are aiding the insurgency in Iraq.

〉〉〉 Enemy Number Three . . .

There are many rivals for this coveted position. Could it be Venezuela's own cross between Fidel Castro and Mahmoud Ahmadinejad, Hugo Chavez? Could it be former KGB colonel Vladimir Putin who goes fishing with the president one day, then seems eager to renew the Cold War the next? What about the platform-boot-wearing megalomaniac Kim Jong-il, who is forever promising that North Korea will behave in return for money? That's a rogue's gallery big enough to concern any great power, but we face a potentially even more dangerous threat in Communist China.

China is the thousand-pound dragon in the room. Our politicians, businessmen, and media like to tell us that China is reforming: its economy is booming; it's a major trade partner and a huge potential market place; its diplomats are helping us talk Kim Jong-il down from the ledge. But it is foolhardy and dangerous to forget that China is also racing to militarize space, rapidly increasing its defense spending, and expanding its navy.

When asked about these alarming developments, Vice President Dick Cheney said, "[T]hey are not consistent with China's stated goal of a peaceful rise."[22] You don't say!

President Bush has pledged to defend Taiwan if China were to attack it. In July 2005, Chinese General Zhu Chengu was asked by an American reporter what would happen if the United States defended Taiwan: "If the Americans draw their missiles and position-guided ammunition on to the target zone on China's territory, I think we will have to respond with nuclear weapons. . . . Americans will have to be prepared that hundreds of, or two hundreds of, or even more cities will be destroyed by the Chinese."[23]

The reporter tried to give General Zhu a way out:

> Presumably, I suggested, he was only talking about the unlikely scenario of a U.S. attack on mainland Chinese soil.

No, the general replied, a nuclear response would be justified even if it was just a conventional attack on a Chinese aircraft or warship—something very likely if Washington honored its commitment to help defend Taiwan against an invasion by Beijing.

A fellow correspondent offered Gen. Zhu another escape route, reminding him that China had a longstanding policy of no first use of nuclear weapons. But the general brushed that aside as well, saying the policy could be changed and was only really intended to apply to conflicts with non-nuclear states in any case.[24]

Some China experts assure us that General Zhu, at the time a dean at China's National Defense University, is outside of the mainstream of the Chinese military. Still, Zhu simply said more directly what the official newspaper of China's army had printed in 2000—a warning to the United States that China "has certain abilities of launching strategic counterattack and the capacity of launching a long-distance strike."[25]

Aside from China's direct threats to America, the Chinese military is a notorious dealer in missiles, chemical weapons, biological weapons, and nuclear weapon technology. In 2003, Paula A. DeSutter from the State Department's Office of Arms Control and International Studies testified before the U.S.-China Commission that, "Chinese entities' record of transferring WMD and missile technologies, and the record of the Chinese government's enforcement of its own laws and regulations to stem these transfers, remains unsatisfactory."[26] In plain English: China is one of the world's biggest arms dealers.

A Congressional Research Service report[27] lists Chinese sales of missiles and nuclear weapons materials to Iran and Pakistan, including sales to the notorious criminal Pakistani nuclear scientist A.Q. Khan, who has personally helped arm Iran, North Korea, and Libya.

The Bush administration, like the Clinton administration before it, knows all this. Yet many of our politicians still live in wishful-thinking-land. Dick Cheney, after expressing concern about China's military build-up, added, "We hope China will join in our efforts to prevent deployment and proliferation of deadly technologies, whether in Asia or the Middle East." Right.

After their dalliances with the nuclear programs of Pakistan and Iran throughout the 1990s, these days China's leaders are cozying up to Sudan's brutal Islamic regime. China's president Hu Jintao visited the Sudanese government responsible for the slaughter of hundreds of thousands in Darfur, and proceeded to extend an interest-free loan to the government to build a presidential palace. He also reportedly forgave all of Sudan's debt.[28] Why would the Chinese government make such an overture to Sudan? One word: oil. China is Sudan's largest oil customer, and also its biggest source of weapons. According to the *Washington Post*, "Chinese-made tanks, fighter planes, bombers, helicopters, machine guns, and rocket-propelled grenades have intensified Sudan's two-decade-old north-south civil war."[29] Remember, our government has accused Sudan of genocide, and Sudan is where Osama bin Laden once had a safe haven. Now China is heavily invested there.

There's No Such Thing as a Free-Trade Lunch

So, if China is our enemy, why do we trade with it? The most obvious answer is: money. Our companies are making their officers and shareholders tons of money investing in China. Plus, our government likes that China buys so much of our debt. Meanwhile, the American consumers love to buy cheap Chinese-made goods. Beyond the money factor, many American politicians, businessmen, and journalists believe that the more China buys and sells with

America, the freer and more democratic, and thus pro-American the government will become. In the words of Dan Griswold, director of the libertarian Cato Institute Center for Trade Policy Studies, "Peace on Earth? Try Free Trade among Men."[30] But columnist Sebastian Mallaby, as avid a free-trade globalist as you're likely to find, wondered whether our trade policy with China was really encouraging a more open society there, given its recent overtures to despotic African countries:

> What does China's policy towards Sudan say about the West's policy towards China? The West is engaging with China on the theory that economic modernisation will bring political modernisation as well; otherwise, the West would merely be assisting the development of a communist adversary. China's Sudan policy is an assertion that this link between economic and political modernisation is by no means inevitable, even in the extreme case. You can construct oil refineries, educate scientists, build ambitious new railways—and simultaneously pursue a policy of genocide.[31]

In theory, it sounds good—the more money China makes, the wealthier its people will become, the greater access its people will have to Western goods, and perhaps the more open they will be to our ideas about freedom and the rule of law. Yet in China this has simply not been the case. In fact, the more the Chinese economy grows, the more powerful the Communist Party of China becomes, because so many Chinese businesses are owned by the Communist Party and the generals of the People's Liberation Army. And consider China's recent moves to enact stricter controls over Internet access, or its continued persecution of dissidents. Are the American corporate profits and the faint hope of liberalizing China worth the costs to American security when our companies sell China technologies that can be used for military purposes? You might remember the

CHEAP GOODS, TAINTED GOODS

〉〉〉 Maybe we should all seriously consider the wisdom of the old-fashioned "Buy American" exhortation now that we have reason to run from China's exports. In a range of products from toothpaste to tuna, China is flooding the U.S. with cheap, yet dangerous goods. Even our children and pets aren't safe. If Fido isn't poisoned by contaminated Chinese pet food, then Little Billy could get lead poisoning from Chinese-made Thomas the Tank Engine trains and Sally hurt by their faulty Easy-Bake (Burn!) Ovens.

Clinton era when China stole advanced military technology from the United States. These days, however, China doesn't have to steal the technology, because it can buy most anything it wants. And it was the Clinton administration that made that possible.

When President Clinton shifted enforcement of export controls from the State Department to the Commerce Department, the business community was delighted.[32] Between 1998 and 2000, Loral Space Technologies, Hughes Electronics, and Lockheed Martin were all investigated for violating export controls in ways that helped China militarize. According to the Congressional Research Service, Loral and Hughes:

> ...allegedly shared their findings with China on the cause of a rocket's explosion while launching a U.S.-origin satellite in February 1996. The companies are said to have provided expertise that China could use to improve the accuracy and reliability of its future ballistic missiles, including their guidance systems. At least three classified studies reportedly found that U.S. national security was harmed.[33]

That harm is carried forward today. China is currently militarizing space. On January 11, 2007, China tested weapons capable of shooting down satellites, trying them out on their own satellites.[34]

The Chinese government has made it clear that they want to be the dominant force in Asia. Everything happening in China today indicates that China wants to join the superpower club—and kick us out in the process.

The People's Liberation Army has pursued building an aircraft carrier over the last two decades, although that project has from time to time been sidelined so that the PLA could instead develop nuclear submarines.[35] Yes, I said nuclear submarines.

The notion that a huge and increasingly powerful China, which was once an empire, will inevitably become more open and less militaristic because it does some business deals with big American corporations and has a huge market for its goods in the U.S., is as naïve as the liberal hope that al Qaeda would leave us alone if we cut off foreign aid to Israel. Remember the old line from Lenin that "the capitalists will sell us the rope with which we will hang them"? Will more of us buy products with a "Made in the USA" label rather than sell the Chinese Communists any more rope?

Returning *POWER TO THE PEOPLE*

❱ ❱ ❱ A Security Policy for All

Presidents and lawmakers, of necessity, surround themselves with foreign policy experts, a class that includes career diplomats, globe-trotting intellectuals, and cosmopolitan activists. It's easy for anyone in such a position to get sucked into the clever, overly ambitious, "bigger-picture" plans that are popular in such circles.

We the people must bring our leaders back to Earth. In our dangerous world, we must demand that our foreign policy stay focused entirely on keeping America safe. This requires enforcing our borders, keeping would-be terrorists out, and arresting or killing those we know are plotting to kill us.

As part of that effort, we must knock down unnecessary obstacles that make it harder for our counter-terrorism personnel to operate effectively. This means resisting the efforts of so-called civil rights groups that challenge our monitoring and enforcement methods that have proven track records. The terrorists are technologically astute and adaptive to changing circumstances, which means that we must constantly look for new ways to follow the flow of information, money, and weapons that may be used against us in the future. We will win some and lose some in court, but we must not roll over for the American Civil Liberties Union and the Council on American Islamic Relations, neither of whom have ever met an anti-terror law they liked.

Our intelligence and law enforcement officers work around the clock to break up terror cells before their plans are carried out, and they need every tool we can give them. They have penetrated terror networks in New Jersey, Buffalo, Seattle, Portland, Northern Virginia, and Florida.[36] But what if, because of legal restrictions, they had not intercepted the home-grown terrorists in Florida who were plotting to blow up the Sears Tower in Chicago? This cell, broken up in 2006, had pledged to wage a "full ground war" against the United States.[37] There are undoubtedly many other groups plotting many other acts of terrorism. Our intelligence officers and law enforcement officials need every available weapon to stop them before they strike.

Discovering and disrupting a terror cell requires more than hard work and flexible strategies, it also requires human intelligence and an engaged public. One on-the-ball video store clerk alerted the Feds to the "Fort Dix Six" who were planning to attack the New Jersey military base. American Muslims have reported suspicious activity to authorities about members of their own community. We must encourage and applaud their patriotism.

Much has been written by former intelligence officials about what is broken in our intelligence agencies. There is no need to rehash that here. And I realize that systemic change of any bureaucracy does not happen overnight. But how is it that in fall 2006, only thirty-three of 12,000 FBI agents nationwide had even a limited understanding of Arabic?[38] Some progress has been made in recruiting translators who work with the FBI, yet the numbers of critical language speakers are still far too low to sift through the information that's out there. How many untranslated transcripts sit in untouched stacks at the NSA, CIA, or FBI? And how many of those contain valuable information that could thwart a future attack on the United States? If we need to pay more to attract Arabic and Farsi speakers, then we should do so. If we need to pay bonuses to agents who become proficient in both, we should do that too. If we need to give incentives for students to study these languages in college and then work for the federal government, we should make the investment. We either pay now or we will pay later—perhaps with a terror attack that makes September 11 seem tame.

⟩⟩⟩ Military Expansion

It's time for all of us to admit that the Clinton slash-and-burn downsizing of our military was a huge mistake. The Soviet Union might be gone, but other threats have taken its place. Given the nature and scope of the threats we face today from terrorists, state sponsors of terror, and traditional power rivals like Russia, China, and North Korea, we must increase the size of our military. The pre–September 11 Rumsfeldian idea of "streamlining" of our armed forces is absurd given the variety of threats we face in the twenty-first century. Today we spend a paltry 3.8 percent of our Gross Domestic Product on military spending. By contrast, during World War II we spent up to 37.8 percent of GDP on our military.[39] Even during the Carter administration, we spent almost a percentage point more than we do today. Smart people such as former Missouri senator Jim Talent believe that the current situation is dire and that we need to invest more now in our military in order to meet our defense obligations for future generations. In a report for the Heritage Foundation he proposed a "4 percent for Freedom Solution," which is a mere two-tenths of a percent rise from current military spending levels.[40] Surely we can afford that. We must.

Our long, difficult engagements in Iraq and Afghanistan have taken a terrible toll not only on our troops, but also on the equipment they use and the planes and helicopters they fly in. Repair and replacement costs, new weapons systems, medical care for our injured heroes, and our ongoing commitments around the globe require that we spend more.

An increase in spending will also allow us to expand the actual size of the military, which we also need to do. Multiple deployments, extended deployments, and our increasing reliance on the Reserves and National Guard have placed an inordinate burden on our military and their families. Sharp military analysts believe that an expansion of *at least* 60,000 troops is necessary. That would bring the number of troops from 513,000 to approximately 573,000. This expansion would ultimately help retention rates, too, as more of our troops would be sharing the burden.

〉〉〉 There's No Place Like the Home Front

At this point, many of you are asking—what can one person do? The threats are myriad. The challenges facing our country daunting. The simple answer is that one person can do a lot. Obviously, military service—active duty, the National Guard, and the Reserves—are all noble pursuits. There isn't one of my friends who served in the military who doesn't treasure the experience. Skills are learned. Friendships made. Personal responsibility encouraged. Love of country instilled.

Yet there are important ways to contribute as civilians, too. Simply being vigilant, keeping our eyes open for suspicious or strange activity, is standing up for the homeland. Remember the passengers on that US Airways Minneapolis flight who alerted airline personnel to the strange behavior of the "Flying Imams"? The Muslim clerics ended up suing the airline and the Metropolitan Airport Commission for "unspecified damages"! Only in our litigious society could this happen. What a joke. Congress has since moved to shield passengers from such suits.

We should also encourage our young people to serve the nation's intelligence community by gaining fluency in critical foreign languages. (As a student toward the end of the Cold War, I studied Russian and did a semester abroad in Leningrad. I thought I might work for the CIA or—of all places—at the UN!)

As Americans it is our civic duty to encourage patriotism and love of country in our younger generations. If our citizens do not learn to appreciate our blessings as Americans, we should not expect them to do much to protect the homefront. America is not just a place where we make a living, raise our families, and shop. It is our country—and yes, it is a "shining city on a hill."

We can do more, each of us, to speak up for the "American culture." Many elites will describe this as myopic and naïve given the wonders of multiculturalism. Nonsense! We have accomplished great things as a nation and everyone living here should be conversant about all the good we have done in our relatively short history. Unfortunately, the "blame America" crowd will never go away. We should start our own "love America" response. We are not perfect, but we are still "man's last, best hope." That's not pride speaking. That's the truth.

We cannot—nor should we want to—change our way of life in order to make our enemies like us more. In February 2007, former British prime minister Tony Blair, warned the House of Commons against the self-loathing tendencies of his critics, saying "We will beat [the terrorists], in my view, when we realize that it's not our fault they're doing it. We shouldn't apologize [heckling]. . . . No,

I'm sorry, we should not apologize for our values, for what we believe in, or what we do."

The Left likes to talk about "root causes" of terrorist attacks. They say that if we take the time to learn and address the terrorists' grievances, we can stop them from attacking us. This approach would work if they were attacking us for mispronouncing their names or for subsidizing pork imports into their countries. In truth, the terrorists hate us for too many reasons for us to "address" these root causes in any meaningful way.

Read Osama bin Laden's own words. In his fatwa shortly after September 11, his list of grievances includes: our blockade against Saddam Hussein's regime, Israel's use of force against the Palestinians, the bombing of Hiroshima and Nagasaki, the very existence of Israel, and our troop presence in Saudi Arabia.[41] His 1998 fatwa (the one that read "We—with Allah's help—call on every Muslim who believes in Allah and wishes to be rewarded to comply with Allah's order to kill the Americans and plunder their money wherever and whenever they find it") listed even more reasons to hate America and the West, including our influence over Muslim states such as Saudi Arabia, Egypt, and Jordan.[42] His 1996 fatwa included charges that our economy was built on lending and borrowing, and our use of alcohol.[43]

Excuse me a moment while I pour another glass of cabernet....

As long as we are the most prosperous country in a world of scarcity, as long as we are predominantly Christian in a mostly non-Christian world, as long as we are tolerant in a world with armed fundamentalists, as long as we are the dominant cultural and military force on the planet, we will continue to be a target. No true American would ever want to abandon any of these things in the hope that to do so would make us safer. There is nothing wrong with America pursuing an *American* agenda. It is not naïve to be patriotic and believe that America really is the best nation on earth.

We should carry ourselves with humility, yet be proud of what we have been able to accomplish in only 230-plus years.

And we must not fall into the politically correct complacency that turned Britain into a breeding ground for Islamic hate. This means that we must not shy away from investigating the activities of private groups—including mosques and "humanitarian" groups when warranted. We must also ensure that our prisons remain houses of incarceration, not houses of radical Islamic indoctrination. Muslim clerics operating in American prisons are winning over new converts at an alarming rate. Former FBI director Robert Mueller, in written testimony before Congress, warned that "Prisons continue to be fertile ground for extremists who exploit both a prisoner's conversion to Islam while still in prison, as well as their socio-economic status."[44] Suspected terrorist Jose Padilla converted to Islam when he was serving time for his gang-banging crimes, and thousands more convert each year. Since when does one have a constitutional right to be tutored in terrorist ideologies in prison? Expect that groups such as the Council on American-Islamic Relations will scream "discrimination" if curbs are placed on prison "ministries" that are actually covers for terror recruiting and radicalization. Too bad. If they were really concerned about the safety of all Americans, CAIR and their left-wing allies would commit themselves unconditionally to our fight against terrorism rather than making the job more difficult.

))) It *Is* About Whether We Win or Lose

Can America ever "win" the type of long struggle we are engaged in now? The answer is "yes." A victory over Islamic radicals won't look like other war-time surrenders, but it is still possible. Winning will require what we haven't demonstrated very much of lately— national unity. This doesn't mean that we don't make room for dissent or that we stifle criticism of our elected leaders. This means that we never give our enemies a reason to doubt that we as a nation are committed to total victory—whatever it takes. When I see the way our media, with sneering condescension, regularly cover our efforts to destroy terror networks, I think we are often our own worst enemy.

Before and during the Iraq war "surge" in 2007, American politicians (mostly Democrats), academics, the dinosaur media, and Hollywood dolts trashed the mission, declared our failure, and even heaped scorn upon our military leaders. Democrat House Speaker Nancy Pelosi called the war a "grotesque failure." Just as the surge was starting, Senate Majority Leader Harry Reid attacked General Peter Pace, the chairman of the joint chiefs, and declared the war "lost." Senate Democrats embarrassed themselves and us when they declared Iraq a lost cause during their inane all-night session in July 2007—more than a month before General David Petraeus delivered his assessment of the surge.

Think of what this cacophony sounds like to the insurgents in Iraq and al Qaeda's acolytes around the globe. From the beginning,

THERE WE GO AGAIN...
THE LESSONS OF REAGAN

》》》 The defense policy of the United States is based on a simple premise: The United States does not start fights. We will never be an aggressor. We maintain our strength in order to deter and defend against aggression—to preserve freedom and peace.... Our defensive strategy means we need military forces that can move very quickly, forces that are trained and ready to respond to any emergency. Every item in our defense program—our ships, our tanks, our planes, our funds for training and spare parts—is intended for one all-important purpose: to keep the peace.[45]

—Ronald Reagan

they must have felt that America's unity would only last so long and only if casualties were kept at a minimum. They must believe that they can try our patience and winnow down our resolve—that they can wait us out. And indeed, it sadly seems like this calculation is correct.

America's foreign policy and military strategy should be focused on one thing—protecting America and her allies. When we fight, we must fight to win. We must elect leaders who clearly understand this and are able to articulate what the stakes are in each conflict. If Americans don't see how money spent and lives sacrificed is keeping us safer here at home, they won't stick with it. A cynical and unsupportive electorate has a terribly demoralizing effect on our troops.

If the GOP doesn't catch on to this soon, the people will move over to the more conservative members of the Democratic Party, such as Virginia's freshman senator (and former Reagan Republican) James Webb. After President Bush's 2007 State of the Union address, Webb, a decorated Marine Corps combat veteran and former Secretary of the Navy, criticized the Iraq war, but not for Howard Dean-like reasons. (Webb's son Jimmy, also a Marine, is serving in Iraq.) Webb contended that Iraq has taken "our energy and attention away from the larger war against terrorism." When Senators Harry Reid or Chuck Schumer say something similar, they sound like politicians, but Webb looks like he'd have no hesitation killing as many terrorists as he personally could. After the president justifies his war with paeans to "the desire for liberty in the broader Middle East," and Iraq's adoption of "the most progressive, democratic constitution in the Arab world," Jim Webb replies by asking, in effect. *But how is this helping America?*

Of course, the counter-argument to Webb is that every jihadist we kill in Iraq is one less potential terrorist we have to worry about at home. Plus the fact that we have thwarted so many plots in this country shows that staying on the offense makes sense. Yet, sadly, we consistently lose the PR battles at home and abroad critical to winning the war.

Traditionally, Republicans have had the reputation as the "Daddy Party" that will keep you safe. If Republicans—those currently in the White House and those seeking to reside there—don't bring the rhetoric and strategy of our wars back to protecting Americans' security, the Democrats could become the new father figure.

The Cold War showed us that Americans *can* persevere through a long fight if we understand what's at stake and how we will ultimately prevail. We were blessed, in Ronald Reagan, with a leader who could clearly explain how his defense policies would deter the Soviet threat, along with why the Soviets were a threat in the first place. Reagan basically ignored the wailing of everyone who was against him—the American media, the university professors, Hollywood do-gooders, the European intellectuals, and the liberals on Capitol Hill. They were all horrified by "Ronnie Ray-gun's" blunt rhetoric and even more so by his "peace through strength" strategy against the Soviet Union.

Reagan ignored the elites and put his trust in the American people, knowing that they were smart enough to see the world as it was, not as the utopianists wished it could be. He was frequently called a "warmonger" or a "tool of the military industrial complex" by the no-nukes gang, yet he didn't care as long as he connected with the American people. He had honed his anti-Soviet views during his years out of politics. In April 1978, Ronald Reagan described our enemy with stirring precision: "There is an evil influence throughout the world. In every one of the far-flung trouble spots, dig deep and you'll find the Soviet Union stirring a witches' brew, furthering its own imperialistic ambitions. If the Soviet Union would simply go home, much of the bloodshed in the world today would cease."[46]

Yes, I want to applaud every time I read that, too. We ache for such clarity and oratory today. Replace the words "Soviet Union" with "Islamic radicalism" and you would be accurately describing the main national security threat we face today. Indeed "much of the bloodshed in the world today would cease" if the Islamic terror networks "would simply go home." We must elect leaders who speak in such blunt terms. This is no time to sugarcoat the threats we face or use euphemistic language such as "the War on Terror," which lacks the power and the descriptive force of "the war against Islamic jihadists" or "Islamic extremists," or "Islamic fascists."

We are in an epic struggle against *Islamic* terrorists whose sole purpose in life is to make America bend to the wishes of a global Islamic state. In their warped thinking, the West will either *submit* or die. Our leaders must articulate it this way and fight the enemy accordingly. And while we fight the Islamists, we need to keep our guard up against other potential threats, whether they come from North Korea, China, or within our own country. And let us never forget that if we do not secure our own borders, the rest of our work will be for naught.

In his famous "Evil Empire" speech, Reagan said, "If history teaches anything, it teaches self-delusion in the face of unpleasant facts is folly."[47] There are a lot of unpleasant facts we must face today. We cannot afford to ignore them. Strength, determination, and a commitment to the values we hold dear, are in the end, our best hope for a peaceful world.

4

JUDGING THE JUDGES

"This morning, I'm proud to announce** *that I am nominating Harriet Ellan Miers to serve as associate justice of the Supreme Court."*[1]

Hearing those words from President George W. Bush just after eight o'clock in the morning on October 3, 2005, put me into a state of momentary shock. Conservatives had been waiting for vacancies on the Court, and this was an opportunity for President Bush to fill the seat of retiring justice Sandra Day O'Connor with a brilliant and experienced jurist who would be a strong force for originalism (faithfulness to the Constitution as written and as understood by its Framers) and judicial restraint (deciding cases based on the law as enacted by the people through their elected representatives, instead of based on the personal views and policy preferences of the judges themselves). There were several sitting federal appellate judges who fit that bill: J. Michael Luttig, Priscilla Owen, Janice Rogers Brown, and Samuel Alito, just to name a few.

Harriet Miers, White House counsel and longtime friend of President Bush, seemed like a nice, loyal, hardworking woman. But no one I respected who had clerked on the Court or argued before the Court thought she was even close to being qualified to serve as a justice. She had been "the first woman" to do this and that (managing partner at a large Texas law firm and chair of the Texas Bar Association), but she had not written any serious articles on constitutional law or demonstrated familiarity with Court precedents. There was absolutely nothing in her record to establish how she would perform as a judge, and whether she had the intellect and fortitude to stand firm against judicial activism on the Court.

As a law clerk for federal appellate Judge Ralph K. Winter, Jr., and afterward for Supreme Court justice Clarence Thomas, I saw firsthand what was required of these judges in terms of intellect and courage. It takes a strong internal compass to withstand the pressures of life on the Court. The legal and media elites are forever hammering conservative members of the Court to "grow" and "evolve" in their legal thinking, away from the text of the Constitution and toward liberal political positions. Conservatives had been burned by Supreme Court justices nominated by Republican Presidents—Presidents Nixon, Reagan, and George H. W. Bush. They "evolved" into voting with the liberal bloc on the Court in landmark constitutional rulings. We could not afford another David H. Souter or John Paul Stevens or Anthony Kennedy on the Court. Been there, done that.

> *Harriet has also earned a reputation for her deep compassion and abiding sense of duty.... When I came to office as the governor of Texas, the Lottery Commission needed a leader of unquestioned integrity. I chose Harriet because I knew she would earn the confidence of the people of Texas.*[2]

I knocked over my coffee as I reached for the telephone to dial a friend who was well connected in Washington conservative legal circles. When he answered the phone, we both said almost simultaneously: "This is a disaster!" One hour later I was behind my radio microphone saying the same thing.

And so began the conservative uprising against the president's second nominee to the Supreme Court. Soon *National Review* writer and former Bush speechwriter David Frum was researching Miers's background and finding little to qualify her for the Supreme Court.[3] Columnist Charles Krauthammer wrote a devastating piece on the matter.[4] *National Review* and *The Weekly Standard* urged the president to withdraw her name from consideration.[5] Judge Robert Bork was horrified by the choice. After meeting with her, Republican senators began to express serious doubts about her abilities. President Bush, notoriously stubborn, was taken totally off guard by the criticism, and remained defiant.

"She's a pioneer woman and a trailblazer."[6]

The White House mounted a rather lame effort to rescue the nomination. A Texas judge who was close friends with Harriet Miers called to assure me that she was a solid conservative. James Dobson of Focus on the Family said he was convinced she was, too. She was an evangelical, so she had to be good, another Miers supporter told me. I was shocked. A person's religion and personal political views should have no bearing on her selection or conduct as a judge. A judge should put aside all personal views, whether religious or otherwise, and decide cases based on faithfulness to the Constitution and principles of judicial restraint.

A few days into the firestorm, a former top attorney in the White House counsel's office called me (at the urging of the administration) to say he, too, had confidence in her. Nothing any of them said came close to convincing me that she was equipped, by either intellect or experience, to sit on the Court. Fred Barnes charged that conservatives opposing Miers were doing so out of "snobbery"[7] because she went to Southern Methodist University, not Ivy League schools. I laughed out loud. The opposition to Miers had nothing to do with her law school pedigree (Southern Methodist is a fine school), but rather her lack of the experience and proven record necessary for the highest court in the land.

The insults and pressure kept coming from the pro-Miers camp, but I kept hammering away day after day, on my radio show. Listeners initially were in a mini-revolt. They thought I was being unfair and should give President Bush "the benefit of the doubt." But a seat on the Supreme Court is too important to leave to "the benefit of the doubt." With life tenure there should be no doubts. There were no doubts among conservatives about John Roberts or Sam Alito. If you guess wrong, the person will be undermining the Constitution from the bench for decades.

Three weeks went by. The president dug in his heels. The tipping point came when a few of Miers's speeches from the 1990s surfaced that demonstrated beyond any doubt her lack of understanding of important constitutional questions. In one speech she said that the principle of "self-determination" informed the debate on issues such as abortion and prayer in schools. "The more I think about these issues, the more self-determination makes sense," she said.[8] Yes, it made sense if you sign on to the loopy notion that the role of judges is to assess what is "self-determination" and what is not. It sounds like Justice Ruth Bader Ginsburg's dissent in the April 2007 Partial-Birth Abortion case, where she said that the right of women to have their babies partially delivered and then have their brains suctioned out is necessary for "a woman's autonomy." It got worse. "Legislating religion or morality we gave up on a long time ago," Miers added. Sounds like someone you'd hear in a women's studies seminar, not from a future justice of the Supreme Court.

On October 27, 2005, the White House announced that Harriet Miers was withdrawing her nomination to the Supreme Court.

I was relieved about the outcome but never felt the same about the Bush administration again. The entire episode was sad and so unnecessary. Had the president consulted any respected conservative thinker before nominating Miers? (Other than that legal sage Harry Reid?) Had he simply grown tired of interviewing prospective nominees, turned to Miers, and said, "Hey, Harriet, you know this stuff—why don't you take the job?"

It hit me a few months later, on the day when Samuel Alito was confirmed to the Supreme Court seat that Miers was originally nominated for: this had been a major victory for conservatism and a quintessential "Power to the People" moment. In 1987, without the existence of an alternative media, Republicans could not rescue Robert Bork's Supreme Court nomination from the distortions of Democrats and the liberal press. But eighteen years later, with the help of the talk radio, cable, and the Internet, the balance of power had shifted and the people were the winners.

These confirmation battles will get more heated as the courts continue to grab more power from the people. The fights over judicial nominees might seem to take place on a higher plane—in the hallowed marble halls of the U.S. Senate and the White House—with only the elite few engaging in the fray. But the Miers battle shows that when talk radio hosts and our listeners, bloggers and their readers, and the conservative network and its supporters work together, we can make a difference. Let's not forget Miers was a Supreme Court nominee backed by a determined president, the Democratic leader, and probably most Republicans. We have a responsibility to suit up and fight for Supreme Court justices with superb qualifications and proven records of faithfulness to the Constitution and judicial restraint.

America to the Supreme Court: Restrain Yourself

What kind of Supreme Court do we want? We aren't looking for a *conservative* Court, a *states' rights* Court, or even a *pro-War on Terror* Court. We want a Supreme Court that practices judicial restraint.

"Judicial restraint" isn't a term you hear that often, because it doesn't fit into the standard political categories of Left and Right, big government and small government—and that's the point. Under our Constitution, judges are not part of the political process. Judicial restraint begins with a judge recognizing what he is not: he is not Congress, he is not the president of the United States, he is not the mayor of a small town in Texas, he is not the commissioner of the PGA, and he is not God.

The "political" branches—the legislature and the executive—are the ones that are supposed to make political decisions, because they are accountable to the people. Judges aren't. So they are supposed to put politics and their own personal preferences aside and uphold the laws the people have enacted through the process of representative government.

To decide cases according to the law, justices of the Supreme Court must decide whether lower federal courts have ruled correctly in cases involving federal laws. Supreme Court justices, since *Marbury v. Madison*[9] in 1803, are also called upon to look at state and federal laws and decide whether or not those laws are prohibited by the Constitution.

When they leave home for work at the courthouse, judges are supposed to leave behind questions such as: "What law would be best?" "How can I help the underprivileged?" Or, "What would maximize societal happiness?" Instead, their job is to ask: "What does the law mean?" "How does the precedent apply?" And, "What does the Constitution say about the matter?" A good judge—a restrained judge—does not set out to make the world a better place. A restrained judge simply does his job, like a neutral umpire. Chief Justice John Roberts said it well during his confirmation hearings before the Senate: "Umpires don't make the rules, they apply them," and the umpire's job is "to call balls and strikes and not to pitch or bat."

You can tell you've got an unrestrained judge when he derisively dismisses "hypertechnical reliance upon statutory provision" [10] (the Florida Supreme Court in the 2000 election); when he refers to his own "conscience" repeatedly in decisions (California's Harry Pregerson on the 9th Circuit); and when he writes things like, "at the heart of liberty is the right to define one's own concept of existence, of meaning, of the universe, and of the mystery of human life" [11] (Sandra Day O'Connor, Anthony Kennedy, and David Souter, upholding abortion-on-demand as a constitutional right). These judges see their duty as substituting their own consciences and philosophical ramblings for the text, history, tradition, and principles of the Constitution.

Oliver Wendell Holmes, a hero of liberal lawyers, said it was a Justice's job to interpret the Constitution "in the light of our whole experience and not merely in that of what was said a hundred years ago." [12] Translation: *The Founding Fathers' plans were fine for the eighteenth century, but the Constitution as written hardly does the trick today.* With that mindset, there is no limit on what runaway courts can do to this country.

This should scare you. A Supreme Court that does not blush at making law strikes right at the heart of our democracy and strips regular people of power. Once the Supreme Court tells your high school that you may not pray at a football game, that's it. You can't appeal the decision. You can't vote the justices out of office. The extreme option of impeachment is available—the Constitution gives federal judges life tenure during "good behavior"—but removal from office has traditionally required a criminal act, not just issuing bad decisions. And lifetime tenure is the very thing that the Founders gave judges to ensure judicial independence in the first place.

Abraham Lincoln put it well in his First Inaugural Address: "If the policy of the government upon vital questions, affecting the whole people, is to be irrevocably fixed by decisions of the Supreme Court…the people will have ceased to be their own rulers."[13] We are perilously close to that point now. Nancy Pelosi said in 2005 after the Court ruled in the case *Kelo v. New London*, "It is a decision of the Supreme Court. So this is almost as if God has spoken."[14]

If the Supreme Court is almost God, then we are not a free country. Alexander Hamilton envisioned the judiciary as the "least dangerous branch" of the federal government.[15] Things have changed.

The Dangers of an Imperial Judiciary

They think they are smarter than the rest of us. They think they are more clever than Congress, more prudent than the president, more intelligent than state or local governments, and certainly wiser than those chumps who wrote the Constitution hundreds of years ago.

For decades, federal courts have been deciding questions that are properly left to the people, on contentious issues such as abortion, prayer in school, religious displays, and now even our war policy. Federal courts have usurped the rightful powers of Congress and state and local governments, labeling their preferred political solutions as newfound "constitutional rights," but then refused to protect us when governments launch illegal assaults on the true rights that are actually mentioned in the Constitution. Many Americans don't realize the extent to which the Supreme Court has usurped power from the people and stolen the decision-making authority of elected officials on the state and federal level. These days, it seems normal to most journalists that five Supreme Court justices in Washington, D.C., should be making laws for the citizens of the state of Nebraska. Most public debates over Supreme Court cases focus on "What is the best policy?" or "What should the state government do?" But that's not the judicial role. The question before the Court in most such cases is really: *does the Constitution prohibit the law in question?*

And the problem isn't just with the Supreme Court of the United States. State supreme courts are also usurping state legislatures and blatantly overthrowing the will of the people, which is how we got civil unions in Vermont and gay marriage in Massachusetts. These initiatives did not come from the people—they came from the courts. A county judge in Kansas even ordered legislatures to increase education spending.[16] Judges on lower federal courts are playing the role of policymaker, banning the Pledge of Allegiance, mandating welfare for illegal aliens, and hatching similar schemes that would earn a politician a pink slip from the voters.

In the last few years some politicians, seeing how serious the threat is from liberal activist judges, have started searching for ways to hold judges accountable and restrain them within the bounds of their job description. This has included talk of impeachment, closer scrutiny of judicial behavior, and prohibitions on the citation of foreign law or precedent in federal court decisions. In response, former Supreme Court justice Sandra Day O'Connor took to the *Charlie Rose* show on public television to complain that "judges these days are under attack both at the national and the state level in the legislative halls, in the press, and I think in the public today."[17] Charlie Rose congratulated O'Connor, saying, "hurray for you for speaking out."

For years, this woman was the swing vote on the United States Supreme Court. During her tenure, she seemed to share the honor with Oprah Winfrey as being "the most powerful woman in America." O'Connor used that power to rewrite the Rules of Golf so that players who couldn't walk the courses could escape the "no golf cart" rule, to dictate when high school kids could and couldn't pray, and to invalidate popularly enacted state bans on partial birth abortion. And we're supposed to applaud her for using government-sponsored television to attack citizens who are fed up with a liberal activist judiciary?

While Justice O'Connor had the privilege of casting the deciding vote in many judicial seizures of our, the people's power, for more than two decades, courts have been stripping away our power for far longer. The phrase "judicial activistm" recently entered the vernacular, but the problem is not a new one, and it won't be solved overnight.

Every American, Left and Right, who wants the people to maintain control over our government and our lives, needs to take this issue seriously, and fight against the imperial judiciary. "We the People"—not unelected judges, should determine our cultural, social, and political priorities. We may change our views on a controversial issue, but we don't want to be forced to do so by nine unelected, unaccountable justices of the Supreme Court.

Judging the Imperial Judiciary: Guilty on Four Counts

The imperial judiciary may not have directly harmed you, but you still suffer. When courts and judges overreach and become lawmakers and executives, they necessarily wrest power from the people and undermine our constitutional order. I hereby level four charges against our activist judges:

1. They invalidate democracy at the state and federal level.
2. They undermine our executive branch's ability to defend us—specifically in the War on Terror.
3. They subvert the foundations of America's laws and our Judeo-Christian moral heritage.
4. They weaken our own Constitution and national sovereignty by relying on international law.

If the judges get to play the role of president, congressman, state legislator, and head scoutmaster, it's only fair that we get to take a turn at sitting in judgment of them.

))) Count 1: Assault and Battery of Democracy

Exhibit A in this case is the 1973 decision *Roe v. Wade*.[18] The justices who ruled with the 7–2 majority in that case should have some pretty heavy burdens on their souls. More than 45 million unborn children have been aborted in the United States since that decision came down, and the one million-plus abortions we still suffer every year.[19] But completely aside from the stunning toll in terms of human life, and purely from a lawyer's perspective, *Roe* is a shameful example of constitutional dishonesty and disdain for democracy and the right of the people, through their state legislatures, to make fundamental policy decisions in our society.

The author of the decision (God have mercy on his soul) was Justice Harry Blackmun. Thirty years after *Roe* was decided, former Blackmun clerk and now a well-respected liberal lawyer Ed Lazarus admitted that "as a matter of constitutional interpretation, even most liberal jurisprudes—if you administer truth serum—will tell you it is basically indefensible."[20]

Liberal Alan Dershowitz, in a book dedicated to railing against *Bush v. Gore*, called *Roe* "judicial activism in areas more appropriately left to the political processes."[21] Even liberal judicial heroes like Laurence Tribe and Ruth Bader Ginsburg have admitted, in various contexts in the past, that *Roe* is a heavy-handed Supreme Court decision that has no substantive basis in the Constitution.[22] Yet in opinion polls, most Americans say they support *Roe v. Wade*. A January 2007 CNN poll found 62 percent would *not* want *Roe* overturned. In 2005 and 2006, that same poll showed 63 and 66 percent, respectively, favoring the preservation of *Roe*.[23] In floor votes, senators say the same thing. The Senate has repeatedly passed resolutions stating that *Roe* was rightly decided and should not be overturned.

Why do these liberal legal scholars acknowledge that *Roe* is a bad decision, yet average, moderate Americans claim to support it? Because the legal scholars know what *Roe* actually did. Almost no one else does. Most people get their information about court decisions from the media, not from reading actual court opinions—and the mainstream media has grossly and consistently (for more than thirty years) misrepresented *Roe v. Wade*. *Roe* did not "legalize abortion," as most newspapers tell the story, and overturning it would not "outlaw abortion." *Roe* overruled the abortion laws of all fifty states, declaring a constitutional right to essentially unlimited abortion, and made abortion largely immune to the democratic process. Overturning *Roe* means nothing more than returning the issue of abortion to the voters where it belongs. Besides turning the Court into an über-state legislature, the justices fancied themselves omniscient OB/GYNs by declaring when unborn children deserved no legal protection (in the first two trimesters) and when they *might* deserve a *little* legal protection (in the third trimester). On January 22, 1973, when *Roe* was handed down, the Court announced a companion decision, *Doe v. Bolton*.[24] In it the justices said a woman's "health" can justify abortion—and not just physical health, but mental and emotional health. *Roe* and *Doe* together practically ensured that abortionists—who have a financial interest in performing the procedure—can never be questioned about their "medical judgment" concerning abortion whenever a woman's "health" is invoked. We live in a country that basically enshrines unlimited abortion in our Constitution.

Every January, tens of thousands of Americans come from all over the United States on *Roe*'s anniversary to march through the slush and the bitter cold in the annual March for Life. The March ends at the Supreme Court building, where the pro-lifers give speeches, wave banners and chant slogans. The Founders might wonder at this sight: why is a public rally aimed at a court? Aren't the courts supposed to operate outside of politics?

Why are Supreme Court nominations the most vitriolic, combative, and poisonous part of our political world? Because it is the closest we the people get to having a voice in the issue of abortion.

Roe is not the only evidence that our justices are more dedicated to preserving abortion than reading the Constitution. In 2000, the Court went even further in a decision called *Stenberg v. Carhart*[25] and ruled that the Constitution prohibited the people of Nebraska from banning partial-birth abortion. (This beyond barbaric procedure involves partial delivery of a baby in its third-trimester, following which the abortionist jams scissors into the base of the baby's skull and suctions out the baby's brains. The dead baby is then removed from the birth canal.) The Court in *Stenberg* held that because the law made no exception for the "health" of the mother, it was unconstitutional. Forget the fact that Nebraska state legislators had concluded that this procedure is never medically necessary to save a mother's life! This holding was a huge blow to pro-life forces in the United States and an abomination to the Constitution. This is the barbarism that *Roe* spawned.

Thankfully, Sandra Day O'Connor's retirement in 2005 and her replacement with Justice Samuel Alito paved the way for *Stenberg*'s (at least temporary) demise. In April 2007, a 5–4 majority in *Gonzales v. Carhart* upheld a federal partial-birth abortion law very similar to Nebraska's law that had been struck down seven years earlier. When the Court allowed the federal law to stand, abortion rights forces in the United States went bonkers. A *New York Times* editorial declared that the Court had undermined its "credibility, its integrity and the rule of law."[26](Does the *New York Times* find a lot of "integrity" in partial-birth abortion?) My personal favorite was a lead editorial in the *Los Angeles Times*, which called the decision (but not the procedure that involves puncturing a baby's skull) "unconscionable." The *Times* noted haughtily that the proper term for the procedure is not partial birth abortion, it is "properly called 'dilation and extraction.'"[27] Properly? A doctor who swears to "do no harm" collapses a partially delivered infant's skull and suctions out its brain and the *Los Angeles Times* is worried about verbal constructions? The Associated Press revealed that it really does think the Court has legislative powers when it reported that "the Supreme Court *banned*" the procedure.[28] Congress—including many Democrats who are accountable to the voters—banned the procedure. The Court merely stood back, as it should, and allowed the people to govern themselves.

Exhibit B in the case against the Court for assaulting federalism and democracy is the issue of term limits for lawmakers. The Constitution's framers intended federal judges to serve for life, but that was not the idea for congressmen and senators. Throughout the twentieth century, however, the cost of campaigns and the perks of office grew to the point that it was almost impossible to defeat a sitting member of Congress. Each year since 1990, more than 90 percent of incumbents seeking reelection in the House have won. On Election Day 2002, only four incumbents lost to challengers. Even in the "tidal wave" years of 1994 and 2006, the House reelection rate was over 90 percent.

If this incumbent dominance were due to popular satisfaction with Congress, we would have nothing to complain about, but it's clear that Americans usually are dissatisfied with Congress's performance. So why do we keep the bums in office? Start with the fact that an average winning house race costs about $1 million.[29] Any would-be challenger who doesn't have a million dollars or can't raise a million dollars is basically dead on arrival. That is enough to keep a majority of Washington lawmakers safe.

Then, throw in redistricting—usually a bipartisan affair that allows both parties to keep their incumbents protected. A classic example of incumbent-protection redistricting came in Virginia in 2002. Republican congressman Frank Wolf's district bordered on the district of Democrat Jim Moran. The state legislature redrew the lines, giving Wolf some of Moran's Republicans and Moran some of Wolf's Democrats—leaving both candidates safer. This goes on all over the country.

Finally, incumbency allows the politicians to buy off the important donors with pork projects, and the activist groups with favors. Also, local newspaper reporters covering their congressmen on Capitol Hill feel pressure to stay on the congressman's good side, or lose access to all information. This means constituents often don't get the bad news back home.

If congressmen can't lose, are they really still responsible to the people they are supposed to represent? To combat this erosion of democracy on Capitol Hill, a movement sprouted across the states to impose term limits on members of Congress. Twenty-three states have passed laws—usually by ballot initiative—limiting the terms of their members of Congress. In 1995, in the case *U.S. Term Limits v. Thornton*,[30] the U.S. Supreme Court, by a 5–4 vote, struck down all of those state term limits, many of which had been enshrined in the state constitutions.

Justice Clarence Thomas dissented, with a straightforward and eloquent nod to states' rights and judicial restraint: "Nothing in the Constitution deprives the people of each State of the power to prescribe eligibility requirements for the candidates who seek to represent them in Congress. The Constitution is simply silent on this question. And where the Constitution is silent, it raises no bar to action by the States or the people."[31]

But still the majority of the Court decided that somewhere, probably in the "penumbras and emanations"[32] of the Constitution, these term limits were banned. Specifically, the majority decided that because the Constitution set *some* criteria for who could be elected to Congress (representatives must be at least twenty-five years old, senators at least thirty years old; representatives must have been a U.S. citizen for seven years, senators nine years; both must live in the state they are elected to represent), that states were not permitted to add to the list of requirements.[33] This argument makes no sense. But, as Nancy Pelosi said, it counts as the word of God. Five justices declared, "Thou shalt not limit the terms of your congressmen," and, like that, the votes of millions of Americans in dozens of states were discarded. Such is the imperial judiciary's assault on the will of the people. If I had the space, I could list dozens of similar cases.

❯❯❯ Count 2: Impersonating a Field General

On November 28, 2001, six days after Thanksgiving, Johnny "Mike" Spann from Wingfield, Alabama, was shot and killed in a prison riot started by Taliban soldiers in Afghanistan. He was the first U.S. serviceman killed in the War on Terror, and memorials to him stand today in Wingfield and in the courtyard where he was killed.

The prison riot erupted into a full-scale battle, and in a couple of days, the Taliban soldiers surrendered. One of those soldiers was John Walker Lindh of Marin County, California, but he wasn't the only American in the group. Yaser Esam Hamdi, also captured, was born in Baton Rouge, Louisiana, and thus a U.S. citizen.

Was Yasser Hamdi a traitor? If he was an American fighting for the Taliban against the United States he was. Hamdi also had Saudi Arabian citizenship and had lived there since he was young. This ambiguity—was Hamdi a traitor or an enemy combatant or both—allowed the Supreme Court to step in and use the Hamdi case to dictate how certain terrorist or treason suspects must be treated.

The Hamdi case[34] is a confusing one, with no real majority opinion, but the key problem is that Justice Sandra Day O'Connor didn't address the issues before her. Instead, she decided Hamdi needed some sort of special trial under complex new rules that she devised, taking it upon herself to micromanage this aspect of the War on Terror.

In dissent, Justice Antonin Scalia agreed that the administration had acted wrongly in the Hamdi case, but accused O'Connor of nearly "writing a new Constitution," and employing "a Mr. Fix-it Mentality." He wrote: "The plurality seems to view it as its mission to Make Everything Come Out Right." He noted also that "As usual, the major effect of [the Court's] constitutional improvisation is to increase the power of the Court...[and] prescribe what procedural protections *it* thinks appropriate.[35]

Even after Sandra Day O'Connor retired, the Supreme Court continued to insert itself into the War on Terror. This time, the suspect in question was Osama bin Laden's driver, Salim Ahmed Hamdan. Hamdan was captured in Afghanistan and transferred to Guantanamo Bay, where the U.S. government charged him with conspiracy to commit terrorism. He was set for a trial before a military commission.

President Bush had established military commissions by executive order. The idea here was a pretty common sense one. Under the commissions' rules, if the government had very sensitive evidence, it could show this evidence to the administrator of the commission and to the suspect's military defense lawyer, but not to the defendant or his private lawyer. This way, a suspected terrorist would not be made privy to U.S. intelligence sources. (Remember left-wing New York City lawyer Lynne Stewart who, while defending the terrorists who first bombed the World Trade Center in 1993, helped them communicate with their compatriots?)

In *Hamdan v. Rumsfeld*,[36] the liberal majority on the high court abolished these commissions, in part citing the Geneva Conventions as authority. While it's clear how this ruling undermines counter-terrorism efforts, it's also another textbook example of judicial activism and overreach.

The *Hamdan* decision was not only wrong, it was even illegal for the Court to be making it. In 2005, Congress passed a law explicitly stating that "no court, justice, or judge" could consider a Guatanamo Bay detainee's petition for *habeas corpus*, or motion that he is being detained illegally.[37] Honest people can disagree as to whether suspending *habeas corpus* for these men was the right thing to do (as they did when President Lincoln suspended *habeas corpus* during the Civil War), but the Constitution makes it clear that such a decision rests squarely with Congress whenever "in Cases of Rebellion or Invasion the public Safety may require it."[38]

So Congress told the Supreme Court, in no uncertain terms: "You have no jurisdiction here." How did the Supreme Court react when it received, on appeal, the *habeas corpus* case of Salim Ahmed Hamdan? The justices decided they *did* have jurisdiction. The majority did not deny Congress's right to strip jurisdiction, they just decided that the language allowed them hear appeals on cases that were brought before the law was passed. Nice try, but an absurd interpretation contrary to all precedent.

Congress has some limited authority to influence the president's prosecution of the War on Terror, even if their motivations are often as political as prudential. The Supreme Court, however, invents authority where it has none, as in *Hamdan*, and further inserts itself into the War on Terror.

❱❱❱ Count 3: Courts Preying on the Faithful

"Congress shall make no law respecting an establishment of religion, or prohibiting the free exercise thereof...." Over the years the Supreme Court and the lower federal courts have made a total mess of those two clauses of the First Amendment to the U.S. Constitution. The word "establishment" has been interpreted over decades of tangled Supreme Court decisions, to include a broad array of government actions that go well beyond efforts to establish of an official state religion. The mischief really escalated at the hands of Chief Justice Warren Burger in *Lemon v. Kurtzman* (1971),[39] where he announced a three-part test for determining if a statute or state action survives Establishment Clause scrutiny. (Any time the Court invents multi-part tests, you know we'll be dealing with a precedent that keeps returning to torment us.)

The three parts: (1) the law's purpose must be secular; (2) the law must neither—in its principal or primary effect—advance nor inhibit religion; (3) the law must not result in "an excessive government entanglement with religion." Is that clear enough for you? The cases following this lemon of a test have been all over the map—a legal mish-mash. The crowning achievement for the ACLU was when the court ruled in *Lee v. Weisman* (1992)[40] that prayer at a school's non-mandatory graduation ceremony violated the Establishment Clause. The Court came close to dispensing with one prong of the ridiculous *Lemon* test five years later, but still couldn't quite bring itself to kill it off once and for all. So with *Lemon* still looming, local and state officials move to expel God from the public square.

A "Happy Easter" banner above a doorway at City Hall would send the ACLU rushing to court to sue for an injunction. Heck, if it could, the ACLU would sue for pain and suffering damages too—because for many of its supporters there is nothing more excruciating than seeing God publicly acknowledged.

When the Supreme Court makes a mistake, its effects are felt throughout the lower federal courts that are bound to follow the bad precedent and, sometimes, even expand upon it. Hence, the Ninth Circuit's outrageous ruling that the words "under God" must be removed from the Pledge of Allegiance. Most people don't closely follow the Supreme Court, so they are shocked when a case like that is decided. The ruling on its face seems outlandish, but really, under these nonsensical and arbitrary "tests" set out by the Court, anything is possible.

The Court can even come up with what amounted to a new geographical proximity test to determine whether a display of the Ten Commandments in a public space can stay or has to go. In two 5–4 decisions involving the displays of the Ten Commandments on government grounds, the Court held that Texas got it right and Kentucky got it wrong.

In the Kentucky case *McCreary County v. ACLU*,[41] the Court, in a majority opinion written by Justice David Souter, ruled that the county had to remove a small framed display of the Ten Commandments that hung in a hallway in two county courthouses. In *Van Orden v. Perry*,[42] the Court decided that Texas could keep its six-foot high stone display of the Ten Commandments on the lawn between its supreme court and its state capitol.

Why would a stone six-foot-by-three-foot monument be less offensive than a barely noticeable 8.5-by-11-inch sheet of paper? Justice Breyer, who cast the deciding vote in each case, listed many reasons in his concurrence in *Van Orden*, including the fact that the monument's "setting does not readily lend itself to meditation or any other religious activity." He also noted: "Forty years passed in which the monument's presence, legally speaking, went unchallenged." He explained that "[t]hose forty years suggest more strongly than can any set of formulaic tests that few individuals... are likely to have understood the monument's amounting...to a government effort to establish religion." Makes you wonder what would happen with a display that was twenty years old. Maybe only five of the commandments would be constitutional.

Another factor that pushed the Texas monument into the realm of the acceptable, according to Justice Breyer, in his concurring opinion: "The display is not on the grounds of a public school, where, given the impressionability of the young, government must exercise particular care." Heaven forbid our young people are exposed to ... gasp ... God! How zany are the Court's religion rulings? Justice Antonin Scalia in his dissent, as usual, hit it out of the park:

> What distinguishes the rule of law from the dictatorship of a shifting Supreme Court majority is the absolutely indispensable requirement that judicial opinions be grounded in consistently applied principle. That is what prevents judges from ruling now this way, now that–thumbs up or thumbs down–as their personal preferences dictate.

The fickleness and creativity of these decisions betray the Court's arbitrariness, but the substance of the ruling—that the Ten Commandments have no place in a courthouse—is just as upsetting. The Ten Commandments, and Jewish and Christian morality broadly, are the foundation of our common law and our Constitution—and a far better, surer, and binding foundation than the shifting sands of fashionable judicial opinion. Despite the Texas victory, the Court has taken it upon itself to strike down any law anywhere that might offend the ACLU. The Court considers its mandate so broadly that not only are endorsements of some *specific* religion deemed unconstitutional, but so are endorsements of "religion over non-religion," in the words of a 1968 Supreme Court case.[43]

Two years before the Texas and Kentucky Ten Commandments cases, a panel of three judges from the U.S. Court of Appeals for the Ninth Circuit, issued an opinion that made front-page headlines coast-to-coast. The panel ruled, 2 to 1, that reciting the Pledge of Allegiance at school was unconstitutional because it contained the words "under God."

The plaintiff in the case, Michael Newdow, undeterred that the Pledge was voluntary, basically didn't like the fact that other kids were near his daughter and implying a belief in God. The Supreme

Court dismissed Newdow's case because his daughter's mother—Newdow's ex-girlfriend—was fighting him for custody and had no objection to the Pledge. This messy personal situation denied us the pleasure (or pain) of knowing how the Supreme Court would have ruled on the merits of the case.

Courts have found school prayer unconstitutional even when it's not lead by teachers and done *way* outside of class. In 2000, the Supreme Court ruled by a 5–4 majority that Santa Fe High School in Texas had violated the Constitution by allowing students to use the public address system to lead a non-sectarian prayer before football games. Almost makes you forget that we live in a country that was born with an "appeal to the Supreme Judge of the world." If this keeps up, they'll find the Declaration of Independence unconstitutional.

❱❱❱ Count 4: Sleeping with the Enemy (Well, Europe)

The final count in our indictment of the American judiciary is the tendency of the Court's more liberal members to look to foreign and international law—sometimes it's not even really "law" but the musings of foreign would-be philosophers—for guidance when they should have their gazes fixed on the U.S. Constitution and federal law. I don't mean to sound as though I'm picking on the lady, but Sandra Day O'Connor again provides the clearest insight into the mind of a justice who forgot what her job was.

In a speech in Atlanta in 2003, O'Connor noted a growing trend of "solicitude for the views of foreign and international courts."[44] She praised such cosmopolitan jurisprudence, saying it would "not only enrich our own country's decisions; it will create that all-important good impression." You can tell a country girl has spent too many evenings at Georgetown cocktail parties when she's worrying about making a good impression on the Europeans.

Chief Justice John Roberts burst that bubble at his confirmation hearings. He explained that "looking at foreign law for support is like looking out over a crowd and picking out your friends. . . . You can find anything you want. If you don't find it in the decisions of France or Italy, it's in the decisions of Somalia or Japan or Indonesia or wherever." This approach is fine if you're picking a head of lettuce, but it's not what judges are supposed to do.

In a 2002 decision on the death penalty, the Court welcomed an *amicus curiae* (friend of the court) brief from a group of diplomats who argued that our use of capital punishment was making it harder for them to earn the favor of their foreign counterparts. The majority of the Court ruled in *Atkins v. Virginia*[45] that the death penalty was unconstitutional for criminals with a low enough IQ to be considered retarded. To buttress the argument that such executions were "cruel and unusual," the Court wrote: "Within the world community, the imposition of the death penalty for crimes committed by mentally retarded offenders is overwhelmingly disapproved."

What "world community" are they talking about? In Afghanistan you can be executed for converting to Christianity. China still has forced sterilizations of mentally retarded teenagers.[46] By "world community," again, the judges mean "Europe." Should we really be looking to Europe to define "cruel and unusual"? Europeans consider a forty-hour work week cruel, and having more than one child with the same woman is certainly unusual.

The story was the same in 2005, when the high court commuted the death sentences of anyone who committed his crimes before his eighteenth birthday.[47] A group of Nobel Prize winners, including Jimmy Carter, submitted an *amicus* brief imploring the Court to "consider the opinion of the international community, which has rejected the death penalty for child offenders worldwide."[48] The Court complied, and in its decision noted, "the overwhelming weight of international opinion against the juvenile death penalty."[49] To guide her decision-making in the 2003 case on affirmative action at the University of Michigan,[50] Ruth Bader Ginsburg set her compass in part according to the 1979 Convention on the Elimination of All Forms of Discrimination Against Women—a treaty the U.S. has never ratified.[51] She praised the Court's pro-racial discrimination decision because it "accords with the international understanding of the [purpose and propriety] of affirmative action."[52]

Also in 2003, the Supreme Court struck down Texas's laws on homosexual sodomy in *Lawrence v. Texas.*[53] Again, the role of a judiciary is not to decide what should and shouldn't be illegal, but to decide, in a case such as *Lawrence*, whether the U.S. Constitution prohibits the law in question. Somehow, the Court found it relevant that the European High Court on Human Rights had ruled that homosexual sex was a protected right.

The Left's love of international jurisprudence is not universal, however. As Justice Antonin Scalia has pointed out on numerous occasions, jurists fond of citing international legal opinions pick and choose those that are consistent with the conclusion they want, and simply disregard the rest. Noting that the United States, thanks to *Roe* and *Doe*, has among the most liberal laws on abortion in the world, Scalia noted:

> When it agrees with what the Justice would like the case to say you use foreign law and when it doesn't agree you don't use it.... [T]hus we cited it in *Lawrence*, the case on homosexual sodomy; we cited foreign law, not *all* foreign law, just the foreign law of countries that agreed with the disposition, but we said not a *whisper* about foreign law in the series of abortion cases.[54]

The Court's reliance on foreign law, like its denial of Judeo-Christian morality, demonstrates a blatant disregard for our own

Constitution and legal system. Our legal tradition differs in many respects from that of Europe. "Innocent until proven guilty" is not a legal principle throughout most of Europe. American courts do not allow "hearsay" testimony while many foreign courts do. Napoleon and the French Revolution shaped the legal systems of much of the Continent—but ours came from the very different English common law.

⟩⟩⟩ Judicial Passivism

Since *Marbury v. Madison*, the Court has been in the business of striking down laws that it judges as violating the Constitution. Here's a pretty straightforward example: if the Congress were to pass a law abridging the freedom of speech, the Court, under "judicial review," would strike it down—and properly so. But increasingly, in cases where government has overstepped its constitutional bounds, the Supreme Court has been committing a sin that is the opposite of its usual judicial activism: let's call it judicial passivism. The same justices who invent new "rights" not contained anywhere in the Constitution also roll over and play dead when our most basic rights—to life, free speech, religious expression, and property to name just a few—are bulldozed by illegitimate government regulations.

One such case involved the now-infamous legal battle over the McCain-Feingold campaign law. In 2001, Senator John McCain finally pushed through his bill officially titled "The Bipartisan Campaign Finance Reform Act" (a.k.a. McCain-Feingold), which banned large political donations to parties, rather than to specific candidates and put restrictions on campaign advertising. McCain-Feingold's restrictions are broadly written, and seriously threaten political speech: the core speech that the Founders wrote the First Amendment to protect.

For example, if the ACLU ran an ad saying, "McCain-Feingold infringes on your right to free speech" within thirty days before the Iowa caucuses, the group would be breaking the law.

When President Bush signed McCain-Feingold into law at 8:00 a.m. on March 27, 2002, without fanfare, he supposedly did so "reluctantly." Senator McCain wasn't invited. (What? No party to celebrate the gutting of the First Amendment?) The White House had put the word out among reporters that the president hoped the Supreme Court would strike down the most blatant restrictions on politicking during an election year. What a wonderful way not to demonstrate leadership on an issue as significant as the reach of the First Amendment—just pass the buck to the Court. George W. Bush had obviously not been following the Supreme Court closely if he was so willing to trust it to do the right thing on McCain-Feingold.

As many serious court watchers predicted, in *McConnell v. FEC* (2003), the Court upheld key parts of the campaign finance reform law, accepting Congress's justification of addressing real or assumed corruption in political campaigns. This was yet another 5–4 squeaker, with Sandra Day O'Connor and John Paul Stevens writing for the majority. The court held that the government's interest in reducing the "pernicious influence" of money in politics justified the law's restrictions of speech. Justice Clarence Thomas, in his dissent, called the law the "most significant abridgment of the freedoms of speech and association since the Civil War."[55] Justice Scalia, in his partial concurrence, summed up the Court's failure to uphold such a key constitutional right:

> This is a sad day for the freedom of speech. Who could have imagined that the same Court which, within the past four years, has sternly disapproved of restrictions upon such inconsequential forms of expression as virtual child pornography, tobacco advertising, dissemination of illegally inter-

cepted communications, and sexually explicit cable programming, would smile with favor upon a law that cuts to the heart of what the First Amendment is meant to protect: the right to criticize the government.[56]

The Roberts Court has since ruled that McCain-Feingold's issue-ad guidelines were too restrictive on a pro-life group's free speech rights.[57]

Another equally unfortunate instance of judicial passivism occurred in June of 2005.

The case was *Kelo v. City of New London*,[58] another 5–4 decision, in which the Court's liberal majority allowed New London, Connecticut's, local government to condemn and take the residences of private homeowners in order to allow corporate commercial development instead. (More tax revenues for the local government, of course.)

The Constitution allows government to seize private property through the process of eminent domain, but only for "public use." (Such "takings" also require "just compensation" for the property owner, and must be executed with "due process of law.") "Public use" has always been understood (surprise) to mean "public"—as in, roads, parks, etc. But New London took away people's homes—including Suzette Kelo's pink Victorian house that she had proudly fixed up—for corporate development.

This counted as "public use," the town argued, because the corporate park would provide economic revitalization (higher tax revenues are good for the "public"). The same Supreme Court that has set about redefining just about every other word in the Constitution decided that it was up to New London to define "public use" however it saw fit. Ruling: Suzette Kelo loses her little pink Victorian house. The Constitution protected her, but the Supreme Court didn't.

What's at Stake

I've discussed these cases to make it clear how important it is for judges to exercise judicial restraint—and judicial responsibility. The elites sure know what's at stake with the courts. They know they can't win at the ballot box, and so they need the courts to bring about their desired social order.

Gay marriage may be the best example. Barack Obama, Hillary Clinton, and John Edwards won't *say* they support same-sex marriage. Voters have considered a ban on gay marriage in seventeen states, and the ban has passed in every state but Arizona. Those who want gay marriage aren't going to accomplish it through ballot initiatives. They also probably can't accomplish it through legislatures—politicians see the issue as radioactive. So, they advance their cause through the courts.

The same is true with the extreme positions on abortion held by NARAL and Planned Parenthood. These types believe that abortion should be legal up until the moment of birth, that taxpayers should be forced to fund abortions for the poor, and that girls should never be required to tell their parents or even undergo a waiting period before an abortion. Such an agenda wouldn't fly on the campaign trail, and so they've had to resort to the courts.

That's why the Left spends so much and fights so hard (and dirty) on Supreme Court nominations. Senators Ted Kennedy and Chuck Schumer in 2002 launched unprecedented filibusters on President Bush's nominees to the federal bench. These were nominees whom the Judiciary Committee had approved, and who had majority support in the Senate, but forty-one Democrats kept the Senate from even holding an up-or-down vote.

On the Supreme Court level, the radical Left is without scruples: it will distort the truth, besmirch conservative nominees, and let's face it, make up bald faced lies about highly intelligent, principled, honest, and patriotic judges just because they are faithful to the Constitution and principles of judicial restraint. In 1991, of course, when they feared Justice Clarence Thomas was going to get confirmed without much of a fight, Democratic staffers on the Senate Judiciary Committee thrust Anita Hill into the limelight to accuse then judge Clarence Thomas of sexual harassment. The Senate Judiciary Committee looked like the Jerry Springer show. When President Reagan nominated Robert Bork in 1987, Ted Kennedy immediately took to the floor and declared that:

> Robert Bork's America is a land in which women would be forced into back-alley abortions, blacks would sit at segregated lunch counters, rogue police could break down citizens' doors in midnight raids, schoolchildren could not be taught about evolution, writers and artists could be censored at the whim of government.

The Left is ruthless in its quest to stack the Court with liberal judicial activists. We can't adopt their tactics—lying, smearing, filibustering, and nominating federal judges who are results-oriented nightmares—so we have to compensate by working harder to oppose these tactics if we want to restore the rule of law and power to the people.

Returning *POWER TO THE PEOPLE*

Judicial power has become so abused, and judges themselves so unreproachable, that it's hard to envision how we can put the brakes on runaway courts. Ye of little faith! There is plenty we can do to restrain the robed wonders.

First, join the battle for good judges and against bad judges. As Judge Bork said recently: "If the Democrats win in '08, the

Supreme Court is gone." He's right. Nothing is more important to the Court than electing presidents and senators who will nominate and confirm justices and judges who will practice judicial restraint, stay out of politics, and respect the role of the people in our democracy. During presidential and Senate campaigns, look at what candidates have done and said in the past on judges. Demand to know what kind of persons they would appoint to the bench, if elected. As in, names. If they will not nominate justices like Scalia, Thomas, Roberts, and Alito, forget it. Don't vote for them.

And if a president violates his promise and nominates another Harriet Miers (or worse) we need to lead the rebellion. We've shown we can win.

We can also work outside judicial channels to fix the messes the Court has made. The errors of judicial "passivism"—as opposed to judicial activism—can be corrected through the normal democratic process. Remember how the Supreme Court in *Kelo* turned a blind eye to private property rights? Well, we can implement that constitutional promise ourselves, through ordinary legislation. Working state-by-state, county-by-county, and town-by-town, we can force state lawmakers and town councilmen to strip governments of the right to use eminent domain except in very narrow circumstances. Twenty-six states have already passed laws to this effect, and dozens of municipalities have seen similar measures. And if your town council proceeds on an eminent domain taking

THE SEVEN QUALITIES OF A GREAT JUDGE

》》》 1. A brilliant mind

》》》 2. Humility

》》》 3. A thick skin

》》》 4. Courage

》》》 5. Top-notch legal training and experience

》》》 6. The ability to listen

》》》 7. The ability to write well

for some pet redevelopment project, organize the campaign to unseat the members supporting this legalized theft.

The same model of legislative reform can work on other issues as well, such as affirmative action. Even when it means undoing the work of wild-eyed activists, who invent fantasy rights that are nowhere in the Constitution. Ward Connerly, founder of the American Civil Rights Institute, has done great work on this front across the country. He is perhaps the most ardent and effective opponent of raced-based preferences in the United States and the genius behind California's Prop. 209. Join in his effort—or others like it that seek to undo the damage done by an aggressively activist court.

We also need to remind our elected politicians not to pass the buck onto the courts. Even some of the politicians who like to complain about runaway courts are relieved when justices take issues out of the political realm. President Bush showed a supreme case of buck-passing when he signed John McCain's campaign finance law while expressing his belief that it was unconstitutional. The president has a sworn duty to uphold the Constitution. President Bush should have vetoed that law, whatever the political consequences. We can't leave these things up to the courts.

The Supreme Court is not God. It gets its powers from the consent of the governed—and it's time we expressed our dissent.

CHAPTER 5

KEEPING IT LOCAL

The more I see of our country, the more I love it.

In the past year alone, I have spoken to various professional and grassroots organizations in Florida, Texas, Pennsylvania, Oklahoma, Colorado, Arizona, Illinois, and California. When I leave my home base of Washington, D.C., to give a speech in, let's say, San Antonio, I usually begin my remarks this way: "It's so great to be back in the United States!" Our capital does seem like a foreign country at times—the home of so many pompous people from political, media, lobbying, and legal circles who have forgotten that outside the Beltway there is this place called America. Most of us who live in Washington actually hail from real America, yet somehow our proximity to the government's halls of power has switched something off in our brains. We think we are the center of the universe, totally blanking on the fact that America is rich because of her state-by-state diversity. Not the politically correct kind of diversity, either. Legislative priorities vary from East Coast to West, Southwest to Northwest, the mountain states to the old Rust Belt. Virginia's priorities differ from New York's. New York's differ from South Dakota's. And South Dakotans have an entirely different view of the world than, say, Marylanders. There's nothing wrong with that. In fact, the states are one of the greatest legacies of our constitutional system. By properly dividing responsibilities between the states and the federal government, we can not only return more power to the people—we can actually make government work better.

What? Laura wants government to work better? Aren't conservatives supposed to be *against* government? Not quite. It is true that I think small government is a good idea. If you want to cut taxes, you will generally get my support. If you say that the federal government wields too much power, I will usually stand up and cheer. But conservatives are not libertarians. We understand that society is fragile and delicate, that borders don't defend themselves, that criminals don't arrest themselves, and that the job of business is to make money, not to preserve the culture. Like the Founders, I want a small but effective government. And too often our federal government fails simply *because* it is federal in nature.

Think about what it means when Congress passes a law, or a federal agency issues a policy. Any federal policy automatically applies to more than 300 million people, spread across thousands of miles from the coast of Maine to Hawaii. (And that doesn't even count Guam or Puerto Rico.) What are the odds that a single policy on a particular issue is going to be the best choice for all 300 million people? That the same policy will work on the crowded streets of Brooklyn as on the open plains of Kansas? That the same policy will please conservative Alabamians and liberals from San Francisco? The odds are not so good. And it's not like Congress is full of Solomons with the wisdom necessary to balance the endless differences across our vast country.

Even worse, as government becomes more centralized it moves farther away from the people. If you don't like what the local school board or city council is up to, you can show up at their meet-

> # THE FORGOTTEN PART OF THE CONSTITUTION
>
>))) "The powers not delegated to the United States by the Constitution, nor prohibited by it to the States, are reserved for the States respectively, or to the people."
> —U.S. Constitution, Amendment X

ings and yell at them. Try doing that to the Senate. Every voter becomes more important as the scale of government gets smaller. If you're a Virginian, your state is represented by eleven congressmen in the U.S. House of Representatives. But in Virginia's General Assembly, at the state level, there are one hundred elected delegates. In other words, your congressman represents ten times as many people as does your delegate to the state house. Who do you think needs your vote more? Who is more likely to have time to listen to you and represent your views?

The Founders never intended members of Congress to be so removed from their constituents. Do you know how many people the Founders thought each congressman should represent? Go look it up; it's in the Constitution. (I'll just wait until you find the answer.) Oh, okay, for those of you who won't look it up (lazybones!), the Constitution provides that the number of representatives shall not exceed one in 30,000 persons. (It's in Article I, Section

2.) It would have been one in 40,000, but George Washington thought that ratio was too large. Think about that. The Founders thought that in a representative government, each member of the House should represent roughly one small town's worth of constituents (by today's standards).

Things have changed since 1787. To have a 1 to 30,000 ratio today, we would need approximately *10,000* members in the House. (I'd like to see Nancy Pelosi try to keep order in those meetings.) Instead, today, each member of the House represents almost 700,000 people. And the House is the part of government that is supposed to be *closest* to the people. In a country of 300 *million* people (and growing) there are only one hundred senators and only one president. How "representative" can such a government be? Not very.

So our federal government has two big problems. One, our country is too large and diverse to be adequately covered by a single set of policies. Two, because the country is so big, it is very difficult even for members of the House to adequately represent the people who elect them. Neither of these problems is going away anytime soon. Certainly the country is not going to get smaller. And I don't think anyone really believes we should have thousands of members in the House of Representatives—talk about "big government." The congressional dining room would become a drive-through and C–SPAN would constitute half of your cable lineup. In light of these facts, how can we truly give "Power to the People"?

Federalism is a big part of the answer. In general, it is far better that issues be decided by a town council than a state legislature, and better that issues be decided by a state legislature than the federal government. Each step up that ladder takes governmental power farther away from the people it's meant to serve and puts more power in unreachable government bureaucracies.

This is not a new concept. Indeed, we often forget that our first thirteen states are actually *older* than the federal government. Con-

YES, THERE IS *LIBERAL* FEDERALISM!

》》》 Now, I know what some of you may be thinking—wait a second, federalism has recently become the big cry of liberals who have grown tired of being in the minority on issues such as stem cell research and greenhouse gas emissions. California and Missouri now spend billions in state tax dollars on embryonic stem cell research. So, yes, federalism can cut both ways. But that's all right. We just need to win the arguments at the state and local level. So what are you waiting for? Keep yourself informed, and get active!

sider this fact: by the time the first U.S. Congress met in 1789, the Commonwealth of Virginia was already 182 years old. Keeping government local, keeping critical decisions at a level where we can control government—instead of the other way around—is a long-standing part of the American experience. As the Supreme Court has long recognized: "[t]he Constitution, in all its provisions, looks to an indestructible Union, composed of indestructible States."[1] Indeed, our Constitution was originally ratified by sovereign states, each of which surrendered only limited power to the federal government. Indeed, the Tenth Amendment of the Constitution specifically provides that "[t]he powers not delegated to the United States by the Constitution, nor prohibited by it to the States, *are reserved to the States respectively, or to the people.*" In short, the Founders believed that the federal government has only those powers given to it by the Constitution. All other political powers belong to the states or the people.

And it is clear that the Founders believed that the powers delegated to the federal government were quite narrow. In *Federalist* 45, James Madison tried to reassure the good citizens of New York that the powers allocated to the federal government would not threaten the states:

The powers delegated by the proposed Constitution to the federal government are few and defined. Those which are to remain in the State governments are numerous and indefinite. The former will be exercised principally on external objects, as war, peace, negotiation, and foreign commerce....The powers reserved to the several States will extend to all the objects which, in the ordinary course of affairs, concern the lives, liberties, and properties of the people, and the internal order, improvement, and prosperity of the State.

You see, that's how our system is supposed to work. The federal government should concentrate on those areas of policy that cannot be dealt with at the state level—primarily foreign policy issues. Most of the key areas of domestic policy should be left to the states.

That makes sense. Because the federal government is so removed from the people, we should use it only when absolutely necessary. Unfortunately, over the 220 years since the Constitution was originally approved, we have wandered far from this original intention.

Who Died and Made You Emperor?

Local control—and even national sovereignty—are not popular ideas among the elites. They look at such issues from exactly the opposite perspective of most voters. We are worried about how we can prevent the elites from taking power from us while they are trying to figure out how to *increase* the power they already have. This is particularly true for those elites who happen to live inside the Beltway. They intend to rule, and they are not going to let any nonsense about "federalism" get in their way.

For one thing, liberals are generally indifferent to arguments that involve the Founders. Once you start mentioning James Madison or the Federalist Papers, the eyes of your typical liberal start to glaze over. Why should we let some dead white guy tell us how to organize our government? (The obvious answer—that these dead white guys *invented* our government, and that they knew more about it than we do—never occurs to liberals.) Furthermore, many well-intentioned, highly educated elites in Washington sincerely believe that they have the best answers, and thus are entitled to exercise ever more power. All those little Americans outside their social circle look the same to them. The only cultural diversity they're interested in is race, sex, and class (because they see the potential for government patronage and voting blocs in these politically correct categories).

They tend to regard concepts like local control, hometown pride, or states' rights as hokey and inefficient at best, and more likely dangerous, bigoted, and racist at worst. To them, the words "states' rights" draw up visions of snarling dogs attacking civil rights protesters. They miss the fact that segregationists hid behind ideas of federalism precisely because those ideas are so powerful and so persuasive; it was their way to avoid the obvious fact that segregation wasn't about states' rights, it was about denying the rights of American citizens.

But when, for instance, the Supreme Court uses an expansive reading of the Fourteenth Amendment to strike down the laws of all fifty states with regard to abortion (as in *Roe v. Wade*), or prohibit prayers over a loudspeaker before a high school football game in Texas (in *Santa Fe v. Roe*), or micromanage the criminal law of the states (the Supreme Court has spent years rewriting the instructions judges give to Texas juries in death penalty cases[2]), we're not talking about upholding the rights of American citizens, we're talking about *denying* the rights of American citizens to govern themselves through their state governments. Why can't the people of Pennsylvania, Ohio, Missouri, and every other state elect legislators who can determine their state's abortion laws?

AN EARLY WARNING

))) "[E]very central government wor-
ships uniformity; uniformity
relieves it from inquiry into an
infinity of details, which must be
attended to if rules have to be
adapted to different men, instead
of indiscriminately subjecting all
men to the same rule."[3]

—**Alexis de Tocqueville**

Why can't the people of Texas decide their criminal justice laws? Why can't the city council of Santa Fe, Texas, decide whether to allow prayers before high school football games? The Founders certainly intended to give them that authority. (Remember: the Bill of Rights imposed restrictions on the *federal* government, not on the states.) The courts, and an overgrown federal government, are taking away our constitutional rights and arrogating them solely to themselves.

The last thing the liberal elites want to do is hand power back to the rubes in Middle America, who clearly aren't sophisticated enough to handle it. They'd rather we transfer power to well-manicured diplomats at the UN, hand-tailored European elites, and Ivy League Manhattan jet-setters (with a few Hollywood celebrities thrown in for good measure).

So they ignore the wisdom of James Madison and the other Founders. Instead, they contend that we have what they like to call a "living" Constitution. They think we should have outgrown the Constitution's strict limits on federal power.

But, hello? The Constitution is still supposed to be the law of the land and it still grants Congress, the president, and the federal judiciary specific enumerated powers, and explicitly forbids the federal government from doing anything else. The Tenth Amendment is perfectly clear on this point. So who's supposed to be in charge here? The Federal Leviathan? The Supreme Court? No. Under our system, the Founders intended that most power would be wielded by we the people *by and through our respective state governments.*

But that's not the system we now have. For a long time, activist judges, overreaching politicians, and an ignorant media have conspired to lift the limits on federal power. They took advantage of the Great Depression to argue that some problems were too big for the states. They took advantage of the civil rights movement to argue that the states can't be trusted. And by and large, they have significantly altered the balance of power in our system.

While our states once had complete control over education policies, criminal codes, and most other areas of domestic policy—just as the Founders intended—now their policies are dictated by Washington. We have huge disagreements in this country over abortion, but we all have to live under a single policy established by federal judges. We have huge disagreements over law enforcement, but the federal courts impose a single code on all fifty states. We have huge disagreements on how to help the poor, but our efforts to fight poverty are dominated by federal welfare programs. We have huge disagreements on education, but all fifty states must yield to the federal "No Child Left Behind" Act.

Consider these facts. In 2006, state government tax collections amounted to just over $706 billion.[4] Meanwhile, the federal government collected over $2.4 *trillion* in revenues.[5] In other words, the federal government had more than three times as much revenue as all fifty states *combined*. Justice Louis Brandeis believed that the states should be "laboratories of democracy," places where many different political solutions can be tried, giving our political leaders the chance to learn from experience. But how can states take the lead on major issues, when the federal government has so much more money? The federal government wins by bribing the states with federal mandates. And so, on issue after issue, the states simply implement policies devised and developed in Washington by federal bureaucrats who don't care about the many differences between Rome, Georgia, and Rome, New York.

Put Them in Their Place

This should all change. By returning control to states and localities, we give more power to ourselves. You want policies that work? Let local people decide what's best for them. Yes, policies in Arkansas will be different from policies in Oregon. But that's okay, because the *people* in Arkansas are different from the *people* in Oregon. Yes, some states will adopt policies that fail. But maybe they can learn from the states that succeed. When the federal government fails, *all* fifty states suffer, and no one learns anything.

Federalism will also relieve the tension surrounding some of our most heated issues. Take immigration. We, the American people, are bitterly divided over this issue. The elites want open borders. Most people want our borders enforced. Because the federal government tends to be much more responsive to the elites than to the people, it has significantly failed to enforce our immigration laws. Meanwhile, efforts to achieve so-called immigration reform at the federal level have been a disaster. But local governments are responding to their constituents on this issue. Virginia passed a bill in early 2005 requiring applicants for state and local benefits—except for emergency aid—to prove they were in the country legally. Arizona voters followed suit using the ballot initiative process (which, notably, is not available on the federal level). Many other states, counties, and towns have taken steps to secure law and order on the immigration question. And they would have done more were it not for federal courts, which stand up for the elites, and occasionally strike down the people's laws (the way they struck down California's famous Proposition 187 that ended subsidies for illegal immigrants).

Imagine if California, Arizona, New Mexico, and Texas were given more responsibility to control their respective borders with Mexico, as well as the resources to fulfill that responsibility that is currently held by the federal government. No longer would voters in those states have to complain to far-off bureaucrats in Washington if they didn't like what was happening at the border. Instead, they could complain to their governors, or to their state representatives. The governors of these states would certainly be much more responsive than the federal government has been. And if they weren't, they wouldn't hold office for long. On the related issue of how we can encourage immigrants to assimilate into this country, local governments are leading the good fight, while the feds look the other way. Arizona voters in 2006 passed an English-only law, and Reston, Virginia, is considering a measure making English the official language of the city government.

Just as state lawmakers are picking up Washington's slack on immigration enforcement, there are also some *lawmen* doing their part throughout the country. In Arizona, Maricopa County sheriff Joe Arpaio is turning his local sheriff's department into a border patrol of sorts, and he checks all his inmates to see if they are "documented." In Hazleton, Pennsylvania, Mayor Lou Barletta, grandson of a legal immigrant, has pledged to make his town "the toughest place on illegal immigrants in America."[6] In August 2006, Barletta pushed through the city council a law to make it illegal to rent an apartment to an illegal—punishable by a $1,000-per-day fine.

Let's consider another divisive issue: public schools. When Ronald Reagan came to Washington, one of the rallying cries from his followers was "Abolish the Department of Education." (I should know, I worked there for Education Secretary Bill Bennett during President Reagan's second term.) In 1980, the budget for this agency stood at $14 billion. When Secretary Bennett tried to cut his budget, Congress wouldn't let him, demanding increases instead. For all his popularity, President Reagan could not resist this tide. After he left office, a new generation of federal lawmakers grew more and more excited about the possibilities of using the federal government to reform the schools. Even the GOP-led Congress from 1994 to 2006 got into the act. By 2006, no one was talking about abolishing this department. Indeed, its budget had increased to $88.9 billion. And our public school system certainly wasn't getting better. Now imagine that all the money spent by our federal government on education over the last few decades—an amount in the hundreds of billions of dollars—had been given to the states to use as they saw fit. Instead of one-size-fits-all policies that have no hope of working across the country, each state could have tailored programs that would fit their history, geography, and people. Rural states like North Dakota would have programs that looked very different from urban states like Ohio. But surely we would be better off than we are now.

Yet we shouldn't be satisfied to return education policy to the state level. Almost every state has an incredibly diverse array of jurisdictions: rich and poor, urban and rural. Our public schools should reflect that reality. Liberals will tell you that local control gives wealthy suburban schools an unfair advantage over poor schools. Don't you believe it. The biggest problem we have is that the one-size-fits-all model doesn't really work *anywhere*. Empowering parents and local administrators will certainly work better than our current practice.

Think about how federalism has helped with respect to the death penalty. Elites on the East and West Coasts have long had attitudes toward the death penalty very much at odds with their neighbors in the middle of the country. But thanks to federalism, some states can keep the death penalty, even while other states adopt a more, shall we say, European approach. As a result the death penalty has not proven to be as divisive an issue as abortion, where a federal solution has been imposed on every state.

Federalism can even help Americans deal with silly and misguided Supreme Court decisions. For example, a few years ago the city of New London, Connecticut, condemned people's homes so that a private company could take over the property as part of a redevelopment project. To most folks, this violates the Takings Clause of the Fifth Amendment, which provides that private property can only be taken for a "public use." But the Supreme Court—neither for the first nor the last time—took a different view, setting off a storm of protests among Americans who didn't want their homes taken for some councilman's pet project. And you know what? Many state and local governments responded, with thirty-four states and many communities passing measures to curb eminent domain abuse.[7]

Vote with Your Feet

Giving power to state and local governments not only boosts our power at the ballot box, but it also enables us to vote with our feet. If your town wants to use tax dollars to pay for condoms for school kids and you're in a minority objecting to this practice, you can move to the next town. On the other hand, if the *federal* government launches such a program, your only escape is to send your kids to private school or home school (though regulators are eyeing those, as well)—and there's *no* escape for taxpayers, other than maybe moving to the Virgin Islands.

As someone who grew up in Connecticut and attended college in New Hampshire, I have seen how voters can exercise a great deal of power simply by crossing state lines. For years, New Hampshire has served as the destination of choice for thousands of taxpayers fleeing Massachusetts's big government and high tax rates. The Census Bureau in 2006 put the per capita tax burden in Massachusetts at $2,628.26—30.4 percent above the national average, the seventh-highest in the country. But imagine how much higher those taxes would be if the people of Massachusetts lacked the option of moving to New Hampshire, which had the fourth-lowest per capita tax burden, at $1,543.79—23.4 percent below the national average.[8] In fact, "Taxachusetts" lost more than 169,000 people on net from 2000 to 2004, to domestic migration, and over half a million since 1990.

That's really voting with your feet.

Laboratories of Democracy at Work

Federalism allows greater opportunity for experience, rather than some "expert's" abstract reasoning, a bureaucrat's convenience, or a politician's demagoguery, to be our guide. A great example comes from the 1996 welfare reform bill—the crowning achievement of the Republican Congress we once had, and certainly the best thing Bill Clinton ever did. This legislation left the states free to come up with their own ways to get people off welfare rolls and into jobs. Wisconsin governor Tommy Thompson launched a program called "Wisconsin Works." Among many commonsense changes to the program, Wisconsin made every one of its welfare case workers an employment counselor. Wisconsin cut its welfare rolls by 71 percent in the first two years after welfare reform—more than double the pace of the rest of the country.[9] Since then, many states have moved to emulate Wisconsin Works.

That's how the laboratories of democracy are supposed to work. If Republicans in Congress had tried to dictate one single approach to get people off welfare, the chances of failure would have been high. But with fifty states conducting fifty experiments in democracy and public policy, it is not surprising that at least one of those states got it right.

More recently, we've seen some states and towns take bold policy steps in education. Utah, for instance, has a universal school choice program, with vouchers for parents of all school-age children. The District of Columbia, over the loud objections of the teachers' union, launched a charter school program, which quickly grew to 17,500 students by 2006, while the suffering D.C. public schools lost enrollment.[10] Allowing states and localities the freedom to try different approaches—freeing them from the federal straitjacket—helps bring a responsive spirit to public policy, even a sense of healthy competition, that benefits the whole country.

It also complements the way we live and is responsive to what is really important in our lives. As Americans, can we truly rectify all the problems of the world, even through global institutions like the UN? Of course not. Even in our own country, if I'm a Mississippian, is it my duty to make sure people in Rhode Island are educating their children according to *my* values?

No. Our first real concern in life is and ought to be for our families and then for our neighbors. We also take pride in our state, are devoted to our country, and do what we can to help others in need around the world, through charitable giving or missionary work. But in our everyday lives it is our neighborhoods, our schools, our local roads, hospitals, police, and fire departments that really matter. We all know that our most important business is our own, by which I mean ourselves, our families, and closest friends. Minding other people's business does us no good.

More and more businesses operate on this same principle. In the modern world, the one-size-fits-all model simply doesn't work any more. When you go on Amazon or Yahoo!, you will often see a page that is especially designed for you. When you buy a car, the dealer helps you pick out the options that are right for you. Naturally, government programs can't be as responsive as private businesses—which is one reason to always prefer private sector alternatives—but they can certainly be a lot more responsive than they are now. And the best way to achieve that goal is to take power—and money—away from the federal government, and return it to states and localities.

Uncle Sam the Crack Dealer

But this raises another question: Why do we have to fight to defend our states and localities? Why don't our state and local governments defend themselves? The Founders would be surprised at the extent to which state and local governments allow the Feds to push them around. Turning back to *Federalist* 45, we see that James Madison was actually worried about protecting the federal government from the states:

> The State governments will have the advantage of the federal government, whether we compare them in respect to the immediate dependence of the one on the other, to the weight of personal influence which each side will possess; to the powers respectively vested in them; to the predilection and probable support of the people; to the disposition and faculty of resisting and frustrating the measures of each other.

In our time, it has not worked out this way. There are many explanations that could be given for this development. But much of it goes back to the federal government having so much more money than the states. Because of this disparity, the federal government can persuade the states to give up their power in exchange for money. Our highway system is a good example of how this works.

In 1956, the federal government began handing out billions of dollars to the states for the sake of building highways. The money came from the Federal Highway Trust Fund, funded by federal gasoline taxes. State-level politicians loved this arrangement—they got more money to spend without having to take responsibility for tax increases.

This was something like the crack dealer giving the kid his first hit for free. Soon, the states were hooked on the federal highway money. That's when Washington started attaching a price. In the 1980s, Washington politicians wanted all the states to set twenty-one as the legal drinking age. But the Constitution does not delegate power to the federal government to legislate a national drinking age. So the federal government persuaded the states to do it instead. In 1984, Congress passed a measure that would cut the federal highway money to any state that didn't set its drinking age at twenty-one. In short order, every state followed suit—they had little choice with millions of dollars at stake.

Now, you may say, "So what? I'm glad we have a twenty-one-year-old drinking age." But that's not the point. There's no limit to the conditions Washington can attach to the money on which the states are now dependent. With Democrats in control of Congress now, who knows what they will impose? They may force every state to ban smoking in cars, or return us to national speed limits of fifty-five miles per hour. The possibilities are endless.

And what is true for highways is true for schools, or for any area where Washington doles out cash. Most obvious of late has been President Bush's No Child Left Behind Act. While this costly bill didn't create a national curriculum, it did seriously extend federal authority over schools. President Bush did this in the name of increased "accountability," which is a noble ideal, but it doesn't justify increasing federal involvement in a local issue. The federal government always attaches strings to the money it spends.

Power to the Global Bureaucracies = Less *POWER TO THE PEOPLE*

Keeping it local means not only preferring local government over state government and state government over the federal government. It means defending American sovereignty against the "globalists" who think we should be ruled by the United Nations. The priorities of the UN are not always our own, or in our own national interests.

One of the UN's latest crusades is to stop global warming by severely curtailing the use of fossil fuels. (You know, the stuff that's burned by the private jets of our eco-friendly entertainers.) As a practical matter, this means that foreign bureaucrats want Americans to use less energy. The main players in this battle are the UN's Intergovernmental Panel on Climate Change (IPCC) and the Kyoto Protocol—a treaty requiring industrialized nations to cut their emissions of CO_2. In 1997, the U.S. Senate rejected this treaty by a vote of 95 to 0. But the will of the American people means nothing to international bureaucrats, and so this issue will not go away. UN types and their European and American allies are particularly excited about the global warming issue because it gives them an opportunity to beat up on the United States. Some global elites see this as the dawning of a new era of world government. Former French president Jacques Chirac gushed in praise for Kyoto, hailing it "this unprecedented instrument, the first component of an authentic global governance."[11]

We got a hint as to what this "global governance" might entail in February 2007 (a couple of days after Al Gore won his Oscar). After the IPCC issued its report on global warming, the UN asked a panel to give policy recommendations. The central recommendation was—surprise, surprise—a global tax on carbon dioxide emissions.[12]

Remember CO_2 is not pollution—it's plant food. Sure, it contributes to global warming, but (except for nuclear power, which the environmentalists still say is evil) there is no reliable way to produce energy without emitting CO_2. And the amount of CO_2 humans produce is dwarfed by what is produced by "nature."[13] But that's not the point. The point is that for many elites around the world, global warming provides the perfect avenue for subverting American sovereignty. No longer, they argue, can nations be left to their own devices. Instead, *global* politicians must pursue *global* policies—and must levy *global* taxes. More than 230 years after Lexington and Concord, foreigners are still trying to tax us without our consent.

Not that any of this bothers people like Al Gore and Hillary Clinton. For them, treaties like Kyoto are just another way to take more power from those SUV-driving voters and turn it over to the hybrid-driving elites. But while liberals and Europeans might not have a problem submitting themselves to centralized, bloated bureaucracies—after all, they're pretty comfortable with such bodies—most Americans do not want any part of such an arrangement. International bureaucrats can't even be honest when they judge figure skating in the Olympics—why would we want them making our laws?

If you want to see what "global governance" will look like, check out the EU. Over the last fifty years, the EU has grown from its roots as an economic arrangement between France and Germany into an unwieldy mega-government that increasingly dominates European life. Remarkably, it's not clear that most Europeans want this to happen. But what the typical European wants doesn't seem to matter. For example, in 2001 voters in Ireland were presented with the Nice Treaty, yet another in a never-ending series of EU accords designed to take power away from the formerly sovereign nations of Europe and deliver it to the EU. The Irish voted the treaty down. Unwilling to take no for an answer, the Irish government simply scheduled another vote in 2002. This time the Irish voters approved the treaty. (They were not given another chance to vote no.)

The EU pressed on, finally putting forward an enormous "constitution" that would significantly revise the relationships between the EU member states and would (surprise, surprise) give more power to the EU. Everything was going fine for the Eurocrats until May 2005, when the French government actually allowed its citizens to vote on this document. They voted it down. A month later, the Dutch also rejected the new constitution. The Euro-elites were crestfallen. French president Jacques Chirac, clearly irritated, said that he accepted his people's "sovereign decision" (how big of him!) but claimed that it created "a difficult context for the defense of our interests in Europe."[14] And, of course, the debate isn't over. As the Irish learned, the Eurocrats don't usually let little things like the voters stand in their way. In April 2007, press reports indicated that the European Commission president was planning to host meetings with other EU leaders to discuss the constitutional project.[15] Not surprisingly, these were described as "closed-door" talks.[16] Because why should the people of Europe know what's happening *before* the elites have decided to tell them? Unfortunately for the European politicians, a document was leaked to the press about what actually transpired behind the closed doors. German chancellor Angela Merkel suggested in a memo that they could recover from the embarrassing defeat of the constitution if they "use[d] different terminology without changing the legal substance." In other words—keep trying to feed the rubes undemocratic centralized rule, just give the dish a new name.

The story of the EU should be a lesson to all of us. Elites like powerful centralized governments. It's easier and more efficient for them—if not for the rest of us. If we want to preserve our national independence, and the federal system left to us by the Founders, we will have to stand firmly against the greedy global bureaucrats.

I'd Like to Teach the World to Tax, in Perfect Harmony. . . .

Another international behemoth, the Organization for Economic Cooperation and Development (OECD) (now, who could be against the lofty goals of "economic cooperation and development"?) is working on the "harmonization" of tax rates and regulations across the Atlantic. Specifically, the OECD is aiming to end "harmful tax competition." But "harmful tax competition" means the U.S. has lower taxes than France, and so businesses prefer the United States, which "harms" France.[17]

The "cooperation" the OECD is talking about means we raise our taxes to European levels. The OECD's plans threaten our sovereignty, our liberty, and our economy. Thankfully, the Bush administration has outright rejected the "harmonization" agenda.[18] If, however, our next president is more keen to cultivate European adulation, you might find the White House joining the high-tax choir of Europe's experiment in socialism.

The OECD's quest for "harmony" is a direct and unapologetic effort to abolish the advantages that sovereignty provides—multiple experiments in governance. The folks in Europe figure they've already worked out the best way to do things, and so it's about time for the rest of the world to get in line.

Returning *POWER TO THE PEOPLE*

The federal government has its proper functions, including national defense, international diplomacy, coining money, and the rest of the specific powers delegated to it by the Constitution. Beyond these constitutionally enumerated powers, the exercise of federal power is unconstitutional. Even good people can be tempted by the allure of limitless federal power. Remember J. R. R. Tolkien's "Ring of Power"? In *The Lord of the Rings* the heroes worked hard to resist the seduction to use Sauron's ring for their own purposes. Similarly, lawmakers must do everything to withstand the desire to use federal authority unconstitutionally.

Should public schools be held accountable for their failure or success? Sure. But that doesn't mean Congress should be the one holding them accountable. Is Wisconsin's implementation of welfare reform a resounding success? You bet. But that doesn't mean it would work everywhere—or that the federal government could effectively administer it.

There are a precious few Washington politicians who walk the walk when it comes to state and local control. We need to make it more common. Currently, lawmakers see little reason to adhere to the commonsense idea that most domestic issues should be handled by states and localities. If more constituents who understand federalism and local control made it clear that we see these principles as crucial, more politicians might start adhering to them.

In order to safeguard our sovereignty, it's pretty clear what we need to do—demand that our politicians clearly and unambiguously tell UN bureaucracts to get lost whenever they start sticking their noses into our business. Former senator Jesse Helms and former congressman Henry Hyde were champions of sovereignty on Capitol Hill. We need new champions—leaders who will take their places in saying no way to the International Criminal Court, the Kyoto Protocol, and any other global schemes that would give the UN or any international body more power over Americans.

Even more important, we need to educate ourselves. Read the Constitution. Read good books about American history. Memorize the Tenth Amendment or write it down on an index card and, as former senator Bob Dole used to do, carry it with you always. No amendment has been more ignored by the judges and politicians in Washington. The Tenth Amendment—with its loud proclamation that Washington may do no more than our Constitution has explicitly authorized it to do—is our best lever to return power to the people. It's what the Framers intended, it's what the Constitution requires, and it should guide the decisions of our elected officials. Why not demand that federal office-seekers take a "Tenth Amendment Pledge"?

When your congressman holds a local town hall meeting and starts bragging about his accomplishments—the new law he sponsored, or the new state project he got funded—ask him specifically what article and what section of the Constitution authorized that law. Write letters to the editor reminding people of the Tenth Amendment. And remember, just because there may be a problem in your hometown doesn't mean that the federal government should come in and fix it. More often than not, the federal government will make it worse!

But if we're going to tell Washington (and often even our state government) to get lost, we need to get much more involved on the local level. Now be honest: When you go into the voting booth on Election Day, do you even recognize the names of the candidates for local judge or county council? When was the last town council meeting you attended? One of the favorite arguments *against* local control is that local governments are incompetent and do not really have the support of the community. A lot of times, this is true. State and local government can be just as corrupt and wrong-headed as the federal government, which is why all government should be limited.

> # MARRIAGE AND "STATES' RIGHTS"?
>
> Some on the Left wonder how Republicans can support something like the Federal Marriage Amendment when it could end up usurping state or local laws that legalize gay marriage. The answer, of course, is that Congress is acting in a purely defensive manner. The federal courts, many fear, are going to use the Fourteenth Amendment to force all states to adopt homosexual marriage as a fundamental right.

But we can also do something very practical about it. It's our duty to address local problems and dive headfirst into local government—maybe by running for town council or serving on a local committee. You want to make your town, city, and country better?

You want the place cleaned up? Get involved, and do it! Run for office. If you're elected, you will do good not only locally, but you'll be positioned to fight against state and federal overreaching.

Fighting the federal beast will take bravery, and at times it will take civil disobedience. If a federal court orders a state to take down its display of the Ten Commandments, maybe the state ought to refuse. If Washington or the state government tell a town they need to open an abortion clinic, maybe the town ought to say no. One factor that allows the federal government and the Supreme Court to grab so much power is that state and local governments surrender. Meekly doing what we're told isn't what it means to be a good citizen. Sticking up for the Constitution is patriotic.

Utah stands as a shining example of good old-fashioned American defiance today. In May 2005, Governor Jon Huntsman signed a bipartisan bill that basically told the federal Department of Education to buzz off. The bill ordered educators in the state to give priority to state programs over the federal No Child Left Behind.[19] This meant giving up as much as $76 million in federal aid. It also meant being harshly criticized by the Bush administration and other defenders of No Child Left Behind. The Education Trust, a liberal group, wrote that such a move would prevent Utah from benefiting from the act, which "aims to raise overall achievement and close gaps between [ethnic and racial] groups."[20] But Utah simply proceeded to address that achievement gap its own way—by offering school vouchers and full school choice to *every* student in the state.

That's what it means to return power to the people.

6

SAVING OUR PORNIFIED CULTURE

started my day in early October 2005 as I had started every weekday for the previous four weeks—in the radiation room at the Sibley Memorial Hospital Breast Cancer Center. If I timed things just right I could make it to the hospital by 7:15 a.m., slip into my hospital gown, get "zapped," get dressed, jump back into my car, drive to the studio, prepare for my radio show, and be ready by the time we went on air at 9:00 a.m. I had only a few more weeks left, and then this phase of my treatment would be over. I really could see the light at the end of the tunnel. On most days I felt fine—though fatigued and gaunt, I still felt much better than two months earlier when I was getting hooked up every two weeks to an intravenous chemotherapy cocktail of adriamycin (nicknamed "the Red Devil") and one called "cytoxin" (that one needed a nickname).

In the late afternoon of this particularly drizzly, gray fall day, I was upstairs in my bedroom resting when I heard a knock on the door. I looked for my wig but couldn't find it, so I threw on a baseball cap to cover my bald, splotchy head. I honestly was worried about scaring people who weren't used to seeing me post-chemo. When I opened my front door, I knew immediately that I should have stayed in bed.

"I'm a stringer for the *National Enquirer* and wanted to talk to you about your ex–..." was as far as this twenty-something got before I cut him off. He clutched a copy of the weekly tabloid, opened to a photo of then *Today* show host Katie Couric and my ex-fiancé, smiling outside a New York restaurant. We were to be married in June but a few weeks after I was diagnosed and operated on, the relationship ended.

I glanced around quickly to see if he had a photographer with him. Lifting my hat up, I said, "As you can see, I am in the middle of something...and I'm not interested."

Half-heartedly he tried again to rope me into talking with him. "Not interested. Don't care," I repeated before closing the door. For the next few days I left my house through the back door in the event there were other ambush attempts. When I look back on this incident, I think—if only reporters were as committed to covering the stories of our brave troops! Yet, of course, the market for juicy "celebrity" gossip of any kind is hot. (And I admit I've picked up these tabloids in the past.) The sadder the story, the better the magazine's sales. I used to laugh about this stuff, but now I was part of the story. Suddenly, it wasn't so funny. I've wondered about that young man working as a "stringer" for that tabloid. Did he feel good about what he was doing? Was his mother proud?

It was the first time that I felt the personal cost of our toxic culture.

* * * * *

Our national celebrity obsession is just one element in our cultural free fall. When we speak of a cultural breakdown the problem seems too big for any of us to tackle. It seems all the more overwhelming because American culture as we know it today is the product of millions of decisions made over the course of generations. Whether you generally dislike or like our culture's current direction will depend on your own life experiences and upbringing. And even if you do believe we are at a critical cultural moment— how do we *win* something as nebulously defined as "the culture war"? Who are the enemies and what do they believe?

For our purposes let's focus on one particular meaning of the word *culture* (from good old *Webster's Dictionary*)—"the characteristic features of everyday existence (as diversions or a way of life) shared by people in a place or time <popular *culture*>." We can't change the past, but we can affect the future in a profoundly positive way if we confront the supremely ugly, sad nature of current trends, while at the same time celebrate that which is good and right.

Let's step outside of ourselves for a moment in the hope of better understanding where we are culturally. Let's say you were asked by a close friend or your church to sponsor a family visiting the United States from a remote farming village in Northern China (or insert the remote village of your choice). You are told that back home this family has little to no contact with the modern world— no TV, no Internet, no iPods, no malls, no multiplexes.

You are tasked with showing them around and giving them a taste of American living. How would you describe American

popular culture to them? When they ask why twenty different magazines lined up on the racks at the local supermarket are devoted to
the latest drinking binge of a Hollywood bad girl—what do you say?
How do you explain why preteen boys are hanging around on the
street corner with their pants hung below their rears, or why girls are
walking down the street wearing skin-tight jeans with their thong
underwear and bellies showing? What do you say when you turn on
a "cable news" channel and the visiting mother asks for a translation
of a crawler at the bottom of the screen that reads "Teacher Nabbed
for Student Sex-capades"? What about when a pop-up ad for
"XXXHot Young ThingsXXX" flashes on the computer screen
when you're showing your guests family vacation photos you just
downloaded? Which non-animated, non-Pixar movie would you
want the whole family to see while they were in this country?

Do you see what I mean? Wouldn't you be frustrated and embarrassed? Does America's popular culture—exported across the
globe—tell the right story to the outside world about who we are
as a country and what we believe? Is there enough good out there
in the popular culture to counterbalance the bad?

It's difficult to face up to this but we must. We owe it to ourselves and to millions of Americans not yet born to survey the dry,
barren cultural landscape and rework the soil. Yes, media executives are making millions churning out trashy films, stupid television, misogynist music, sleazy magazines, and porn-laden Web
fare. But they are only partly to blame—after all, we are buying this
junk. This is really dumb and destructive. We are poisoning ourselves and future generations.

The "Just Turn It Off" Defense Debunked

When parents or concerned citizens complain about some specific
television program, commercial, or music lyrics, liberals usually

throw out one of two arguments. First, they will claim that every-thing under the sun is protected by the First Amendment (except talk radio, but more about that later), and that any attempt to regulate content is censorship. Second, they say "just turn it off—no one is forcing you to listen to those lyrics, or watch that television show."

The "turn it off" defense is disingenuous and pathetic and should stop no one from demanding more from our entertainment, media, and advertising industries. Mothers and fathers should be able to sit down with their children and watch the World Series or Super Bowl without gripping the remote out of fear of what might fall out, pop out, or stick out next. We all should be able to drive down the highway without seeing billboards pushing treatments for erectile dysfunction or an adult 1-900-SEX-LINE. We should be able to live in a country where the dominant culture doesn't feel empowered to elevate the freakish fringe while insulting the intelli-gence and values of the mainstream.

Let's also not forget that when the Left is outraged by some entertainer's hate speech, the "just change the channel" line loses its appeal. Did they take that approach when radio host Don Imus made his racially insensitive remark about the Rutgers women's basketball team? No, instead they wanted him gone, and no expression of contrition on his part was going to satisfy them. For thirty-five years conservatives have been trying to get liberals to admit that the culture has become polluted with negative stereo-types, sexualized content, and coarsened language. For thirty-five years, those concerns fell on deaf ears. In fact, conservatives were ridiculed as prudes set on stifling artistic expression. What about Imus and his "expression"? Are the liberal P.C. police immune to the charge of "liberal hypocrisy"?

I constantly hear stories from fed-up parents about the cultural minefield through which they tiptoe every day. My friend Raymond was watching television early one Sunday evening with his seven-year-old son when a commercial came on that seemed innocent enough. It showed an older guy watching sports on television. A woman enters the scene and the two of them go to another room as the sports broadcast continues. At the end of the commercial the announcer says, "In cases of erections lasting more than four hours, contact a physician." Cut back to Raymond's house: "Daddy, what's an erection and why is it bad if it lasts more than four hours?" his son asked.

The "just turn it off" argument doesn't fly when the bombardment of sexual imagery is everywhere you turn. "Honey, can you go get the mail out of the mailbox before you go to soccer practice?" a mother asks her twelve-year-old son. She notices it's taking him longer than usual to walk to the mailbox and back. Ten minutes later it all makes sense when he drops the pile of mail on the kitchen counter, and on top is the Victoria's Secret catalogue. The cover shot features a gorgeous brunette in pink bra and panties with the "come hither" look.

SEE SEX YOUNG, HAVE SEX YOUNG.

>>> One recent university study found that "exposure to sexual content in music, movies, television, and magazines accelerates white adolescents' sexual activity and increases their risk of engaging in early sexual intercourse." In fact, white youths who were subjected to repeated exposures of sexual content were 2.2 times more likely to have sex between the ages of fourteen and sixteen than those who viewed much less of such material. "Some, especially those who have fewer alternative sources of sexual norms, such as parents or friends, may use the media as a kind of sexual superpeer that encourages them to be sexually active," the report concluded.

Source: Jane D. Brown, Kelly Ladin L'Engle, Carol J. Pardun, Guang Guo, Kristin Kenneavy, and Christine Jackson, "Sexy Media Matter: Exposure to Sexual Content in Music, Movies, Television, and Magazines Predicts Black and White Adolescents' Sexual Behavior," *Pediatrics*, Vol. 117 No. 4, April 2006, 1018–1027.

I know what some of you are saying at this point: "Oh, come on, Laura. Sex has always been used to sell stuff—clothes, cars, perfume, everything." That may be partially true, but sex in advertising has never been as prevalent, explicit, and marketed toward kids as it is today. Is there no difference between an ad featuring a pretty girl ordering lunch at McDonald's and one for Carl's Jr., where ex-con sex video star Paris Hilton is sudsing up a car in a bikini? And are we really supposed to believe that Pizza Hut can't sell pizza without having Jessica Simpson strutting her stuff in a sexually charged commercial modeled after her inane character in the *Dukes of Hazzard* movie? In the ad she vamps her way through a doorway in a tight dress, approaches a teenage boy sitting down with his mouth hanging open. She leans down, chest-first, close to his face, and says "one's going to pop right into you" as she drops a "pizza bite" into his mouth.

Short of living in a Saddam Hussein spider hole, there is no escaping the barrage of sexually charged images being pushed by big corporations and their marketing firms. The hugely popular clothing retailer Abercrombie & Fitch thought it was being edgy and hip in late 2003 when it filled its 280-page "Christmas Quarterly" with photos of barely dressed teens. (What an innovative way to commemorate the birth of the Baby Jesus!) Many of the most overtly sexual photos were group shots with the beautiful young models in various stages of undress. Why would anyone have thought that these portrayals were encouraging group sex? Maybe because one of the catalogue's featured "commentaries" was by a sex educator who extolled the virtues of engaging in threesomes and group masturbation in college.[1] There was a massive uproar about this, and eventually Abercrombie pulled the catalogue. But even today the A&F stores showcase huge posters of young people in sexually suggestive poses. The company's Internet home page is no better—the last time I checked it, the first image that pops up is a black and white close-up of a girl who can't be more than fifteen on her back with a shirtless teen boy lying on top of her. The folks at A&F left out the obvious headline: "Buy from Our Store and You'll Score."

Many magazine covers and billboards feature people with perfect bodies wearing next to nothing or clothes that leave nothing to the imagination. Over time, how does that affect the way all of us judge ourselves and others? How much pressure does this put on young girls (and boys) to look and dress a certain way? Sadly, we aren't surprised to read that girls as young as six years old are being diagnosed with anorexia.[2] The objectification of men and women has gotten progressively worse, and it is getting harder to escape.

When the "just turn it off" argument wears thin, many in the entertainment and media industry claim that they "are only giving the people what they want." I can't tell you how many times I have been told "but it gets huge ratings" whenever I criticize the creeping tabloidization of cable news.

That line of reasoning is a total punt. Did the viewers of MSNBC, FOX News Channel, and CNN band together to implore news directors that they wanted nonstop Anna Nicole Smith coverage in February and March of 2007? Did I miss the e-mail write-in campaigns urging certain shows to keep up the fine reporting on the Natalee Holloway disappearance in 2006? Was America really demanding hundreds of hours of programming devoted to the Paris Hilton incarceration, the Scott Peterson murders, and the Mary Kay Letourneau teacher-student sex case?

This is not giving people what they want or need, it's giving people what they'll take. It's giving them what's easy—easy to produce, easy to market, easy to cover. Friends tell me that they find themselves getting "sucked into" these stories—it almost becomes a "tragedy TV" addiction. You get a little taste and you keep going back for more because it requires little critical thinking and has next to no impact on your life. Still I think that most people, given the option, want more from the media.

As much as we want to stay above it all, the daily media bombardment affects us. The danger is that we become inured to it, and ultimately cave to the crud in our culture. We simply cannot allow this to happen. But take heart, because there are measures you can take to minimize your family's exposure to the excrement that companies try to pass off as information or entertainment. Of course, you have to accept the fact that you will be engaged in hand-to-hand cultural combat 24/7— but isn't your family worth it?

Remember, when we have powerful technology that can reach us almost anywhere—with advertisements, pictures, and language that play to the lowest common denominator—there is simply no "turning it off."

The only alternative is to turn it around.

Sex, Sex Everywhere

You've heard the acronym "TMI," which stands for Too Much Information. I find myself constantly saying "TMI" under my breath whenever I catch one of those non-newsy segments on the network morning shows: "Up next: Senior sex: you'll be surprised to find out what goes on at the retirement home." Sex-related topics that were once addressed privately (or written about in a few magazines such as *Cosmopolitan*, *Playboy*, and *Penthouse*) are now unavoidable on television, in films, theater, magazines, and of course on the Internet.

It's a Sunday ritual for many Americans to go to church, have fun outdoors, and at some point to relax and read the newspaper. Inside many of our Sunday papers is *Parade*—one of the most widely read magazines in America. I always thought it was innocuous enough—some celebrity tidbits, health articles, recipes, profiles. But the March 18, 2007, issue featured a cover story titled

"Have Better Sex at Any Age," as part of the "Live Longer, Better, Wiser Special Issue." The article started this way: "Face it, as liberated as we Americans claim to be, most of us keep our under-the-cover preferences just that—under covers. Why?"

In other words, all of you who bristle at these sorts of articles just need to lighten up. What was once sacred and private and ideally between husband and wife, is now written about, discussed, and analyzed endlessly. TMI!

The sad truth is that the culture puts an enormous amount of pressure on young people to be sexy and to perform sexually. The sexualization of young women starts them down the road to "Pornville" at an early age. And the story is not any better for boys and young men who are taught by the culture to objectify women as a type of sport.

For the moment, let's just focus on the print media. Magazines marketed to young people help shape more than fashion, entertainment, and music tastes. They sell lifestyles—alternative lifestyles, promiscuous lifestyles, living-without-consequences lifestyles—all the while selling a phony message of empowerment and well-being.

"Oh, Laura, how bad can these teen mags really be? What's wrong with selling a little fashion, makeup, and fun?" One section of *CosmoGirl!* online shows us how far these mags are willing to go. Advice columnist Marina Khidekel has some "new dating rules!" and urges girls to "[f]orget your mom's romance advice."[3] Tune out that old nag who birthed you, girls! What does she know about boys? Remember, "these are the modern up-to-the-minute rules that CG!s (CosmoGirls!) like you live and love by every day."

CosmoGirl! is unabashedly explicit about undermining parental authority. Still don't think it's a big deal? Then check out Marina's blog on CG! online, where she posts a "what kind of sexy are you?" poll for girls. "You have a certain something that just draws people to you! Find out what it is—and how you can use it to get the guy you want!" Purrrrr....

Girls are essentially taught to commodify themselves in order to get the boys. The other "teen magazines" are not much better. The teen models look like they are in their mid-twenties, and most of the clothes are wildly inappropriate for teenagers—halter tops with bare midriffs, short shorts, the mini-est of miniskirts, and spaghetti strap clingy tops with breasts on full display And to think I was wearing Laura Ashley into my college years! Loser.

The message to girls from all quarters: Sex it up, sweetheart, or the boys won't like you and the cool girls won't invite you over. And you don't want to be one of those pathetic girls sitting with the Math Club at lunch, do you? Whatever you do, keep mom and dad in the dark. They are waaaay unhip and just get in the way of your getting to hook-up heaven.

This is all great—for hormonally charged boys and perverted men. But I thought this was supposed to help girls. I can't tell you how many mothers tell me that girls today are more aggressive than the boys. Heck, the guys don't have to worry about convincing girls to hop in the backseat anymore. The girls are dragging the boys back there themselves. Is this what all those self-esteem exercises in school were supposed to achieve? I guess mom's old rules are out the window. Question is: are our young girls better for it?

Magazines marketed to adolescent and teen boys also rely overwhelmingly on sex to sell. I thought magazines like *GQ* had crossed the line until publications such as *Maxim*, *FHM*, and *Stuff* came on the scene. Their publishers somehow manage to pass themselves off as "men's lifestyle magazines." They are often displayed on the general men's interest rack. But how do *Outside* and *Men's Health* compete with a magazine baring the pop star Fergie on its cover (wearing only a black bra-shirt and panties) with the caption "Death of Sexy." Another can't-miss story highlighted "Forbidden Sex Tonight!" Hit the *Maxim* Web site and it's porn central—girls kissing girls, girls licking the backs of other girls to promote their "Girls Like Spring Break" and the "ultimate lingerie guide." Take a quick glance through any one of these magazines and you'll find mostly sex-related articles and sexy photos of near-naked women with a few fitness and cultural articles tossed in as window dressing.

Recently I was killing time before a flight out to the West Coast and decided to stand and observe the *Maxim, Stuff,* and *FHM* aficionados. The interested parties were virtually all in their teens (fourteen and up) and early twenties. In one of the more disgusting episodes, a fifty-ish father with the perfect tan in a can bought himself a *Playboy* and bought his teenage son a copy of *Maxim.*

So much for "father knows best."

In the race to degrade women and debase young men's tastes, these magazines have to compete with rappers. If you don't already know that some of the worst misogynists in the entertainment business come out of the rap world, then you must be over forty or living under a rock. The number-one downloaded song in America earlier this year was Akon's "I Wanna F— You" (from his album *Konvicted*). This follows in the grand tradition of rap lyrics that for years have demeaned women and glorified violence. Another subtle title is by Eminem protégé 50 Cent, whose hit "Surrounded by Hoes" wouldn't be at the top of your list to play at your daughter's wedding. Then, from the grandfather of filth, we have Dr. Dre's "Bitches Aint Sh*t." Very uplifting. But what do you expect when a song like "It's Hard Out Here for a Pimp" can snag an Oscar?

These "artists" have been given a platform to spew their vile message courtesy of some of the biggest music companies in the world. One of the worst offenders is the corporate behemoth Universal Music Group (yes, of NBC-Universal), which owns the labels Interscope, Geffen Records, and Universal Motown. Their singers include 50 Cent, Snoop Dogg, Ludacris, and many others who have become very rich by poisoning young minds with gutter lyrics that would never be uttered by a man who has any respect for himself or for others. Women are commodities to be dehumanized, sexually exploited, and tossed aside until the next one comes along. While some rock and pop is also sexually explicit, nothing approaches the putrid content that has emerged from many of the most popular performers in rap.

Can it get worse than this? Don't be surprised—it already has, and it's only a telephone call or a mouse click away.

Welcome to Pornville!

It is the single biggest money maker on the Web. Its profits are bigger than ABC, CBS, NBC, and ESPN combined. It makes more money than all the studios in the American film business. I'm talking about the $12 billion a year "adult entertainment" industry. According to one estimate, of the $1.6 billion that Americans spent on pay-per-view or video-on-demand in 2006, about a third went to "sex-related entertainment."[4] The figures are staggering across the board in the porn/sex recreation industry. Strip clubs, exotic sex toys, porn DVDs, and Internet porn have grown steadily, and with that growth has come acceptance.

This business is so big that there is actually a porn trade show that takes place every year in Las Vegas (of course). It is organized by AVN Media Network (I don't even want to know what the acronym stands for) and is a multi-day event featuring panel discussions, screenings, open forums, booths, and workshops. Paul Fishbein, the president of AVN, and other "leaders" in this field have told the *New York Times* that their industry is thriving, and adapting to new technologies.[5] Fishbein crowed that a new porn frontier was opening up with women between the ages of thirty and seventy now appearing in hard-core films. Take that, AARP.

As porn moved away from the peep show and into your computer and television, it lost much of the shame that once surrounded it. Now images and dialogue once reserved for seedy XXX theaters are making their way into traditional American cinemas. Fishbein noted that the idea of putting older women in pornos actually came from a huge teen blockbuster: "The flashpoint for this in our culture was the teen movie *American Pie*, where one of its most famous scenes involves one of the kids and his friend's mother."[6] *Koo-Koo-Ka-Choo, Mrs. Robinson.*

For all the crusading against the tobacco industry, attacked for marketing cigarettes to young people, where are the protests against the porn dealers and the entertainment industry for trying to get kids addicted to these cultural pollutants?

PORN AND POLITICS

》 》 》 That champion of women's rights Hillary Clinton happily accepted a $2,300 campaign contribution in 2007 from the ogling octogenarian Hugh Hefner. Odd, since Clinton had returned *Hustler* publisher Larry Flynt's $1,000 check years earlier. Like there's any major difference between the two!

Hefner contributions (as of 4/28/2007):

$108,000 Democrats
$1,000 Independents
Zilcho for Republicans!

Flynt contributions:

$38,199 to Democrats
$2,775 to Republicans

Gee, I wonder why the political favoritism!

This business has become so mainstream that the porn phenoms of yesterday are dissolving into "legitimate" media tycoons. Jenna Jameson, probably the biggest skin flick star ever, racked up millions for having sex in front of the camera in the early 1990s. Now, according to *Forbes*,[7] she heads up her own adult entertainment empire called ClubJenna that includes her personal porno production company and Internet club (revenues of $30 million in 2005 alone). Was it that long ago when an aging porn star retired quietly to Scottsdale? Well, not anymore. Today, porn is not a scarlet letter, so much as it is a reference letter. As a woman in the sex-related entertainment industry, Jameson can easily be considered edgy and alluring by traditional media. Radio shock jock Howard Stern features her as a regular guest (no shock there), but what was startling was that her autobiography, *How to Make Love Like a Porn Star*, was a *New York Times* bestseller. She has also appeared on influential cable shows such as *The O'Reilly Factor*. Jameson has said, "I've always embraced my hard-core roots, but becoming a household name was an important thing to me."

Congratulations, Jenna.

If Jenna the porn queen is accepted by the dominant culture, hasn't the dominant culture become pornified? Just ask porn princesses Tera Patrick and Stormy Daniels, who were given roles in a huge 2007 box-office hit starring Will Ferrell, *Blades of Glory*. Or check out the career trajectory of former porn stars Kirsten Price, Nautica Thorn, Sasha Knox, and Chanel St. James, who are now featured in the FOX reality show *My Bare Lady*. The FOX Reality Web site describes the show thus: "Four former adult film stars head to a prestigious London acting school to see if they can do something in front of a camera other than be naked: Virgin cast. Naughty past."[8]

Doesn't putting out the welcome mat for these gals and Jenna risk presenting young women with a false sense of empowerment? Life in ClubJenna seems like so much fun! They don't see the dark side of the porn industry—the damage done to families when fathers and husbands become addicted to this smut. They don't recognize the sheer degradation that pornography is to everyone involved—the participants, and the viewers, whose minds, expectations, and proclivities become contaminated by porn.

That used to be called perversion, but the way porn is being mainstreamed, it's no wonder that there are plenty of women and girls who think that being part of the sex entertainment industry affords them more "control" over their lives and "financial independence" and even "stardom." We used to think that selling porn meant selling your soul. Now it means getting booked on legitimate television shows to discuss your "business strategy." Case in point: Joe Francis, the founder and president of the "Girls Gone Wild" franchise. You've seen the DVDs marketed endlessly on late-night cable television. He has been indicted on tax evasion charges and charged with misdemeanor sexual battery, but still has been chatted up by everyone from CNBC's Donny Deutsch to FOX News Channel's Neil Cavuto. Hey guys, his marketing strategy doesn't take a Harvard B-School grad to figure out: Convince drunk young women on spring break to flash, french kiss each other, and simulate sex on the dance floor while a perverted cameraman rolls tape. (GGW staffers get a $1,000 bonus for filming girls who are just celebrating their eighteenth birthdays.) When not in jail, Francis regularly makes the gossip pages. He has been profiled in major newspapers such as the *Los Angeles Times* and—get this—even had the temerity to complain that one of his personal sex tapes made its way into the public domain.

Of course many of these porn entrepreneurs have taken their lead from Hugh Hefner, the granddaddy of "adult entertainment." His Playboy Enterprises has grown from just magazine publishing to a way of life. He is one of the richest men in Hollywood, adored by the "it" crowd. Many so-called legitimate actors and actresses pay homage to "Hef" and make regular pilgrimages to the Playboy

Mansion in Los Angeles. HBO's Bill Maher is a proud regular. E! Television chronicles the exploits of the harem at the Playboy Mansion in a hideous reality show called *The Girls Next Door* (featuring Hef's three twenty-something "girlfriends"). Hefner has done cameos in countless films and shows up on chat shows such as CNN's *Larry King Live.* He is right about at least one thing: "I think that *Playboy* is mainstream, and has been for a long time. You know, it is the largest selling, most popular men's magazine in America and around the world."[9]

Sadly, this is true.

People like Hugh Hefner and Larry Flynt (the founder of *Hustler* magazine) are guilty of cultural fraud and untold moral outrages yet they are still making huge bucks. What's worse, we as a nation are co-conspirators in their slime crimes. Yes, Hefner, Flynt, and all their wannabes produce the porn fare, but millions of our citizens buy it—and laugh it off as harmless fun. After making their fortunes peddling "run-of-the-mill" smut, many of the top porn moguls stepped things up a notch and segued into hard-core obscenity. So today, not only is it hard to distinguish the porn from the norm, but the worst hard-core pornography is knocking at the door of every home that has an Internet connection.

> # DIRTY OLD MAN ALERT!
>
>))) "[T]he major message of my life and what I hope to be remembered for is someone who managed to change the social sexual values of his time absolutely."
>
> —Hugh Hefner, on *Larry King Live,* November 29, 2005

That is the legacy of Hefner and Flynt—they have legitimized filth. My mother used to use a three-word term to describe these types of characters: Dirty Old Men. Oh, I'm sorry, writing that is considered in poor taste today. What pornographers do is fine—it's calling them "dirty" that's in poor taste. Shakespeare had it right: what's foul is fair, and fair is foul.

Porn has been around for a long time, but it has never been so easily accessible as it is today, thanks to technology and favorable federal court rulings. If it's dirty, it's downloadable. And if the porn industry has its way, it will soon be available on a cell phone near you. Talk about "reaching out and touching someone"! Every hotel and motel in America that offers porno movie rentals is complicit. Hilton, Marriott, and Holiday Inn hotels all tell their porn patrons not to worry—the final bill will not reveal their little secret to anyone.

And for those porn consumers who are tiring of the same old adult fare in their hotel rooms, there may soon be new, exciting product offerings. In early 2007, the *New York Times* reported that "Gregory Clayman, the owner of the live-action company Video Secrets, predicted that the industry would soon be selling not just videos on demand in mainstream hotels, but images of people having sex live over the hotels' entertainment systems."[10] He told the *Times:* "We feel that live, right now, is coming of age. We are planning to make the jump to hotel rooms."[11]

The "Do not disturb" sign has given way to just plain "disturbing"!

Our Celebrity Obsession

How does a no-name heiress with no talent suddenly become a fixture on the celebrity landscape and a veritable pop culture icon? How does a woman with virtually no vocal gifts become a platinum selling recording artist? How does a nonstop party girl and mediocre actress become an A-lister?

Two words: sex and scandals.

Personal responsibility, manners, and grace are not traits in entertainers that attract the attention of shows like *Hard Copy* or *Access Hollywood*. The tabloids and the tabloid culture they have spawned thrive on showcasing the lowest common denominator—celebrity sexploits, drug and alcohol abuse, other criminal activity, and infidelity. It's part of our pop culture today to revel in the moral and physical degradation of entertainers. The more depraved and debased celebrities become, the more television profiles and ink they get. Bad boys Paul Reubens (Pee Wee Herman), Rob Lowe, and Hugh Grant gave way to bad girls Paris Hilton, Lindsay Lohan, and Britney Spears. Look ma, no underpants!

Lest you forget, Paris Hilton was just another skinny blonde rich girl until a hard-core porn video filmed by her ex-boyfriend started making the rounds. Paris pushed the story that she was a victim. If so, she turned this trick on the public by using the entire episode to enter Hollywood. Doors previously shut were suddenly opened for her. Now she's a mainstream star with her own fragrance line, fashion label, bestselling book, and let's not forget her moronic reality show. She is stopped for DWI and *Access Hollywood* is there to get the scoop, but rarely reports with a disapproving tone. After all, the worse Paris behaves, the better the story, the higher the ratings. She's being released from jail? Send a camera crew!

Most of what kids see is a smiling, glamorous twenty-something driving an expensive car with a Chihuahua—so she must have done something right! I hate to think of how many pre-teens think that Paris, with her $5,000 handbags and countless party invites, leads a charmed life—even when she spends some of it behind bars.

The sad saga of Britney Spears—who went from sexpot to potbelly, from M-I-C-K-E-Y to A-L-A-N-O-N—was chronicled in countless magazines and television reports. Stories like hers would have been covered primarily by entertainment shows and magazines twenty years ago. Now they have worked their way into television newscasts, newspapers, and general interest magazines. If only we saw the same wall-to-wall coverage of uplifting stories from our military in Iraq or Afghanistan as we saw of Britney's meltdown or Anna Nicole Smith's tragic life and death. Why must we see every depressing twist and turn in the life of a young woman careening out of control? Is this what we really crave? Does it make us feel better about our own lives when we see the rich and famous flaming out so spectacularly? An entire industry has been created so that we may witness a mother of two abuse herself, as she stumbled in and out of parties and clubs. Already divorced twice before the age of twenty-five, Britney Spears capped off a terrible run by shaving her head, getting tattooed, and going to rehab. Of course the entertainment rags, and the morning shows, were all abuzz about this poor little rich girl. It was shameful.

When *Newsweek*'s cover story "Girls Gone Wild"[12] hit the newsstands—with the cover photo of the partying triad of BFFs (best friends forever Hilton, Lohan, and Spears)—many of us were wondering why it took the editors so long. On the magazine's Web site, *Newsweek* stated it this way: "Paris, Britney, Lindsay, & Nicole [Richie]: They seem to be everywhere and they may not be wearing underwear. Tweens adore them and teens envy them. But are we raising a generation of 'prosti-tots?'" This sounds like it came straight off the Concerned Women for America Web site. "Like never before, our kids are being bombarded by images of oversexed, underdressed celebrities who can't seem to step out of a car without displaying their well-waxed private parts to photographers."[13]

Excuse me, *Newsweek*, but—duh!

A "double-duh" for this conclusion from one of the authors of a study by the American Psychological Association: "The consequences of the sexualization of girls in media today are very real and are likely to be a negative influence on girls' healthy development.... We have ample evidence to conclude that sexualization has negative effects in a variety of domains, including cognitive functioning, physical and mental health, and healthy sexual development."[14] In February 2007, the APA's Task Force on the Sexualization of Girls released a report that stated the obvious: "Throughout U.S. culture, and particularly in mainstream media, women and girls are depicted in a sexualizing manner."[15]

Britney Spears wears a leather dominatrix outfit in her *Toxic* video, Jessica Simpson struts out for Pizza Hut in her high-thigh Daisy Dukes, and Christina Aguilera hits the town looking like she's hitting the stage at a strip club—and our girls are taking it all in by osmosis. Madonna was a pioneer in this horrible farce, beginning with her sexually charged performances of "Like a Virgin" in 1984. Another hit was "Papa Don't Preach." (She started preaching herself when she had children of her own and began releasing children's books.) She made hundreds of millions of dollars from her twenties through her forties, with her sexualized lyrics and trampy clothes. I wouldn't have been surprised if she won the Pulitzer for her 1992 book aptly titled *Sex*. (Madonna shared her sexual fantasies, complete with photos.)

No amount of yoga and Kabbalah in her fifties will change the fact that Louise Marie Ciccone or Madge or whatever she calls herself now has had a net negative effect on the culture. (And this is coming from someone who danced like a madwoman at college fraternity parties to Madonna's early hit "Material Girl"—if only women's biggest problem today was materialism!)

Today, the entertainment industry is littered with young men and women who make Madonna appear tame by comparison. They have eating disorders (Mary-Kate Olsen, Nicole Richie), they "hook up" when filming a movie (too many to mention), they revel in binge drinking (ditto), and they joke about taking ecstasy (hip hopper 50 Cent: "I got the x, if you into takin' drugs"). This behavior is splashed all over the Internet, chronicled on the E! network, and covered endlessly in the tabloids. Our teens know more details of these celebrity trainwrecks than our nation's founding.

Young people with strong families and a strong faith may see this behavior for what it is and steer clear of it, but what about others who aren't so lucky?

We're All Celebrities Now— Bring on the Raunch!

Isn't it wonderful to know that as long as you have computer access and a camera, you, too, can be a celebrity and behave badly? MySpace and Facebook are just a few of the social networking sites that have brought out the worst in people. With thousands of young girls scantily clad, revealing intimate details of their lives, it is a treasure trove for perverts, stalkers, and assorted freaks.

Becoming an Internet celebrity requires little more than showing lots of skin and revealing more than any of us should ever know about your sexual exploits. Just ask Tila Nguyen (a.k.a. Tila Tequila). *Time* magazine described her as "the queen of the massive social-networking Web site MySpace."[16] She is a former *Playboy* cyber-playmate and now you can see her touching herself on her MySpace page. She blogs, sings, struts, dances, and poses—and it's all about sex. She has more than 1.9 million MySpace "friends" and her page has been viewed more than 50 million times.[17] Warning: don't log on unless you want to hear her "song," "F*** Ya Man."

MySpace boasts that it has 106 million accounts in the U.S. alone.[18] Many of these are harmless billboards for aspiring rock bands, artists, and even presidential contenders. But other MySpace users have nefarious intentions or simply a bizarre, pathetic need to be "viewed" by millions of strangers online. Young people—and even many parents—see no real problem with posting intimate photographs and personal details on these social networking sites. The National Center for Missing and Exploited

Children reported recently that 58 percent of teens do not see any danger in this.[19] Ironically, 39 percent of teens on MySpace or Facebook report being harassed online.[20] Let's hope there's not any overlap between the two groups!

It has become painfully clear that the quest for "celebrity" status or notoriety can come at a very high price. Freaks and nutjobs sit at their keyboards looking for a cheap cyber thrill—or worse. A sting operation set up by New York's Suffolk County netted eleven men who made Internet contact with what they thought was a fourteen-year-old girl. (The "girl" turned out to be Miss America Lauren Nelson.) Sadly, this predatory behavior happens every minute of every day in the U.S. *Dateline NBC*'s Chris Hansen has publicized this sicko phenomenon (maybe too much so) on his show *To Catch a Predator*. Perverts, one after another, are caught trying to meet underage girls for sex. It's hard to watch, but an eye-opener.

Our TV Wasteland

For decades, conservatives have been complaining about how out-of-control, sexualized, and downright stupid the popular culture has become. Everyone from Phyllis Schlafly to Pat Buchanan has written extensively about the personal, moral, and physical perils of the sex-without-consequences mindset. They argued that the situation wouldn't be so bad if this lifestyle were not celebrated in the popular media. The American Left dismissed this as the prudish rantings of stodgy paleo-cons. The counter-culture has, over time, become the dominant culture and they want to keep it that way. Year after year, television and magazines pushed the envelope with their sexual depictions and content.

In 1993, David Caruso showed his butt on *NYPD Blue* and there were a few gasps. Today there is little public outrage when television comedies regularly include jokes about "threesomes." The goal posts keep shifting. The outrage over Ellen DeGeneres's first on-screen kiss seems positively quaint now given the rest of the sexually steeped content that manages to make its way into television dramas and sitcoms.

FX's *Nip/Tuck* is advertised as the "most provocative show on television" and they mean to prove it. As a matter of course, the show features prolonged kinky sex scenes, including one that showed the two male leads and a woman (who had a child by one of these characters, and was married to the other). Normal! *Nip/Tuck*'s plot lines touch on everything you'd expect from your plastic surgeon: incest, gender reassignment surgery, and (I'm not kidding) Joan Rivers begging for more cosmetic help.

In the post–September 11 world FX decided to explore the lives of firefighters. What they came up with was *Rescue Me* starring Denis Leary. Somebody sound the four alarms, please. The language is foul, the sex nonstop, and it's not just boys and girls. The partnerings on this winner have included men and men, women and women, and even men and women who are really men. I'm sure this sort of thing is going on in every firehouse in America. Forget them, rescue *us*—from this show!

Reality TV is little better. *Big Brother* and *Fear Factor* are just two shows that rely on public humiliation as their dramatic staple. "Reality TV" has created a new breed of trashy celebrity—people who will do anything on camera for a buck and their fifteen minutes of fame. I confess that a few years back I watched a few episodes of some of the popular reality shows. After spending a few hours watching *Survivor*, I actually would have preferred to be stranded on an island of my own—preferably one without television reception. Then I tuned in to *The Bachelor* for comedic relief. Seeing woman after woman blubbering over a man she had just met a few weeks earlier was too much to take. I simply cannot understand the mindset of someone who would agree to be filmed making out with someone he or she barely knows. Will the women who don't end up happily ever after with the dream bachelor want to show their children the DVD of their performance? "Mommy, why does that strange man who is not Daddy have his tongue down your throat?"

Other horrific reality fare includes shows such as *The Swan*. Watch as the ugly girl has her jaw reset and gets a new set of boobs! See her smile with her new plumped-up lips! Cheer as the middle-aged woman who lives in a trailer park gets her face stretched and tightened! No wonder young women are so body-obsessed today. The culture is sending out a constant message— physical perfection is what matters most. Young people are programmed to feel that outward beauty trumps everything. It's what gets you noticed, gets you famous, gets you rich, and gets you accepted. "It's out of style to admit it, but it is more important to be hot than smart...effortlessly hot,"[21] wrote Kat Jiang, when she was a senior at Newton North High School in Massachusetts. She was profiled in a front-page *New York Times* story on girls' struggle to find meaning in our hyper-competitive academic and social environment. Her sentiment is startling, in part because she is an academic star who nailed a perfect score of 2400 on her SATs.

Returning *POWER TO THE PEOPLE*

Many of you have told me that you feel powerless to change the culture for the better. Given the corporate power behind our major media companies and the prevalence of the sexual images and raunchy language all around us, it's easy to get discouraged. But thanks to the efforts of conservative cultural activists, faith-based organizations, and dedicated parents, we have already made some progress. There is good news to report. Teen pregnancy rates are down.[22] Teen drug use is declining.[23] And more young people are waiting at least a little bit longer to have sex.[24] Yet there are still plenty of battles to be fought. The most powerful forces in our popular culture today work to rob our children of their innocence and get them hooked into a lifestyle that will bring them untold regrets and heartache.

What can one mother in Omaha do to get the fashion industry to listen to parents who don't want their twelve-year-olds dressing like call girls? What can one father do to keep sex-laden ads off television during family viewing hours? Most parents try to instill good values, strong faith, and character in their children but feel like they're fighting a lonely, losing battle given the corporate- and government-sanctioned assault on their kids.

But do not despair—there are concrete steps we can all take to turn things around.

》》》 Educate the Young—or the Pornified Culture Will

All of us must do everything in our power to help our young people reject the noxious elements of our culture. The most important step is faith, putting God first in our lives. I'll talk more about the indispensability of faith in the closing chapter, but for now suffice it to say that the best way to provide your children with a solid foundation that even the savviest marketers of smut can't undermine is to give them a solid—and that means a sincere and educated—foundation of faith. The most important school your children go to is your church or temple—make sure the instruction resonates.

The next step is to fill your home with great music, great books, and classic films. Start early enough in exposing your children to quality and substance, and they often will voluntarily say no thanks to the likes of Akon, *American Pie*, *The Real World*, and lurid stops on MySpace or Facebook.

My own experience bears this out. My family was by no means rich, but we were rich in music. My dad was (and still is) a Frank Sinatra devotee and was always playing Sinatra in his car or in the house. My favorite was "High Hopes." He loved the jazz greats, too, so I heard a lot of Oscar Peterson, Art Tatum, and Ben Webster. My brother Brooks was self-taught in his appreciation of classical music from Tchaikovsky to Bach, and so it didn't seem foreign to me at all. My brothers Jimmy and Curtis played records ranging from classic Elton John to Rogers and Hammerstein. I came to appreciate aspects of many different musical genres. Well, maybe not my mom's favorite—Bobby Vinton—but nobody's perfect. She made up for Bobby V. with her love for big band music from Tommy Dorsey and Benny Goodman. I loved hearing her tell me stories of her trips to New York City when she was in her early twenties, the country was at war, and everyone was taking the A-Train. Even with all this exposure to great music, I still had my detours into teenybopper pop silliness but back then it was entirely harmless. Compare Donny Osmond's "Puppy Love" to Justin Timberlake's "SexyBack." If I had tried to buy a song with the title "Hips Don't Lie" (Shakira), my mother would have gone ballistic.

The point is, what I was exposed to musically as a kid shaped my taste in music as an adult. (That's why you hear a lot of Sinatra played as bumps on my radio show.) The same was true with films—long before DVDs my mom and I popped popcorn and watched such golden oldies as *My Girl Friday*, *Ben Hur*, *Robin Hood*, and my favorites—*The Sound of Music* and *The Wizard of Oz*. These were family events for so many in my generation and should continue to be so in our homes today. Watch a film together as a family and afterward discuss the plot, the characters, the deeper meaning—what made you laugh, cry, love it, or hate it. You can't imagine what a positive effect this will have on your son or daughter's future ability to discern the garbage from the greats.

I hear a lot of parents complaining about the increasing amount of homework children are getting in school. So how could there be any downtime for you to teach your children to love reading for fun? I like the rule that my friend Patricia DeSanctis enforces in her home—you can't see the movie if you haven't read the book. It always makes me smile to hear a girl or boy say, "Laura, the book is way better than the movie!" The film-watching experience is transformed from a passive activity into something richer and more textured. All things considered, would it not be better if our children spent more time reading books than reading homepages on MySpace or sending text messages on a tiny cell phone screen? You can make that happen.

❱❱❱ Be Your Own Movie Mogul

Right now someone reading this book has the talent to write a great screenplay or television pilot or has the money to support someone who does. Millions of us are tired of spending 120 minutes at a movie, only to be complaining about its hypersexualized, hyperpoliticized, or sophomoric content as we walk out of the theater. We can't believe how little there is to watch on televisions that have hundreds of channels. Again, grousing about content only gets us so far. We have to create our own alternatives—and support the alternatives that are already out there.

As we saw with the wild success of *The Passion of the Christ*, which Mel Gibson made outside the traditional studio system, great films will draw diverse and huge audiences. Many of those who bought tickets to see *The Passion* hadn't been inside a movie theater in years. The film made $400 million globally—despite how the cultural gatekeepers of the Left tried to smear it. Gibson started his own production company called Icon Films so he could make the types of films that Hollywood wouldn't.

Another new player on the scene, Walden Media has produced such hit family films as *Narnia: The Lion, the Witch, and the Wardrobe* and *Charlotte's Web*. The film *Amazing Grace*, released in 2007, told the inspiring story of William Wilberforce and managed to turn a healthy profit. These are films that won't make you cringe when you watch them with your family. They remind me of the films I watched as a kid—before the culture decided that teaching brattiness, cynicism, foul language, and lechery was healthy.

Disney, after many years off the reservation, returned to its roots when it realized that the only films making money were those fit for family consumption. This hugely underserved segment of our population not only showed up, but returned with their children again and again—then bought the DVDs. Disney/Pixar animated features such as *Finding Nemo*, *Toy Story*, and *The Incredibles* are just a few of the mega-releases of the last ten years. Yet the fact that the best films are animated should also tell us something about the state of filmmaking today. The movie industry seems to think it's okay to produce a wholesome story as long as it's in the form of a cartoon or computerized fantasy, otherwise who among the young cynics would believe the plot? Answer: a lot of people.

⟫⟫⟫ Be Your Own Filter

Sometimes just exposing your children to quality entertainment isn't enough to stop them from straying into unhealthy pop culture terrain. That's where the Mom and Dad Filters come in. For reasons that I do not fully understand, some of my friends who are parents have a hard time saying no to their kids. I take my lead from families with whom I am close and who somehow manage to make it all work. Sometimes by saying no.

Betsy Hart, in her terrific book *It Takes a Parent*, calls the "just say yes" phenomenon "Pushover Parenting." I call it PlayStation parenting. I know parents who, when worn out by moody adolescents underfoot, actually tell them to go use their PlayStation. They don't even know what kind of games their kids are playing. Are they age appropriate? What is the violence rating? Is there any sexual content involved? There is evidence to suggest that repeated exposure to these violent and sexed-up images numb our children to violence and can lead to horrific real world actions. If we can keep our children away from this, perhaps we can stop the acts of violence and perversion that are becoming all too routine in the lives of our young people.

Being the filter for the young people in our care requires that we take the time to do our research before we say yes to the film or television show they want to watch, the music they want to download into their iPod, or the Web site they want to visit. Again, this takes a little time, but you will be glad you made the investment. Plus, there are all sorts of helpful online resources for you to use to navigate our choppy cultural seas.

Whatever you do, don't rely on the Motion Picture Association of America with its increasingly meaningless film ratings. Some of what passes as "PG-13" today would have been rated "R" fifteen years ago. My friend Becky uses screenit.com as a resource to determine a film's suitability for her nine children. With more Americans building "media rooms" in their homes, DVDs and movies on demand are increasingly replacing trips to the theatre. All the better for the Parental Filter. At

IT'S HIP TO BE UNCOOL

》》》 If you care that your children, their friends, or even *your friends* think you are uncool for saying no to a film, a clothing purchase, a music download, or a Web site, then you have work to do. You have to get to a point where being called an "old fogey" or "unhip" is a badge of honor. If the kids and the immature adults in your life say "but everyone is wearing it/listening to it/watching it!" it's a safe bet that saying no is the right thing to do.

home you can trust your teen to see the movie he said he was see-ing, but you can also verify it.

Filtering out what your children run across on the Internet is tougher. But many families have told me that the first thing parents must do is to set up, if at all possible, one computer area in the home where you'll be able to better monitor the sites the kids are visiting. A lot of my friends also put passwords on the computers so they cannot be used unless they are present. Rebecca, a married mother of two teenage boys, told me that her boys are not allowed to bring their laptops behind closed doors and away from her supervision. She tells them ahead of time that she has monitoring software installed on every computer in the home and that every few days she will review every Internet site they visited.

Gulp!

Certainly avail yourself of all the technologies that are designed to keep parents one step ahead of the porn peddlers. There are numerous pop-up blocking programs and ones that prevent access to certain types of Web sites. But don't depend on technology to save you when technology is what disseminates these XXX images in the first place. Thankfully, every television sold today allows you to block the channels you don't want your children to watch. My friend Pam, who has an eleven-year-old girl and an eight-year-old boy, told me recently that while all of these measures help to some degree, nothing is a substitute for being there. "It's exhausting," she said, "but either I do the parenting or the pornographers will."

❯❯❯ Drastic Times Require Drastic Measures

There are a small but growing number of families who are swearing off television altogether—or coming close to it. My friends Steve and Beth, who have three sons and a daughter all under the age of fourteen, put strict limits on TV watching. The kids are not allowed to watch any television at all during the week.

The parents set the example by not watching any themselves. A few select shows or parent-approved DVDs are saved for non-school nights. I know it's hard, but shouldn't we try to live without television for two weeks every now and then?

When my brother Curtis moved to a new house recently, he didn't bother getting cable hooked up at all. "After a few weeks, I realized I really wasn't missing much of anything," he laughed. Very funny—at least until I was visiting him for a few days and had to prepare for my show. No TV!? Somehow, I ended up having more time to prepare and the show went on without a hitch.

Uncle Sam vs. the Smut Kings

Shouldn't the government work for us and not *against* us as we try to keep our children beyond the reach of the pornographers— away from their cameras and away from their products?

Yes!

When the fight is between those who want to combat child pornography and those who want to protect the First Amendment rights of pornographers, the latter usually win out. In 2002, the Republican Congress passed and President Bush signed a law to prohibit the sending of e-mail messages that offer child pornography, but it was shot down in the Supreme Court.

In 1998 Congress passed the Child Online Protection Act, which would have made it a crime for Web sites to have material deemed "harmful to minors" by "contemporary community standards" available to children. Such sites would have had to verify the age of the user (via a credit card or some other means). Sounds good, right? Well, the federal courts did not agree. The law was challenged by the usual suspects, and every step of the way judges struck down the law down as unconstitutional, citing the First Amendment.

Pornographers and their pals argue that parents should use filters on their computers rather than the government getting involved. Conveniently for them, that lets them off the hook completely and leaves them free to invest in ways to get around the latest filters. Justice Department attorney Peter Keisler made a commonsense point in support of the act, "It is not reasonable for the government to expect all parents to shoulder the burden to cut off every possible source of adult content for their children, rather than the government's addressing the problem at its source."

We must demand that our politicians appoint judges who understand that the First Amendment was never meant to cover pornographic expression—its primary purpose was to protect *political* speech so that our government would always be held accountable by the people. How did we get to a point in our country when the Supreme Court does more to protect the rights of pornographers than it does the rights of political activists who want to buy advertising time before a federal election?

Cleaning up our culture's toxic spillage is sometimes a simple matter of law enforcement, because laws are being broken. Every once in a while we hear about federal authorities raiding porno studios to verify that all actors and crew are adults, but enforcement seems far from consistent. The porn industry is now required by law to keep more detailed records. But pornographers say they are being unfairly targeted. After all, minors are more exposed to pornography today than at any time in our history, courtesy of the Internet, and if the government allows that, why should the pornographers themselves be punished?

At an annual porn industry convention called Internext, panelist Michael Price, the owner of Price Communications, told the audience that while some in the business were concerned about protecting children, "unless the government intervenes, I don't see this industry policing itself."[25] Being a conservative does not mean that you resist all action taken by the government—and this is one area where conservatives and moderate Democrats should be able to find common ground. Our government needs to do more to protect children.

People Making a Difference

Where government fails, the people of America usually step in to offer creative solutions. More Americans are putting pressure on the big media companies that make huge profits from filthy music. Al Sharpton and others drove Don Imus off the air for one racially tinged remark, so why is it okay for corporate executives and their musical geniuses to make piles of cash from music that uses the same language relentlessly? Why is it acceptable for presidential candidates like Barack Obama and Hillary Clinton to legitimize the rap industry's most egregious offenders by appearing with them in public, and even raising hundreds of thousands of dollars with their help? Why is it "censorship" to demand that rappers clean up their acts, while it was "the free market at work" when Imus was forced off the air?

Race hustlers like Al Sharpton threaten boycotts and we see the corporate suits crumble. How about American parents taking a page from Reverend Al's playbook and doing the same thing to wake up the media companies who traffic in music that degrades and defiles women on a regular basis?

Movements start with one person who has an idea and the courage to pursue it. Taking back the culture will require hundreds of such movements across our nation. There are many people who are already doing the hard work. They deserve credit for doing more than complaining (or writing) about our cultural death spiral. You should get involved too.

〉〉〉 The People Supporting the Heroes

We understand by now what is wrong with our culture, but do we know enough about what is right with it? Do we know the stories of our military heroes? I was traveling home from Colorado in early 2007 and noticed a group of about fifteen World War II veterans gathered at the gate. They had their baseball caps on with their ship names or unit names on them. I struck up a conversation with one who had fought at Iwo Jima and another who was one of the "Band of Brothers." Their escorts, all of whom seemed to be in their twenties and thirties, told me that they were part of the Greatest Generations Foundation. This Denver-based non-profit organization is dedicated to preserving the stories of our war veterans and making it possible for them to travel to the battlefields where they fought. Those vets—many in wheelchairs and using walkers—were going to the World War II Memorial in Washington, D.C. Courtesy of TGGF, many others are traveling to Normandy and the site of the Battle of the Bulge to share "battlefield remembrances." We ought to do more to preserve the memory of our real heroes instead of clogging our memories with stories about plastic celebrities. Why not celebrate the veterans in our own families? Why not make sure our kids can tell the difference between a real hero—the one with medals on his chest—from a Hollywood celebrity?

The People vs. the Fashion Industry

Brenda Sharman left her lucrative lingerie modeling career to start a movement called Pure Fashion, which is aimed at promoting an alternative to the trashy clothing lines—the low-rise jeans, midriff-baring tops (if you can call these tops at all), and micro-minis that are the current adolescent norm. In 1999 Brenda and other moms in her native Georgia decided that they couldn't wait for the fashion world to change—they had to take positive action for their daughters' sakes. Through their participation in fashion shows, mentoring programs, and weekend retreats, hundreds of high school-age girls have learned that you can have cool clothes that are also modest. The last slate of fashion shows brought together 10,000 attendees coast-to-coast. The program's purpose goes beyond just influencing the fashion industry and marketers. The overarching goal of Pure Fashion is to help high school girls make wise life choices. For more information go to www.purefashion.com. Modest clothing designers have set up shop to fill the fashion vacuum and are starting to do a brisk business.[26] Amen!

The People vs. the Hook-Up Movement

In 1998, young people heard President Clinton describe what he did with Monica Lewinsky as "not hav[ing] sexual relations with that woman." Soon after, reports began to trickle in from school health surveys across the country that more students were engaging in oral sex, believing that it was not sex at all. That is just one learning curve that abstinence advocate Pam Stenzel confronts on a daily basis. She is one of the most sought-after speakers on teen abstinence in the United States. More than 500,000 students over fifteen years old have heard her message, and tens of thousands more have read her books. Most forty-two-year-old lecturers on this topic might find it hard to connect with their audience, but Stenzel's straight-talk presentation of facts about STDs, pregnancy, and low self-esteem are riveting for old and young alike.

Pam Stenzel's work has a faith-based component, but even secular groups are popping up on college campuses to tackle the "hook-up" culture that is all the rage. (Hooking up, which is a staple in so much of our entertainment industry, involves young people having recreational sex with no strings attached, a.k.a. "friends with benefits.") Harvard students Sarah Kinsella and Justin Murray started a group called True Love Revolution, which promotes abstinence and has close to a hundred members. The group is not religiously affiliated, but that doesn't mean it hasn't been the subject of scorn and ridicule on campus. Feminists, predictably, are upset by this group's message, which included Valentine's Day flyers that read, "Why wait? Because you're worth it!" When almost three-quarters of college students report that they had sex in the past year, it takes some guts for students to ask if it's time to take a time-out.

The People vs. the Pornographers (and Their Enablers)

A priest friend of mine told me recently that several of his parishioners had become addicted to porn over the last few years, and that the habit was ruining their lives. One penitent was so desperate that he actually brought his television remote control into the confessional and said, "Please, Father, take this from me." (The next week he gave the priest his laptop computer.)

Finding a hotel that does not offer X-rated movies on its in-room pay-per-view can be a challenge. Places of lodging offer the raunch because it makes them big money. But now there is help for those of us who would like to support businesses that just say no to porn— regardless of how much money they are losing. Cleanhotels.com is a search engine (affiliated with Priceline.com) that lists porn-free hotels, motels, and inns. Users are encouraged to e-mail the Web site if the "clean" conditions at a hotel changes.

The Web site was started by former self-described porn addict Phil Burress, president of the Cincinnati-based Citizens for Community

Values. Did you know that the Omni Hotel chain does not offer pornography in its in-room television listings? Good for Omni. Let's reward the hotel chain with our business.

The People vs. TV Trash

If you want to change the culture, you have to engage with the culture enough to lodge your protests when appropriate. When you see a television show that offends your values or morals, make a note of the advertisers and take the time to call or write a letter sharing your outrage. Ditto for the big music companies that pump out the putrid lyrics in some of our popular music. The squeaky wheel gets the grease—so squeak away! In egregious instances advertisers will pull important dollars from these offensive shows if they hear from enough of us. That is the first step toward de-funding the cultural waste altogether. More than any grassroots organization in America, the Parents Television Council (PTC) exposes the worst and promotes the best of today's television offerings.

Brent Bozell founded PTC in 1995 and the group is an invaluable source of information for parents who need guidance to determine the suitability of television programs for children of all ages. The group's overall goal is to "foster changes in TV programming to make the early hours of prime time family friendly and suitable for viewers of all ages." Plus, PTC drives the Left bonkers.

Another indefatigable warrior in this fight is Bill Donohue of the Catholic League. If you see a bastardization of Christianity in the popular culture, chances are Donohue has sought to shut it down. He's an attack dog—but he's our attack dog.

You have no excuse now. You now know how corrosive the culture has become. You understand the horrible effects this is having on our young people. So now let's do something about it.

7

SCHOOL'S OUT... OF CONTROL

I t was early Saturday morning in January 1983, and my roommates Andrea and Dianne were still sound asleep. Weekends at Dartmouth College were noted for one thing—parties—so nine o'clock in the morning might as well have been five o'clock. The hallways of most dorms were quiet and empty.

My roommates awoke to someone's loud, repeated banging on our dorm room door.

Still in her pajamas, Andrea opened the door a crack to see a recognizable figure—the thin, goateed, bedraggled-looking College Music Department chairman William Cole. She knew this was not a good thing.

He was irate. "I'm looking for Laura Ingraham!" he snarled. "Is she here?!"

"Uh—she's not here. Do you want to leave a message?" Andrea asked sheepishly.

"Did you see the article she wrote about me in the *Review*?" he shouted, not really expecting an answer.

He was referring to my latest column in the conservative student weekly the *Dartmouth Review*. The title of the piece was "Professor Cole's Song and Dance Routine," which I had written after auditing one of Professor Cole's very popular classes called "American Music in an Oral Tradition." The course was a notorious "gut" class—meaning you were pretty much guaranteed an "A" for showing up and writing legibly on your final exam. But more interesting than that was Cole's use of a music class to promote his own Marxist-socialist views about America. He asked students what they knew about poverty, railed against racism (Cole was black), and was generally the typical unhinged lefty commonplace on liberal arts faculty departments at American colleges and universities.

"You tell her—if she doesn't show up in my class to apologize on Monday for what she wrote, then I'm going to have her brought up on charges on campus," Cole warned my roommates.

I was in New York for the weekend when I got the call from Andrea, who was a tad shaken up. "You better get back here," she said. "We had an unexpected visitor this morning."

Needless to say, on Monday morning, I never showed up to "apologize." But the *Review* did send another reporter to "audit" this Cole class. The content was even more precious than the class I had covered the week before. Professor Cole immediately asked if

I was present in the class, and when I wasn't, he started in on a tear against me. I was thereafter referred to as the "motherf**king, c**k-sucking reporter!" (followed by various lovely iterations of that).

Cole then announced that because I hadn't come to apologize, he was canceling class—indefinitely!

Three days later the *Review* published a cover story detailing Professor Cole's profanity-laden rant. It was a blockbuster. We mailed out a special letter to the 40,000 Dartmouth alumni, informing them of the situation. The College began to receive irate telephone calls from across the country.

But the professoriate couldn't have been happier. At the next Dartmouth faculty meeting, Professor Cole received a standing ovation. Months later, Professor Cole sued the *Review*, some of its officers, and me for $2.4 million.[1] Several years later Professor Cole left campus for greener pastures.

This little Dartmouth drama was my official introduction to the concept that didn't yet have a name—political correctness. It was a mindset that eschewed excellence, critical thinking, and accountability in favor of forced sensitivity and racial and ethnic pandering. College administrators, professors, and most students were too frightened (or too politically attached to left-wing causes) to stand up to this craziness.

I am sorry to report that things in the sphere of education—from elementary schools through universities—have only gotten worse. The people paying the bills (taxpayers, parents, alumni) feel less empowered than ever to change the status quo.

* * * * *

When children and young adults do not receive a well-rounded, serious education, they are being robbed of the power that is rightly theirs. "Knowledge is power" may be a cliché, but it's also true. A good corollary would be, "thinking skills are power." Without these skills, how can we develop into responsible, mature adults? A real education doesn't simply teach us facts; it teaches us how to love learning and separate the profound from the phony.

Education is also character development. Virtues and a good education go hand in hand. A moral grounding teaches us self-control and the importance of making good decisions. A solid moral education, like a good academic education, is crucial to making us responsible, informed adults. That's where the term "liberal education" comes from. A proper education equips students to be free men and free women—it empowers them and prepares them to use that power.

This means *everybody* needs to worry about our nation's lagging education. And it *is* lagging. The Organization for Economic Cooperation and Development (OECD) studied the academic strengths of fifteen-year-olds in all its member countries, and the results are not flattering for American schools. In science, mathematics, and "problem solving," the United States is below average, while in reading, we are just about average. In all four of these categories, we rank the lowest among all English-speaking countries—and fifteen countries, including Canada, France, and Japan, rank above the U.S. in all four categories.[2] In math and problem solving, the United States is in the bottom third of all OECD countries, behind Latvia.

Things are getting worse. In both reading and math, high school seniors did worse in 2005 than in 1992, on the National Assessment of Educational Progress (NAEP) exams—with scores showing a steady decline over those thirteen years.[3] (This was despite the fact that the NAEP started making accommodations for learning disabled students in 1998.)

How did things get this bad? The problem here is that the people have lost power at the hands of the educrats. The teachers' unions guard against any efforts to enforce quality standards on teachers. The unions and the politicians they sponsor fight to the death against school choice, which would allow you, the parents, to choose where to send your children to school. Politicians, if they do anything at all, assure us that the answer is spending even more of our money on schools (which usually pays for more bureaucracy). Even the well-intentioned politicians misguidedly try to fix things by centralizing control over the schools in state and federal bureaucracies.

Our children aren't getting the education they deserve because educrats bully parents into ceding all decisions about what and how our children are taught. To truly restore American education, we need to restore power to the people.

Call Off the Union Thugs

The chief culprits in the collapse of our schools are the teachers' unions. The National Education Association (why does everything with the initials NEA involve using our money for junk?) has 3.2 million members, and spent more than $300 million in 2005 alone. The American Federation of Teachers boasts 1.3 million members, and had a budget in 2005 of nearly $200 million. That gives teachers' unions a half-billion dollars in spending money per year—which means quite a bit of clout. Most of that money is not spent educating your child—at least not in the way he or she should be educated.

And before you say, "But Laura, you're being awfully hard on teachers," I should tell you that I am a major fan of teachers. My brother and sister-in-law have given three decades combined to the teaching profession. I still remember the devoted, wonderful teachers who taught me English literature, Spanish, Russian, and yes, even, advanced algebra at Glastonbury High School in Connecticut. Good teachers are true blessings to our society. They deserve, more than anyone else, the title "public servant." But teachers' unions are largely dedicated to ensuring that teachers are not rewarded for their skill or success.

The AFT and NEA exist almost exclusively to defend the tenure system and oppose merit pay. Almost all public schools follow the hiring, firing, and wage rules demanded by the unions. In most public school systems, teacher pay depends only on two factors: (1) how long the teacher has been teaching, and (2) whether the teacher has an advanced degree or has undergone teacher training. But these two factors do not necessarily a good teacher make.

Teacher training does not equal student learning. Many studies over the last decade have concluded that a master's degree in education, while it will earn a teacher a pay raise, will not make the teacher better at educating students.[4] In 2000, economists Dan Goldhaber and Dominic Brewer found, amazingly, that students do better if their teachers do *not* have an education degree.[5] Makes you wonder: what are they teaching at these teaching schools?

Not much—according to a 2006 study by Dr. Arthur Levine, president of Columbia University's Teacher's College.[6] The general thrust of his research is that teaching schools are boondoggles that take the money of would-be teachers, give them sub-par training, then hand them degrees that translate into higher pay. Levine found:

> On most campuses, teacher education is regarded by university professors and administrators inside and outside the education school as one of the poorest-quality campus units owing to low admissions standards, particularly for future elementary school teachers. Moreover, a majority of teachers are prepared at the education schools with the lowest admission standards and least accomplished professors.

Teacher seniority—the only other factor in most schools' pay scale—also has little relationship to student achievement. Many studies suggest that teachers improve over their first three or four years on the job, but after that, teachers do not measurably improve on average—even though their pay does.[7]

You don't have to be a raging capitalist to realize that if teachers don't get pay raises for teaching well, and if they don't get fired for teaching poorly, you'll end up with a whole lot of bad to mediocre teachers. Of course it's not the easiest thing in the world to judge who's doing well and who's not, but the teachers' unions deny that there's any difference. NEA resolutions repeatedly reject "any form of merit pay," for K–12 teachers. At the union's annual meeting in July of 2006, the NEA issued a resolution stating: "[P]erformance pay schedules, such as merit pay or any other system of compensation based on an evaluation of an education employee's performance, are inappropriate."[8] In other words, paying good teachers more than bad teachers is out of line. John Stossel, in a withering exposé of the NEA, filmed a teacher exclaiming "there's no such thing as a bad teacher."

Good teachers make a big difference.

I still remember Mrs. Remmer, who introduced tenth graders to *Moby Dick* and *The Scarlet Letter*. These books were tough going—but classics that I'll never forget because of her love for literature. It was infectious.

A study published in 2005 turned up results that "show large differences among teachers in their impacts on achievement and show that high-quality instruction throughout primary school could substantially offset disadvantages associated with low socioeconomic background."[9] Translated: some teachers are better than others at teaching. They convey a joy for learning that even the most cynical and easily distracted students can appreciate. If teachers are bored by the subject material, or think they should be acting on Broadway or collecting Pulitzers, the student will sense it and tune it out. This is especially true in disadvantaged neighborhoods.

Firing bad teachers is anathema. NEA resolutions demand that if a school has to lay teachers off, the district should "exclude performance evaluation from consideration."[10]

While they make a nice target, teachers' unions don't get all the blame. "Education professionals" and curriculum innovators shoulder some of the culpability. Some people seem to think we have to reinvent the wheel every few years when it comes to education. We don't. Through thousands of years and dozens of cultures, we have developed a few tried and true ways to turn out well-rounded, intelligent, independent men and women fit to be citizens in a free country. "Classical education" is one method, with its roots in ancient Greece, but there are many other proven ways of teaching children.

Such proven methods are terribly old-fashioned, though. These days, feel-good fads based on boosting "self-esteem," and the notion that there are "no wrong answers," crowd out sound, traditional ways of teaching kids. "Whole Language," a 1960s and 1970s fad that eschewed teaching rules of grammar and phonics, has been widely discredited as a way of teaching reading and writing, but it still lingers. In 1985, the National Council of Teachers of English condemned grammar drills in the classroom, calling them, "a deterrent to the improvement of students' speaking and writing."[11] Twenty years later, we have an adult populace that, through little fault of its own, has no idea where to put a comma or when to use whom instead of who. Diagramming sentences is even more verboten in some classrooms. One Atlanta resident wrote in to the *Atlanta Journal-Constitution* that "As a new substitute teacher, I just received a letter from Fulton County schools warning me not to correct 'grammer.'"[12]

The embrace of "ebonics" as a first language is another example of recent educational nuttery. It's bad enough when rappers like 50 Cent and Snoop Dogg use this language in their "music," but when the teachers started adopting it in their curricula in the 1990s, we knew something had to be done. Back in 1996, the Oakland school district declared that 28,000 of its students spoke a foreign language—ebonics. This difference was not a result of culture, the district claimed, but the genetic makeup of African Americans. This meant Oakland needed to hire teachers fluent in ebonics to teach black students. What had been a joke in the movie *Airplane* fifteen years before ("Oh, stewardess! I speak jive.") became educational reform in the mid-1990s. Oakland soon abandoned that idea, and the school board doesn't really like to talk about it much.

But ebonics has tried to make a comeback. Rochester City School District in upstate New York sent a newsletter to teachers encouraging them to use ebonics—they call it "Black English Vernacular." "We need to embrace the diversity they bring into our schools," a school district official said. And by "diversity," she meant "bad grammar." This proposal was nipped in the bud once it got some press coverage from local media and my radio show.

Ideologues and Pedagogues

This will come as no surprise to anyone: liberals use public schools to grind their ideological axes. Nobody should say public schools don't teach values—it's just that the values they teach are a disdain for America, a dislike of capitalism, and an embrace of the Hollywood approach to morality. In other words, they are indoctrinating our children.

World history curricula usually amount to a yearlong study of how Europe and the United States have oppressed the rest of the planet. European history is an extended diatribe against the Catholic Church. American history classes are one long story of how the white man oppresses women, minorities, immigrants, animals, and the environment at home, while waging unjust wars of empire abroad. It seems FDR, JFK, and Jimmy Carter are the only

HOW BAD CAN A P.C. CURRICULUM GET?

》》》 Really bad. In England, some teachers are dropping any discussion of the Holocaust in their classes so as not to offend Muslim students raised by parents who deny that the genocide against the Jews ever occurred. Some courses also opted against discussing the medieval Crusades, citing the same sensitivity concerns (for Muslims, not Christians).

Source: Laura Clark, "Teachers Drop the Holocaust to Avoid Offending Muslims," *Daily Mail*, April 1, 2007

white American males to come out of the average high school U.S. history course looking good.

For many years now, the quality and objectivity of our school textbooks, tests, and teaching materials have been gutted by special interest groups demanding changes and wimpy state legislators who bow to the pressure. The publishers end up altering the textbooks to accommodate the various left-wing (and some right-wing) grievances so that they don't lose fat state contracts. The real losers in this, of course, are our children. History and literature are distorted through content manipulation. Language is altered in ways that are just plain goofy. Words such as *snowman* are banished from reading materials in favor of the non-offensive *snowperson*. Heaven forbid the word *devil* appear anywhere in a textbook. Depictions of women as traditional housewives are no-no's. And don't even think about using a drawing of an American Indian in traditional warrior garb.

In a second-grade civics textbook titled *Social Studies People and Places*[13] youngsters are introduced to outstanding figures who have shaped America's history. There are twelve biographical sketches in the book, complete with illustrations. If the kiddies were looking to get acquainted with the likes of Hamilton, Washington, and Jefferson—they'd better look elsewhere. Dead white guys need not apply. Instead, the kids are treated to the full multicultural show. Full-page sketches celebrate the contributions of such extraordinary Americans as Rosalynn Carter (a forgettable

First Lady if there ever was one); Cesar Chavez (the migrant union activist); some female Mexican American baseball team owner; and Ieoh Ming Pei (the architect responsible for such wonders as the National Museum of Modern Art and the Javits Convention Center in New York, of which a *New York* magazine writer once noted, "If the walls of the Jacob Javits Center could talk, they'd probably say something like, 'It ain't easy being ugly.'").[14]

Okay, I'm not going to say that these people should be left out of history books altogether (well, maybe Cesar Chavez), but with only twelve pages available to highlight Americans who have made a lasting influence on our government and our way of life, are these the best examples to present to our youngsters? What ever happened to Henry Ford, the Wright Brothers, Susan B. Anthony, and General Patton? Boring!

Education historian Diane Ravitch, in her book *The Language Police*, exposed with painstaking research how these politicized and sanitized textbooks shortchange children. She testified before Congress that all mass-market publishers "of textbooks and tests have compiled what they call 'bias guidelines' or 'sensitivity guidelines.' Major publishers, for example, tell writers to be careful about using the words 'America' or 'American' because they suggest 'geographical chauvinism.'"[15]

The result of the politically correct censors' crusade? The materials our kids are supposed to learn from are just plain dull, not to mention inaccurate.

What are parents facing here? Education consultants and administrators who put "diversity" and "sensitivity" before learning. The wacky thinking behind our textbooks shines through in the comments of Sue Stickel, the deputy superintendent for curriculum and instruction for the California Department of Education: "I think our textbooks should, to our greatest capacity, be free of any type of stereotyping. We need to make sure that all ethnicities are represented. We need to make sure that both males and females are represented. We need to make sure that our materials cover the full gamut." So there you have it—being inclusive is more important than being right.

Forget Internet Filters— We Need Public School Filters

Not content to advance the political correctness racket, public schools now have turned into sex education machines. And we're not just talking about the basics of the birds and the bees. In this brave new education world, the birds and the bees are mating with each other! What is being offered is avant-garde sex ed. It involves teaching children about abortion, "transgenders," and cross-dressing. Oh my!

Dorothy, I don't think we're in Kansas anymore.

In Alexandria, Virginia, where a sex-ed class has been mandatory since the early 1980s, the school board recently decided to spice stuff up with some edgier material. The course includes the history of abortion, stressing how abortion was legal at the founding of the country. Some of the abortion material was lifted from Planned Parenthood literature.[16] How's that for an unbiased educational source!

In liberal Montgomery County, Maryland, similar antics are occurring. Late in the 2006–2007 school year, the county school board pushed through a pilot program for a sex-ed curriculum in which students, including eighth graders, were taught to "develop" their own sexuality as well as their own "gender identity," defined as "a person's internal sense of knowing whether he or she is male or female."

In Lexington, Massachusetts, Tonia and David Parker were surprised when their five-year-old son brought home a workbook from *kindergarten* teaching him about gay marriage.[17] The Parkers filed a lawsuit, together with their Lexington neighbors Joseph and Robin Wirthlin, who objected to their son's second-grade teacher reading the class a story titled "King and King" about two princes falling in love.

The Parkers and Wirthlins, being Christians, objected to the government using their money to push moral teachings on their children that contradicted the moral teachings of their religion. The school district joined forces with the ACLU, the Massachusetts Teachers Association, and a gay activist group called the Human Rights Campaign to defend this curriculum.

A federal judge sided with the ACLU and the school district, sending the message that parents' right to raise their children as they see fit has no bearing on what they are taught in public schools. U.S. district judge Mark Wolf ruled that "teachings that contradict a parent's religious beliefs do not violate their First Amendment right to exercise their religion."[18] Unfortunately, given the state of our courts, the judge was well within federal court precedent to rule that "diversity is a hallmark of our nation. It is increasingly evident that our diversity includes differences in sexual orientation." Still, it sounds more like something you'd hear from the gals on *The View*, rather than from a judge on the bench.

Even more striking, Judge Wolf ruled that parents had no right to opt their children out of the objectionable portions of class. So, while a girl with ethical objections can get out of dissecting a frog with no problem, a kid with religious objections had better learn to enjoy the romance of two princes.

A high school in Newton, Massachusetts, celebrated "To B GLAD Day," the acronym of which (TBGLAD) stood for "Transgender, Bisexual, Gay, Lesbian Awareness Day." At one point, three "transgendered" speakers addressed the students, and one panelist, who described herself as an "androgyne in between both genders of society" declared, "Gender is just a bunch of stereotypes from society, but I am completely personal, and my gender is fluid."[19]

These bizarre stories may be the most sensational, but we shouldn't skip over the basic problem here: sex and school don't mix. Basically, whenever possible, *parents* should be the sex educators of their children. Is a classroom—usually co-ed, with peers, ex-girlfriends, crushes, and bullies surrounding you—a good place to learn and ask questions about intimate and personal things? And shouldn't parents have real control over what their children are being taught?

School officials in Deerfield, Illinois, seemed to think that parents should be the *last ones* to know about what went on in their children's sex-ed classroom. In March 2007, freshmen were required to sign a confidentiality agreement promising not to tell anyone—including their parents—what went on in sex-ed.

The Deerfield curriculum came from the Gay, Lesbian, Straight Education Network (GLSEN), which gives workbooks to school administrators urging them to take "direct action" to "enhance the environment for LGBT [Lesbian, Gay, Bisexual, and Transgendered]" students, with the aim of making the school "healthier." And not to be missed: the GLSEN "lunchbox." "Packed in an actual lunchbox, this comprehensive training program offers a menu of exercises and activities. . . . " This lunchbox, yours for only $129.95 plus shipping, comes with GLSEN "Safe Zone" stickers. And to think all I got in my "Little House on the Prairie" lunchbox was PB&J and a box of raisins!

One GLSEN workshop for teachers was titled "Girls Will Be Boys and Boys Will Be Girls: Creating a Safe, Supportive School Environment for Trans, Intersex, Gender Variant and Gender Questioning Youth." If you're confused, join the club.

Then there's a GLSEN children's play with the musical number "In Mommy's High Heels," sung by a boy being teased for his dressing proclivities:

> They are the swine, I am the pearl
> They'll be beheaded when I'm queen!
> When I rule the world! When I rule the world!
> When I rule the world in my mommy's high heels![20]

There are worse stories of what GLSEN and their cohorts have sneaked into public school classrooms, but I'll save that for the *Power to the People: The Author's Cut*!

These are not a bunch of unattached episodes. A 2003 article in the Manhattan Institute's *City Journal* explored what was going on:

> For the last decade or so, largely working beneath public or parental notice, a well-organized movement has sought to revolutionize the curricula and culture of the nation's public schools. Its aim: to stamp out "hegemonic heterosexuality"— the traditional view that heterosexuality is the norm—in favor of a new ethos that does not just tolerate homosexuality but instead actively endorses experimenting with it, as well as with a polymorphous range of bisexuality, transgenderism, and transsexuality.[21]

These programs are all pitched in the name of "tolerance"—an idea, that when correctly used, is a good one. But *tolerance* is one thing; promoting, publicizing, and propagandizing for a point of view is quite another. Can you imagine how a similar campaign to promote traditional Judeo-Christian values would be received in our schools? It would be branded as theocratic, narrow-minded... and the old standby, fascist.

Universities Universally Wacko

If things are bad at elementary, middle, and high schools, they are simply awful in many of our colleges. You think you know the sad state of affairs in American academia? It's worse than you think. From the abandonment of academic standards to the censorship of religious and patriotic expression and the infiltration of leftist politics into instruction, American colleges are accelerating in the decline that began in the late 1960s.

Some people, however, seem happy with what's happened on college campuses. On May 31, 1969, young Hillary Rodham delivered one of the three commencement addresses at Wellesley College. In it, she reminisced about the principled protests her class had held against the power structure at Wellesley. "We protested against the rigid academic distribution requirement. We worked for a pass-fail system."[22] In other words, her grand cause in the 1960s was to make schoolwork easier.

Well, if you look at colleges across the country, she's succeeded. Most top colleges have no core curriculum at all. The requirements that remain in place are often so loose that a student can easily graduate without having read a word of Shakespeare or Aristotle. Most top schools, however, do have diversity requirements, and no end of ridiculous course offerings.

Did you know you could get an Ivy League education taking any thirty courses you want, each on a pass-fail basis (Hillary's dream come true!)? Brown University has no core curriculum and no distribution requirements. At Oberlin, the only course requirement is the cultural diversity requirement, consisting of three courses.

THE UNKINDEST CUT OF ALL

>>> An English major at Yale, Princeton, Dartmouth, or most top schools can graduate without reading a word of Shakespeare. The American Council of Trustees and Alumni studied 70 schools, including the 25 top colleges in the country according to *U.S. News & World Report*, and found that only 15 of those 70 required their English majors to take a course that included Shakespeare. Harvard was the only Ivy League school that required the Bard for its English graduates.

Source: "The Vanishing Shakespeare," The American Council of Trustees and Alumni, April 2007

Every academic year, Young America's Foundation ranks the twelve most bizarre classes offered on campuses across America. Some of the weirdest: "The Phallus," "Queer Musicology," "Adultery Novel," "Sex Change City: Theorizing History in Genderqueer San Francisco," "Drag: Theories of Transgenderism and Performance" (I promise, no more sex changes or cross-dressing this chapter), and "Lesbian Pulp Fiction." All of these were just from academic year 2006–2007.

Doing away with the classics of Western culture, from the ancient Greeks to Jane Austen, and replacing them with these faddish sex-obsessed and race-obsessed classes cheats our students and our culture. We lose a common cultural foundation, and graduates miss out on the enduring wisdom of these classics, now considered archaic by much of the academic establishment. If knowledge is power, if a classical education is a gift, then the sort of "education" that's offered on most American college campuses—an "education" that makes us dumber, weakens our cultural ties, and drills us in radical Left obsessions—is a rip-off.

The Bad Kind of Diversity

While most colleges foist a "diversity requirement" on their students, there is no such requirement in their hiring practices. Again, the general point here won't surprise you: college faculties are overrun by liberals. But the numbers surprised even me.

Over the last few years, a handful of national magazines, alternative student papers, or individual economics students have combed through county elections records and polled teachers to find their party affiliation. In California, economics major Daniel Klein at U.C. Santa Clara studied the voter registrations of nearly 1,500 tenure-track professors at Berkeley and Stanford. At Berkeley, he found 9.9 Democrats for every Republican. Stanford, comparatively, was a conservative school with a 7.6:1 Democrat-to-Republican ratio. At these two colleges, Klein found 352 Democrats teaching social sciences, and only twenty-one Republicans—a 16:1 ratio.[23]

It's not just California, either. David Horowitz and Eli Lehrer conducted a broad study of 150 departments at thirty-two elite colleges, and turned up similar results.[24] They found ten Democrats for every Republican. The most bipartisan campus was Northwestern University with a 4–1 Democratic edge. Brown had thirty Democrats for each Republican. In the departments Horowitz and Lehrer studied at Williams, Oberlin, MIT, and Haverford, they found zero Republicans. Bill Clinton's cabinet was more bipartisan.

This matters. Putting aside the radical professors, there are thousands and thousands of liberal or center-left professors who, even with the best intentions, are incapable of presenting a balanced picture to their students. How could they, when they have no exposure to conservative peers in their academic circle? It is impossible for universities to center themselves on a classical liberal education when there is no right and, in truth, very little center among the faculty and the administration. One result is the sort of idiotic course offerings we see, eschewing Socrates for the Simpsons.

But liberals defend this. The imbalance is not a problem, argues University of Pennsylvania professor Michael Berube, who wrote a book titled *What's Liberal About the Liberal Arts?*[25] He contends first, that it's fine that the Left dominates academia because the Right controls government and the media (yeah, you got that right, CNN is a right-wing operation). Maybe now that Democrats have both chambers of Congress, Berube will be open to more balance on campus? Don't count on it—his next answer is that liberalism is really just tolerance, and so being open-minded means being a leftist. It's got to be nice to believe that everyone who disagrees with you is a de facto bigot.

Berube is a self-described liberal progressive, which makes him a moderate in academia. At the extreme left end is the likes of former University of Colorado professor Ward Churchill. On September

12, 2001, Churchill penned an essay titled "Some People Push Back: On the Justice of Roosting Chickens." The piece infamously called the victims of September 11 "little Eichmanns," referring to Adolf Eichmann, devout Nazi and top aide of Adolf Hitler. A couple of years later, he expanded this argument into a book.

Naturally, this upset a lot of people, including the Colorado taxpayers who were paying his salary. Then governor Bill Owens argued that taxpayers shouldn't have to subsidize such filth, an argument greeted by cries of "censorship" from liberal magazines and Web sites and the National Coalition Against Censorship. Four professors from the department Churchill had chaired—the ethnic studies department—held a news conference after the book came out, sticking up for Churchill's "freedom of expression and First Amendment rights."

These weak arguments are not only dodges, but they are offenses against the English language. It is not *censorship* to refuse to pay someone who says horribly offensive things. The First Amendment doesn't protect anybody's right to live off the taxpayer dole. The taxpayers were Ward Churchill's bosses, and they had every right to fire him. And they *did* fire him, but not for calling innocent New Yorkers Nazis. They fired him because he faked his résumé and displayed "serious research misconduct," among other things.

Like many in academia, Churchill's devotion to free speech is pretty self-serving. He has repeatedly stated in public that the Constitution actually *prohibits* Columbus Day parades. Nobody ever said Ward Churchill's vile words should be illegal—we just argued they shouldn't be subsidized by taxes. Churchill, on the other hand, has argued that celebrating Columbus *should* be outlawed. Intolerance is the new tolerance.

Other professors less notorious than Churchill brought the same message to their state university campuses. Dana Cloud at the University of Texas on September 12, 2001, engaged in the typical liberal soul-searching, trying to find out how *we* are to blame for the terrorists' anger. One of her arguments—and I am not making this up—was that our absence from a UN conference on racism may have spurred al Qaeda to attack us. Her exact quote:

> Few people I have spoken with have thought about the role that the U.S.'s refusal to participate in the UN World Conference Against Racism in Durban, South Africa (where questions of Israeli racism against Palestinians arose) may have played in intensifying Arab anger at the United States.[26]

We should find it encouraging that despite all of the Professor Clouds and Churchills in academia, Ms. Cloud still only found a "few people" who thought this way. Ms. Cloud has also not gotten traction with her proposed new pledge of allegiance, which includes:

> I pledge allegiance to the people of Iraq, Palestine and Afghanistan, and to their struggles to survive and resist slavery to corporate greed, brutal wars against their families, and the economic and environmental ruin wrought by global capitalism....[27]

After appearing on my radio show, Ms. Cloud received e-mails arguing for her firing. She called this "McCarthyism" and "censorship." Once again, I will defend the liberty of Dana Cloud to say anything she wants—especially on her blog, "TXcommie"—but I don't think taxpayers should be forced to pay her salary if they think she's a fool.

Conservatism = Hate Speech

Keep in mind all this talk about academic freedom and the decrying of censorship, and then take a look at the way conservatives get treated on campus. Jim Gilchrist and Marvin Stewart, two members of the Minutemen—a group that patrols the Mexican border—learned firsthand what illiberal education means. When they spoke at Columbia University at the invitation of the College Republicans, they were shouted at, heckled, and booed throughout. When that didn't shut them up, the protesters rushed the stage, setting off a fight and prematurely ending the talk. One student told the *New York Sun*: "These are racist individuals heading a project that terrorizes immigrants on the U.S.-Mexican border.... They have no right to be able to speak here."[28] ¡Muy bueno!

At Georgia Tech, student Ruth Malhotra learned the hard way about what you get for speaking out as a conservative on campus. A Christian and a campus Republican, she anticipated being shouted down by angry liberal classmates, or even unfairly punished by leftist professors, but she was surprised when the administration piled on, too. Ruth came on my show and told the story:

> The first day of my required public policy foundations class I'm told that if I attend a Conservative Political Action Conference the professor would fail me. I didn't take her seriously.... The weeks and months passed, I received failing grades, derogatory remarks every week in class toward Christians, specifically directed toward me. One day when I tried to speak out in defense of President Bush's tax cuts her response was "George Bush hasn't done anything for you—he's too busy pimping for the Christian Coalition."

Ruth complained to the head of the department, and continued to take her complaints all the way up the chain of command. She got no satisfaction, and it's no surprise: the Georgia Tech administration that ignored Ruth's complaints is the same one that instituted a wide-ranging speech code on campus (more on that below).

Ruth's experience is not unique. Conservative campus newspapers are regularly stolen and thrown out. If a prominent conservative speaks on campus, he should be on guard for pie-throwers at best, and violent thugs at worst.

Conservatives find some pleasure in bashing left-wing academia, but there's a real sad side to all of this. Think about what it means for our country when our Ivy League schools, which are supposed to produce some of our top citizens, are so utterly out of touch with the values of the rest of the nation. Consider the implications when colleges stand behind hateful frauds such as Ward Churchill.

The anti-conservative, illiberal thinking that pervades our university life today results in a loss of credibility of American academia, especially our top colleges. This has dire consequences for our culture and our future.

Returning *POWER TO THE PEOPLE*

Education may be the key battlefield in our war to bring power back to the people. It is both crucial and utterly winnable. On top of that, the education battle is where regular people—moms, dads, taxpayers, voters, and students—have the most direct influence. You are the go-to-guys in this one.

This battle has two fronts: K through 12 and colleges and universities. And there are two strategies you can take—engagement or withdrawal—which one is best depends on your particular situation. We can do what the Left did decades ago and try to take over the institutions. Or we can build and develop our own institutions, however big or small. I'm not going to pass judgment or make this decision for you, but I can show you some strategies to deploy whichever route you choose.

❱ ❱ ❱ Schoolhouse Brawl

Public schools in this country have huge problems, but that's not a good enough reason to give up on them. We can bring the public

VOICE OF THE PEOPLE

From C. Richards, Satellite Beach, Florida: "I don't know how much parental involvement there is anymore in public schools. Up until last week I was working in our local twenty-four-hour Wal-Mart. After what I saw in my four years there, I came to the conclusion that many parents just didn't care about their children at all—keeping them out at dinnertime, bedtime, or any other time that it was convenient for them. The children didn't seem as important to them as their lives. So why would these parents go to a parent conference or get involved in school? This was confirmed to me by fellow associates who were also teachers."

schools in line with the needs and wishes of the people, but it will take hard work.

First, realize that even if you don't have students in public schools, you still have a dog in this fight. They are spending your tax dollars and supposedly educating the future leaders of your community and your country. You have a right to speak up, although administrators and activists may try to dismiss you. If you go to a school board meeting or a public school forum, and someone suggests you should keep to yourself because you're not a public school parent, borrow a line from Ronald Reagan, and point out, "I'm paying for this microphone." If your property taxes are paying the honorarium of some smut-peddler in the public schools, you ought to object—at public meetings, in op-eds to your local paper, in letters to the editor. Don't be afraid to call a reporter, and spur some media attention if something crazy is going on.

If you *do* have children in public schools, it is your parental duty to get into the trenches. Start with the PTA meetings. Too many PTAs across the country are feel-good groups that hold bake sales in order to buy books for the library (often with marching orders from the school board or the teachers). Why not turn your PTA into the local watchdog of education? Ask about curriculum. Ask about reading lists. Make sure the teachers are challenging the students, and not just trying to get by. If the teachers need help, give it to them. But also fight them tooth and nail if they try to dumb down the curriculum or sex it up.

Fighting back is effective, as parents will tell you in Evesham, New Jersey. The school district in this Philadelphia suburb had introduced a video into the third-grade curriculum called "That's a Family!" Promoted as teaching tolerance and diversity, the video described how families could be different and still be families. (You can probably guess where this one is going.) At one point, a sweet little girl on the video explains, "My name is Abby, and I'm nine years old. This is my mom; her name is Betty. And this is my other mom; her name is Kim." A minute later, a young boy declares, "It's really cool to have two gay dads." Another kid explains: "The reason I live with my grandparents is because my mom and dad were on drugs for quite a long time." You can understand why some parents would like the right to explain these sorts of scenarios to their children themselves.

Parents in Evesham turned out for a school district screening of "That's a Family!" and didn't like what they saw. Following their protests and complaints, the school district polled parents, and decided to stop showing the video.

Lesson: you have to show up for the big game to have a shot at winning.

Remember the confidentiality agreement students in Deerfield, Illinois, were supposed to sign to keep their parents from finding out what they were being taught? Most public school administrators would rather that parents just stayed out of school matters— except maybe chaperoning school dances or donating goods for school auctions. But the parents in their community would not be intimidated into silence. Concerned parents formed a group called the North Shore Student Advocacy, and took out a full-page ad in the local paper.[29] The issue has now gotten press in the *Chicago Tribune* and *Washington Times,* and the group Concerned Women for America has jumped into the fray.[30]

Needling the school administrators is important, but knowing what goes on in your child's *classroom* is what counts. Talk to your children's teachers. The teachers I've spoken to say their number-one wish is more parental involvement. And watching the finale of *American Idol* with your child doesn't count!

))) Government Class

Another culprit in our failing schools is negligent local government. Don't get me wrong—we don't want mayors grading kids' papers and city councils assigning homework, but public schools belong to the voters and the taxpayers. Local, county, and state governments are our trustees. Just as local government is responsible for making sure the fire department is doing its job, our officials have a duty to check on our schools. Too many are failing at that duty.

There are some basic measures local politicians can and should take that they often don't. First, they need to ask: can our graduates read, write, add, subtract, multiply, and divide? The embarrassing fact is that many school districts are turning out graduates who lack the most basic knowledge and skills.

Local governments can also lean on school boards and principals to hire better teachers. The numbers earlier in this chapter make it clear—schools prefer credentials over quality. This needs to be reversed.

Governments have the ability and the obligation to reject union demands that harm education. Rewarding good teachers and firing bad teachers are pretty basic liberties a school district should have. The politicians have the power to protect the freedom of school districts to hold teachers (and administrators) accountable. Voters have the power to force the politicians to stand up to the unions.

We need to fight for quality education on every level—at the individual school, at the school district, at the county, state, and federal level. But in this fight, we must remember that education is a local issue. If you have a liberal school board in a conservative state, it may be tempting to try to call in the state government to set things straight, but it also could backfire. Centralizing power and weakening local control is a very dangerous game.

Here's a cautionary tale about federal involvement in education: Ronald Reagan's chairman of the National Endowment for the Humanities was Lynne Cheney, now wife of the vice president of the United States and a solid conservative. Seeing how many students lacked basic knowledge of American history, she launched a program under the first President Bush to draft national history standards. The project didn't get finished until the Clinton administration. The result was an embarrassing smorgasbord of politically correct drivel dedicated to making America—especially white, male America—look evil. Thankfully, what Mrs. Cheney had initiated were only non-binding standards, and so no harm was done. But it teaches a lesson: calling on Washington, D.C. to fix our schools is like calling on Paris Hilton to rebuild your car transmission.

Which brings us to No Child Left Behind. President George Bush made the No Child Left Behind Act a centerpiece of his campaign. Part of that was political. No Republican wants to be accused of "not supporting education," and No Child Left Behind fit into Bush's compassionate conservative model. Part of it was idealism— George W. Bush really wanted to improve education without simply throwing more money at the schools as most politicians would. The idea of NCLB was to force schools to improve student achievement one way or another. This would involve *measuring* student achievement, which in the end meant more standardized tests. Failing schools could lose federal funding if they didn't improve. NCLB would impose something like marketplace incentives on schools.

Passing NCLB was one of President Bush's early victories, but we knew it was trouble when we saw Ted Kennedy at the Rose Garden bill-signing ceremony.

Six years later, NCLB looks like a mistake. In early 2007, some of Bush's staunchest supporters introduced a bill to fix some of its problems. Conservatives, specifically, did not like how Kennedy and other Democrats who helped pass the legislation had turned the bill into another federal spending bonanza, resulting in more federal control of education. Since NCLB passed, federal education spending has gone up 25 percent, but educational achievement has flatlined. NAEP test scores have not improved. Kennedy and his friends say they need more money. Conservatives respond that the law needs to be crafted to provide more local autonomy—as Republicans did with welfare reform in the 1990s. In any event, more of the same—federal money and federal control—is not the solution.

Decentralization of textbook decisions will also help. Remember the lame, watered-down, politically correct textbooks I discussed earlier? The current politicized process of textbook procurement is only going to get worse without reform. As Professor Diane Ravitch has argued, states should get out of the textbook selection process and let the individual teachers pick the materials that fit best for them. We also need to foster more competition in the textbook publishing industry. It is increasingly difficult for smaller publishers to stay in the game when they have to hire countless diversity mavens and sensitivity monitors to stay atop the ever-changing requirements of state departments of education. Get rid of those bureaucrats, let teachers (and parents) choose, and we'll have more—and better—textbooks to choose from.

❱❱❱ Choose or Lose

After I discussed some of these education issues on the air, one listener—a former school board member—wrote in to say that what she saw on the front lines convinced her to home-school her children. Other parents read these stories and decide the only option is to pull their children from the public schools, take on some additional debt, and send their kids off to private schools with better track records.

While it's not the *only* option, removing your kids from public school is an option every parent needs to keep in mind, even if it imposes the financial strain of having to afford a private school or the enormous commitment required to home-school. It might mean dropping that European vacation or driving that 1992 Ford Taurus for another few years. No matter how huge the sacrifice, this is your children's future we're talking about. Handing your children over to the educrats in some school districts could constitute gross negligence. Not all good private schools cost $20,000 a year, either.

Private school students usually do better than public school students. Private school students outperformed their public school counterparts in both reading and math, according to a 2003 survey of scores from the NAEP test.[31]

The private religious school advantage can also be significant. After Hurricane Katrina, the difference between Catholic schools and public schools in New Orleans was easy to see—the Catholic schools were actually *open*. In March, a National Public Radio reporter checked out how the schools were recovering. What she found won't surprise you: "Before Hurricane Katrina, 64,000 students attended 123 public schools in New Orleans. Now 9,000 of them are back, mainly in charter schools." Comparatively, thirty of the city's forty Catholic schools had reopened.[32]

If you do go the private school route, don't be dazzled by prestigious names or fancy campuses. Look for substance. Look for high academic standards, but also for high moral standards. Schools should reinforce and build upon your values. And virtue is more than students raising money for the Sierra Club! Religious schools fit that bill for many parents (though some religious schools can be as radical as public schools, so be on guard).

The less expensive, but far more ambitious route is home-schooling, which used to be the province of hippies, but is now an option for thousands of parents across the U.S. It's not as scary as you might think. First, ignore the stereotype that home-schooled kids end up anti-social. Do you really think our public schools are turning out perfect ladies and gentlemen? Most communities have home-schooling networks that field basketball teams, host field trips, and even have dances. Home-schoolers don't stay inside all day—in fact, many report having more, not less, time for extra-curricular activities.

On the academic front, there's even more support out there for home-schooling. In addition to the networks of other home-schooling parents, there are dozens of Web sites, books, computer programs, and even magazines dedicated to helping home-schoolers. Parents who do this admit it's not easy, but usually say it is worth it.

))) Be Pro-Choice . . . for Students

What do you do if your local grocery store has bad service and poor quality and does not respond to your complaints? You drive a bit farther down the road to the better one. What do you do if your local school has bad teachers and poor quality and won't respond to your complaints—in many cases you just grin and bear it.

If you can't afford private school, and you're just not the right fit for home-schooling, you might be stuck with your local school. That's why we need school choice—an indispensable element in returning power to parents. There are many different ways local and state governments can provide school choice. To begin with, parents should be able to choose which public school or charter school they want their child to attend, rather than abiding strictly by the borders of school districts. This gives parents more control over their children's education, but it also can send a powerful message to school boards and principals. If one school starts losing all of its students when parents elect to drive farther to some other school, any decent educator will realize something is wrong.

Charter schools are a key aspect of this sort of school choice. Charter schools are public schools—funded by tax dollars, and chartered by the local government—but they operate independent from the school board. This gives the schools more latitude, the ability to craft their own curriculum, and the freedom, in some cases, to hire non-union teachers—and pay them according to merit. Not all states or cities have charter schools. But they should.

The next step in school choice is freeing up the money. Vouchers are the most well-known—and most despised by the educrats—form of school choice. In a voucher system, parents receive one voucher per school-aged child, approximately equal to the cost of educating that child in the public schools. If the parent sends the child to a public school, that voucher money goes to that school. But with the voucher in hand, all parents have the resources to help defray the costs of private school. Not only does this enable parents to improve their children's education, it applies competitive market pressures to schools. Just as grocery stores must meet customer demand or go broke, under voucher systems, the public school monopoly would be broken up and these schools would have to compete for students.

It's no wonder the teachers' unions hate vouchers. Check out this charming language from those NEA resolutions: "The Association also opposes any governmental attempts to resegregate public schools through any means, including vouchers, charters, and other school-choice initiatives." Yes, that's right. Trying to help poor and middle-class students go to decent schools is "resegregation." The unions have clout—remember their $300 million budget. The national Democratic Party largely does the NEA's bidding, as do many state parties. Winning school vouchers is a tough fight today, but halfway measures—such as tax deductibility of private school tuition—can do wonders. We need to press our lawmakers to stand up to the unions and fight for school choice.

We have had success. In Utah, for example, the state recently passed a law providing vouchers to parents of all students. Utah's schools had been underperforming pretty badly. This injection of competition should jumpstart the schools. To return power to parents, we should push for similar laws in every state, with the knowledge that we will be fighting the educrats the whole way. The teachers unions in Utah immediately launched an initiative to repeal the school choice laws, using the PTA as an arm of their anti-school choice signature drive and sending home petitions with students.[33]

The might of the teachers' unions and the hurdles facing any would-be reformers are enough to make you wish the government had never gotten into the education industry in the first place. This is the essence of the arguments put forth by the Alliance for the Separation of School and State. Marshall Fritz, who runs the Alliance, argues that education is the proper role of parents and associations voluntarily joined—such as a church, a home-school association, or a private school (which would be more affordable if we weren't already paying taxes for bureaucracy-bloated public schools). The Alliance urges all parents to pull their kids from public schools and dreams of a day where the government is out of the business altogether.

⟩⟩⟩ The Old College Try

Fixing our universities and colleges will be quite an ordeal—but it's important and worth the struggle. The tactics appropriate and possible for state colleges will differ from those for private colleges. Both can be fixed if the people stand up to the ivory tower elites.

First, we need to shed our Stockholm Syndrome when it comes to elite colleges. What the *New York Times* thinks is the best possible education might not be what you think. We shouldn't play by their rules. Think long and hard about this question: will your children really be better off after four years at Brown—studying "queer lit" from angry Marxists—compared to four years at a less prestigious college with a real moral foundation and an adherence to traditional education? Consider Grove City, Providence College, or Wheaton College instead of Middlebury or Smith.

Second, alumni need to fight for their alma maters.

Remember my Dartmouth story at the beginning of the chapter? Well, if the College's Board of Trustees were not so monolithically left-leaning at the time, I wouldn't have been in such a mess. Now, things are starting to change at Dartmouth. In 2004, Silicon Valley CEO T. J. Rodgers, a fierce defender of the free market, won a seat

ALL-AMERICAN COLLEGES

》》》 The Intercollegiate Studies Institute researches American colleges from a more traditional perspective, and they have produced a new book called *The ISI Guide to All-American Colleges* featuring "Top Schools for Conservatives, Old-Fashioned Liberals, and People of Faith." Of the 52 schools ISI lists, here are some of the strongest:

University of Chicago, Chicago, IL
The Citadel, Charleston, SC
Cooper Union, New York, NY
University of Dallas, Dallas, TX
Providence College, Providence, RI
Rhodes College, Memphis, TN
St. John's College, Annapolis, MD
University of St. Thomas, Houston, TX
University of the South, Sewanee, TN
Thomas More College, Merrimack, NH

on the Dartmouth Board of Trustees. He got on the ballot the hard way—gathering 500 signatures of alumni—and ended up beating the favorites who were endorsed by the college administration. Over the next few years, former Reagan speechwriter Peter Robinson and conservative law professor Todd J. Zywicki and former Clarence Thomas clerk Stephen Smith all followed Rodgers's path. Sick of the hard left tack the school was taking, the alumni swept them all into office.

Slowly but surely, seat by seat, these independent candidates are taking over the board of trustees. With trustees who are not hand-picked by the administration, real checks and balances will return to this college.

Third, we need to quit criticizing and actually jump into the ring. We can't balance out the ideology of college faculties if conservatives don't apply for academic jobs. Paul Krugman, who is almost always wrong about everything, got it partly right when explaining the political imbalance of college faculties: "The sort of person who prefers an academic career to the private sector is likely to be somewhat more liberal than average, even in engineering." In other words, liberals are more willing to take lower-paying jobs in order to sway young minds. If we continue to cede that territory, we'll be in trouble.

Students need to fight back, too. Don't be cowed or intimidated by illiberal, left-wing professors. I never let them stop me. Say and write what you believe, and invite speakers who disagree with the school's orthodoxy. The most important thing you can do is to speak out. Most Americans would be *shocked* to learn what goes on at your campus. At Georgia Tech, Ruth Malhotra went public with her fight, and author David Horowitz commended her courage. But he explained that standing up has its consequences:

> Most students just get out of the way. Because she has stood
> up at Georgia Tech she has received a series of death threats,

threats of violence, and the administration at Georgia Tech, which is a disgraceful administration, has done nothing to protect her.

You have to be bold but careful. The administration, the faculty, and the most active members of the student body are going to be watching you closely, waiting for you to slip up. If they catch just one tasteless joke, one factual error, one out-of-line outburst from you, they will use it to destroy you.

One last resort: sue the bastards. Ruth and her fellow College Republican Orit Sklar took the Georgia Tech administration to court over the campus speech codes, which were broad and vague, and even laughably hypocritical. For instance, when the school sponsored a performance of the vulgar *Vagina Monologues*, the College Republicans protested by making placards with lines from the play. The administration made them paint over the lines because they were offensive! The students won in court, with the judge striking down Georgia Tech's unconstitutional speech code.

At state schools, we have some more powerful tools at our disposal. These schools are supposed to belong to the people, not to the radical Left. While we don't want politicians micromanaging universities, we do want them to ensure quality and balance on campus. And to the inevitable cries of "academic freedom," we need to respond that academic freedom must have its limits within the bounds of decency and honesty.

We also can apply pressure directly as voters, without bothering with the politicians. If Ward Connerly could pass a ballot initiative in California banning racial quotas in the state schools, why can't the citizens pass similar initiatives to curb some of the more egregious efforts to indoctrinate our children?

Public schools, private schools, and even our universities need our help—whether they know it or not! They can be salvaged.

They *want* to be salvaged. For only an educated populace is a free populace.

8

THE REVENGE OF THE "LOUD FOLKS"

When my nameplate kept disappearing off my office door at CBS News in Washington, D.C., I should have known I wouldn't last long at the "Big Eye." It was the fall of 1996, and I had only been hired as a political analyst a few months earlier.

I really had no idea what I was getting into. As a practicing white collar criminal defense attorney and freelance columnist, I had only done a few television appearances here and there—Charlie Rose, CNN, etc. A friend and CBS producer Bill Owens had introduced me to CBS News president Andrew Heyward at the annual White House Correspondent's Dinner, and we hit it off. The next thing I knew I was offered a job.

From Day One, I was a fish out of water in the television news business. I didn't come from their world and I didn't buy into their worldview. They knew it and I knew it. As a conservative lawyer who had worked for the Reagan administration, and clerked on the Supreme Court for Clarence Thomas, I didn't fit the CBS mold of the earnest, idealistic, liberal, "citizen-of-the-world" type attracted to the news business. I might as well have dropped in from a blinking spaceship from Saturn. One of the closet conservatives at the network told me that most of the producers and on-air talent thought the top brass's decision to hire me was a "pathetic sell-out to the Right."

My mother used to tell me that she worried about me working at CBS. "Who will be your friend there? Who will look out for you?" she asked protectively. Her instincts were right as usual. But I was just a rookie and kept thinking, "Any day now Paula Zahn is going to speak to me!" (In the New York bureau, I was told not to enter the make-up room until she was out of the chair.)

In 1997 I turned in a script I had written for a piece I filmed on abortion for the Sunday CBS News. "You can't use the term pro-life," a producer said to me, after reading my draft.

"Why?" I asked, incredulously.

"Because it's CBS policy—'anti–abortion rights activists' is what we use," she said flatly.

"Why?" I asked again.

Irritated that she had to provide an explanation, she snapped: "Because we do not want to appear like we're taking sides. We don't use 'pro-choice' either. For them we use 'abortion rights activists.'"

This job was definitely not going to work out.

While I was still negotiating with CBS, a new cable network named MSNBC contacted me about becoming one of their on-air "friends." The deal was that I would appear on MSNBC three days per week and write columns for msnbc.com. It wasn't much money, but I thought it sounded fun and different. So soon I found myself working for two different television networks simultaneously.

Compared to my CBS experience, my time as a political analyst and on-air host at MSNBC was idyllic, but still rocky. When we launched the cable network's first live television show out of Washington in August 1998, MSNBC execs told us we wouldn't have teleprompters for months. This was the supposedly new, cutting-edge high-tech news outlet and they couldn't get their act together enough to get teleprompters? So my producer Lia Macko and I improvised with an easel and a big white pad of paper. Every day Lia would write the show topics on the pad with a big magic marker and flip the pages segment to segment. Guests thought it was a gag. A few months later we got prompters. I still have the pad.

The episode was a sign of things to come, a sign that the "new media" was maybe not so "new" after all. NBC's partnership with Microsoft was supposed to revolutionize the news business. I thought weaving humor and cultural stories into a traditional news show was a way to live up to that ethos. Yet sure enough, my producer and I ran into resistance from NBC executives on everything from whether we could book the cast of *Gilligan's Island* to whether we could cover the Juanita Broaddrick rape allegations against Bill Clinton. (NBC's own Lisa Meyers did the story and we still had to fight tooth and nail to air the piece on the show.) My personal favorite was the day when I was chastised for asking one of NBC's top political reporters a question about Iranian weapons. It was the main story above the fold that day on the front page of the *New York Times,* but it was not on the list of pre-approved questions. Oops!

I remember watching CBS anchor Walter Cronkite as a kid and thinking how wise and knowledgeable he seemed. Then I grew up and saw the wisdom of what my parents knew; most of what we see on television is filtered through a relentless, if unthinking, liberal bias. Every time Cronkite said, "That's the way it is" to close the broadcast, one of my parents would say "No, Walt, that's the way you *think* it is." I remember years later when Cronkite retired, and Dan Rather took his place, my dad slapped a bumper sticker on his car that read "Rather Not." I felt the same way after working at CBS.

I owe an eternal debt of gratitude to two news executives—Jon Klein of CBS News (now president of CNN) and Steve Capus of MSNBC (now president of NBC News). If both of them hadn't fired me, I wouldn't be hosting a radio show heard by millions today. I left television for a true "new media" experience. And I love it.

Breaking the Liberal Monopoly

Today, unlike in the past, we don't have to rely on CBS, NBC, ABC, or the *New York Times* for the news. That quasi-monopoly—run by the elites for the elites—is now happily broken thanks to countless new media outlets. Hundreds of talk radio shows, thousands of news Web sites, and tens of thousands of blogs now spread news, information, a diversity of opinion, and even expert investigative reporting all around the world.

The old saying was "never pick a fight with people who buy ink by the barrel." Well, in the last decade, we've picked that fight, and we are winning it. Blogs, the Internet, and talk radio are vital weapons in our fight to wrestle power away from the elites and put it back into the hands of the people.

Talk radio is indispensable to circumventing the mainstream media's filter. For Americans who don't share New York City or

Hollywood values (in other words, most of us) talk radio at its best provides an entertaining and intelligent forum for discussing and analyzing politics, culture, books, and ideas—and without the time constraints that television has. While the dinosaur media starts with the idea that morality is hypocrisy, tradition is bigotry, and bigger government is the answer to everything, talk radio is full of voices that know that morality is essential, tradition is wisdom, and big government is the problem.

If we continue to build and harness the power of the new media, we can keep the old media a bit more honest. The new media can strip power away from the media elites and apply competitive pressure, thus bringing back to the people the all-important power over the flow of information.

On the flip side, new technologies present our culture with all sorts of new threats and pitfalls. While the new media can give the old media a run for their money and call them out on their omissions and distortions, the instantaneous nature of today's news media multiplies inaccuracies and errors as fact-checking standards give way to a rush for the scoop. In politics, substantive journalism often gives way to "gotcha" journalism. More important, new Internet technologies create new risks for children and teenagers, running the gamut from new ways to waste time to new avenues for child predators. But the new media can also be a forum for whistleblowers, and that's a public service.

Pulling the Plug on Akon

When I began watching the two-minute video clip a friend sent to me with the title "Caution—disturbing," I didn't know what to think. Was this a sick spoof on rap music? Or could it really be one of the global rap superstars carrying out what appeared to be a simulated rape of a young woman on stage? He had pulled her out of the audience, and was throwing her around the stage like she was a rag doll, thrusting his pelvis into hers. Perversely, the audience in this club (which turned out to be in Trinidad) seemed to be loving this. By the end of the violent bumping and grinding, the rapper dropped her on stage like a piece of trash. Her body went limp and lifeless until she was carted off by a security guard.

The only person who needed security that night was that young woman—who turned out to be fourteen or fifteen, and the daughter of a minister.

The rapper is not some local thug on the Caribbean hip hop scene. He is Akon—who dominated the music charts over the past year with his CD *Konvicted*. When news spread of his onstage "performance," the explanations ranged from "this was part of a dance contest" to "how could he have known she was fifteen?" to "what was she doing in the club, anyway?"

I kept thinking of our soldiers in Iraq and Afghanistan. If one of them were involved in similar behavior caught on videotape, the outcry would be deafening from the same media elites who were strangely silent on Akon. Breathless articles would be written, asking whether the military "culture" somehow encourages or condones this misogynistic treatment of women. The dinosaur media didn't cover the bad behavior of Akon, so much as it covered *for* him.

When I discovered that Verizon Wireless was not only sponsoring Akon's nationwide "tour" but had partnered with him in February amidst huge fanfare to launch their new V-Cast phone features, I knew my listeners would be outraged. Verizon's top marketing executive had hailed Akon as "a multi-talented global superstar." Akon and Verizon Wireless were not just about ring tones anymore.

Then the new media kicked into action. Michelle Malkin and Debbie Schlussel started blogging about this, and on May 2, 2007, I started discussing the Akon-Verizon relationship and the "dance"/simulated rape incident on my show. How could Verizon not have done due diligence on this guy? The Senegalese American Muslim not only puts out some of the filthiest lyrics in the rap industry, he served time in prison for armed robbery, and, on a New York radio station, had bragged about having three wives.

Calls that I placed to Verizon's corporate headquarters went unreturned. But thousands of my listeners who phoned and e-mailed Verizon expressing their outrage did get through. The message was clear: if Verizon didn't terminate him, my listeners would terminate their Verizon accounts.

Two days later, on a Friday afternoon, Verizon Wireless quietly announced that it had terminated its sponsorship with Akon. He lost millions of dollars. (After Akon was cut loose from Verizon, he apologized for his onstage behavior. Now if he'd only apologize for his hit "I Wanna F— You.")

It took the *New York Times* six days to report on this stunning corporate reversal. (I guess this initially didn't qualify as "all the news that's fit to print.") The piece began with a list of other celebrities who have had problems but hadn't been dropped by corporate sponsors.[1] (As if Keith Urban's stint in rehab is comparable to Akon's proud promotion of filth!) The *Times*, always revealing its bias toward the cultural Left, referred to the "chill" that Verizon's decision was sending through the music industry. A few weeks later, when writing about the Gwen Stefani/Akon concert tour, the *New York Times*'s music critic Kelefah Sanneh dismissed Akon's critics as "harrumphers."[2]

The people, spurred by voices in the new media, had won one battle in the culture war, and the old media didn't like it one bit. They liked it better when they were the nation's sole cultural gatekeepers.

Now look at what this pesky public—who clearly doesn't understand the nuanced artistry of performers like Akon—has done! They have mucked it all up!

We can only hope that a "chill" turns into a freeze—freezing out lyrics and behavior that degrade *everyone*. Better name for Akon: a con man.

Did You Get the Memo?

The real media sea change occurred when diligent bloggers, promoted by talk radio and conservative Web sites, blew a hole so huge in dinosaur media giant Dan Rather's last big story that it sank his career. On Wednesday night, September 8, 2004, two months before the presidential election, CBS's *60 Minutes* ran a segment featuring memos purportedly written in 1972 by George W. Bush's commanding officer in the National Guard. Dan Rather used the memos as evidence that our commander in chief had been AWOL from a cushy National Guard post during Vietnam, and that Bush's powerful family connections had pulled strings to cover for him.[3]

Four hours later, someone writing under the name "Buckhead" made a post on the popular conservative message board Free Republic. He explained that the spacing and lettering on these memos did not look like the work of a 1972 typewriter. "Buckhead" wrote, "I am saying these documents are forgeries, run through a copier for 15 generations to make them look old. This should be pursued aggressively."[4]

It *was* pursued aggressively. One reader forwarded the post to blogger Scott Johnson at the popular blog Powerline. Another pro-Bush blog, Little Green Footballs, joined the frantic charge. The conservative blogosphere was soon abuzz parsing the superscripts, proportional spacing, kerning, and signatures of these memos.

Hundreds of blog posts and comments dissected these memos around the clock over the next few days. On Saturday, Charles Johnson at Little Green Footballs put to rest any doubts about these documents: they were forgeries.

Johnson created an image file that flashed back and forth between CBS's document and a verbatim document he had made using Microsoft Word at its default settings.[5] With this comparison up on a Web page available to the whole world, it was clear to any unbiased observer that the documents were forgeries. After days of stubborn and embarrassing defenses of his reporting, Rather eventually had to back down (sort of). If this had been the 1996 election, Rather's report might have gone unchallenged.

This is just one striking and famous example of how blogs and the Internet can create citizen journalists and citizen fact-checkers to do the work that CBS producers—too blinded by the prospect of a sensational scoop that could defeat Bush—failed to do.

The old media types complain that the Internet and the twenty-four-hour cable news channels encourage the press to rush into reporting unconfirmed, and often false, stories. This danger is real, but on the flip side, the blogosphere can make journalists more honest. When Dan Rather says he ran the memos by experts to determine they were authentic, that's not good enough anymore. He now has to run them by the whole world.

These thousands of fact-checkers behind keyboards created a headache in 2006 for Reuters and one of its freelance photographers named Adnan Hajj. In August 2006, Israel launched missile strikes at Beirut in retaliation for Hezbollah's kidnapping of Israeli soldiers. Reuters released a picture by Hajj of the Beirut skyline showing many plumes of smoke rising up from different parts of the city. The photo created the impression that repeated missile strikes were devastating the whole city.

But someone on a photography discussion board noted that the plumes all looked strange, with repeating patterns. Another photographer forwarded this message board to widely read blogger Michelle Malkin. Once Malkin posted the comments and the pictures on her Web site Hotair.com, another blogswarm ensued. Other readers in the comments section shared their knowledge of Photoshop software, scoured the wires for similar pictures, and researched Adnan Hajj's past. This decentralized cooperative effort yielded far more accurate results than an organized investigation ever could have. In the end, Reuters told all of its clients to kill the picture, and it removed every Adnan Hajj picture from its Web site.[6]

Blogs also give a potential megaphone to voices that would never make it past the gatekeepers of the mainstream media. For example, the courage, struggles, suffering, and victories of our soldiers, sailors, airmen, and Marines may get play in history books, but they usually get ignored by the contemptuous old media. Blogs have fixed that. For instance, former army major Matthew Burden launched a blog he called BlackFive. This blog tells the stories of troops fighting, recovering, and dying in Iraq. He tells the stories from an apolitical, but patriotic and pro-military perspective.

Burden launched his blog after his good friend, Matt Schram, was killed in action in 2003. Schram had successfully fought his convoy out of an ambush in western Iraq but had received mortal wounds in the process. Burden learned there was a reporter for a mainstream outlet in the convoy Schram helped save. The reporter, though, never thought it worthwhile to tell Schram's story. Burden realized that there were hundreds of such stories to be told, and so his Web site, and now his book, *The Blog of War*,[7] serves as a clearinghouse for underreported stories of war heroism. BlackFive.net collects these stories from the soldiers' hometown papers or even from the troops' own blogs, and broadcasts them to the world.

Blogging from the front-lines is also new to this war. Instead of relying on the Peter Arnetts of the world to tell us how horrible things are in Iraq, we can get the full story today from the ground.

Any serviceman who can find an Internet connection for his laptop can give the world his view of the war. It's not that our enlisted men are unbiased and all-seeing—it's that their voices have been silenced, or at least heavily filtered, in the past.

Blogging and talk radio have not only expanded what we know about the world—they have *changed* the world, especially in the realm of politics. If John Kerry had run for president in 1992 on his military record, he likely would have gotten away with it. The brave Swift Boat Veterans for Truth probably would have condemned him, but they might not have gotten much attention.

In fact, for weeks after the Swifties started telling the less flattering aspects about John Kerry's Vietnam performance, the mainstream media ignored them. But when Swift Boat veteran John O'Neill and Jerome Corsi published their book *Unfit for Command*—itself published by "dissident publisher" Regnery (my publisher too)—it was seized on by the Drudge Report, Human Events Online, talk radio, and the blogosphere. The American public finally learned the devastating big scoop that the old media had ignored—that most of Kerry's Swift Boat comrades did not support his run, that two of Kerry's Purple Hearts were for self-inflicted injuries, and that his antiwar activities after the war provided aid and comfort to the enemy.[8] Only after everyone already knew these stories about Kerry in Vietnam, thanks to the new media, did the old media ever address them—and then most of their reporters and pundits tried to deny them, and blacken the reputations of these former Swift Boat commanders.[9]

Of course, the Left understands and uses the power of the new media, too. The left-wing blogosphere—led by Web sites like DailyKos—has become a powerful PR force for the Democrats. These sites generate both policy and income for Democrats they deem worthy. On issues ranging from national health care to carbon credits, they have moved the Democrats farther to the left. (If that's possible!) Move on...to the left...dot com!

Meanwhile, conservative blogs and Web sites have to fight not only the lefty bloggers and the old media, but they have to fight to keep squishy Republicans honest as well. Just look at the invaluable role conservative blogs, Web sites, and talk radio played in taking down the ludicrous nomination of Harriet Miers to the Supreme Court.

Internet Dangers

Any new invention that brings great promise also usually brings great peril. With the Internet this is easy to see. The Web presents dangers to our culture, our children, and our own souls. We will need to heighten our vigilance in the face of these dangers.

For all of the salutary effects of the new media—Akon losing his coroporate sponsorship; Dan Rather losing his job—the instantaneous nature of the Web and the twenty-four-hour news channels makes our media sloppier. Since Adam and Eve, rumor mills have been getting facts wrong, but these days cable news outlets are likely to rush these rumors onto the air for fear of being scooped. This means we, as news consumers, need to be careful about believing what we hear, but we also need to start rewarding accuracy over speed.

Among the favorite destinations for younger Internet browsers are social networking Web sites such as MySpace or FaceBook. In themselves these sites are neither good nor bad, but they certainly provide some dangerous temptations. These sites showcase a strange blend of vanity, narcissism, and exhibitionism, with young people posting their personal life stories for total strangers to read.

The counterpart to Internet exhibitionism is Internet voyeurism. Millions of YouTube viewers watched the personal travails of "LonelyGirl15," who claimed to be a sixteen-year-old girl named

Bree (but turned out to be a nineteen-year-old actress). Her videos discussed her first kisses and fights with her parents. While LonelyGirl15 wasn't really exposing her private life to complete strangers, Net voyeurs can get their cheap thrills by reading what millions of kids in chat rooms or with MySpace pages are revealing about themselves. It's no wonder that one in five children who regularly use the Internet told one survey that they had "received an unwanted sexual solicitation via the Web." About 3 percent of American children reported receiving "an aggressive sexual solicitation" in the past year. Another study found that a quarter of all children were exposed to unwanted pornography online.[10]

Even for adults, the Internet poses real risks. For one thing, it can make us less social. We already have a problem of alienation from our neighbors and the atomization of our society, and the Internet can make that worse by sucking up our time and replacing real social interaction. And aren't you tired of people who hide behind e-mail—using it to avoid people or obligations? Internet addiction also appears to be a real problem, and some organizations have even started setting up clinics to treat the e-dicted. The bottom line: use the Internet, but don't let it use you.

Talk Radio—the Voice of the People

The impact of talk radio is even bigger than the Internet, because while Internet use is concentrated among younger people, talk radio reaches virtually all of America. Whether the shows are nationally syndicated or local, you can see talk radio's influence all over the country. Never was the power of talk radio more apparent than during the "Great Immigration Debate" of 2007, when the Senate tried to buffalo the people with a "comprehensive immigration reform" bill that would have given amnesty to between 12

and 20 million illegal aliens in the United States. A few enforcement provisions were thrown in as window dressing. With a grand
bargain struck in May behind closed doors by a bipartisan coalition (and with the support of the White House), it seemed like the
fix was in for a fast-track to legalization. The open borders crowd
boasted that they were going to vote it through by Memorial Day.
Republican senator Jon Kyl of Arizona was the White House's
quarterback in the Senate. Over the last few years I had done two
fundraisers for Kyl, breaking a rule I set for myself against doing
such events, because he was a conservative and a stand-up guy. I
was stunned that Kyl had taken on the role of legalization facilita-
tor since just months earlier, he had come on my radio show pledg-
ing to filibuster any legislative attempt at amnesty.

This was time to drop the niceties—as dramatic as it sounds, the
future of the country was at stake. I knew the day was going to
come when the GOP had to finally come to terms with this issue.
Actually, I looked forward to finding out who really cared about
"the American people" and who just liked to *say* they "cared about
the American people." I knew I was about to embark on one of the
most protracted, toughest fights of my media career. I knew that if
there was any chance of stopping this madness, I'd need to light a
fire under my audience, arming them with facts and arguments.

I spent most of the six weeks leading up to the final June 28 cloture vote dissecting all angles of the bill. My Web site listed the "flip-
pable" senators and several times an hour I urged my millions of
listeners to get involved: "It's your country, now do something
before it's too late." I was so impassioned about this that I started to
lose my voice and my sleep. *They can't defy the will of such an overwhelming majority of the people, can they?* I kept asking myself this
question. Even when I was off the air and tired, I felt we were in
good hands with other dedicated radio hosts and with Web sites such
as HotAir and RedState, which did a tremendous job of informing

people about the four-inch-thick monster piece of legislation. *National Review*'s Web site and others also provided a constant stream of updates, and important analysis of the potential political, cultural, and financial fall-out of the massive legalization scam.

A groundswell was building and it was as if the elites in Washington were in an information blackout. They charged ahead reviving "comprehensive reform" and in the process they lobbed some verbal hand grenades at the people who were exposing their chicanery. Senator Lindsey (affectionately known as "Let 'em in") Graham ranted against the "loud folks" (read: the people calling his office, and hosts like me urging them to do so). In a girlish huff, he asked, "Are we going to let talk radio control the debate?"

That's infinitely better than you, George Soros, and La Raza controlling it, Senator.

Graham and other shepherds of the bill continued to pour gasoline on the border fire by insulting millions who believe in the rule of law. Also on the anti–talk radio warpath, Senator Trent Lott made a complete fool out of himself several times on national television and radio—leading the voters of Mississippi to wonder whether it was something in the hairspray. Presidential contender John McCain, one of this bill's original sponsors, watched as his White House aspirations went up in smoke. (Months earlier Graham had already endorsed McCain—whoops!) Seeing conservative support for this immigration package continue to slip away, the White House dispatched press secretary Tony Snow to defend the indefensible. I love Tony, but on my show, he simply could not make a coherent case as to why we should not simply enforce our existing immigration laws. He had no good answer. Nor could he answer why we should link enforcing of our laws with the alleged "reform" of legalizing and offering temporary work status to illegal aliens. When I asked him if he had seen the just-released Rasmussen poll showing that 85 percent of the GOP was against the bill, he said no.

Although I felt bad for my friend Tony, I realized the figure could be 99 percent and it still wouldn't have mattered to the president.

During these weeks, the talk radio listening audience kicked into action—the Senate was bombarded by telephone calls, e-mails, and faxes. By some estimates more than 95 percent of the public response was against the McCain-Kennedy-Kyl-Bush-Martinez nightmare bill. Certain senators were getting very irritated by all of the hullabaloo talk radio had created. Living up to his reputation for aloofness and pomposity, Senator Arlen Specter dismissed the public outcry, claiming that "you can't tell what the American people think simply by those who object and those who call." So how are the people supposed to tell their senators what they think? Smoke signals? Telepathy?

In the end, despite millions spent by Latino lobbying groups, the chambers of commerce, and George Soros, the bill went down in flames because the people rose up in a passionate fury against what they knew would be an unworkable, totally ineffective approach to this big problem. They jammed the Senate telephone system on the final day of debate and we received reports that office staff was "overwhelmed" and "exhausted."

A few weeks before the bill collapsed in a cloture vote, President Bush cockily told reporters, "I'll see you at the bill signing." Ignoring the president's bravado, the new media were not cowed or demoralized. We kept on fighting. Citizens from coast to coast did what many of them had never done before—they called Washington and made their voices heard. It was a true "Power to the People" moment that simply never would have happened if Americans didn't have a choice in information and news sources. Talk radio and the blogs prevented the Democrats from signing up millions of new voters, helped avoid a national security nightmare, and stopped another massive surge in illegal immigration. Mission Accomplished.

The (Un)Fairness Doctrine . . .
Back from the Grave

Given how effective conservative talk radio has been in mobilizing the electorate, is it any wonder that politicians and left-wing activists are trying to figure out how to regulate it out of existence?

California senator Dianne Feinstein (one of the authors of the failed immigration bill) is one of many Democrats itching to drop the hammer on conservative talk radio. She said that "there ought to be an opportunity to present the other side . . . I do believe in fairness." Lie of the day! Lie of the day! What she believes in is government restricting political speech that does not support her agenda. So the Democrats, having lost the ability to convince America to favor their left-wing social and economic agenda, want to neuter their political opponents by blunting their most effective means of communicating to the people. How "liberal" of them. Feinstein remembers fondly "when there was a fairness doctrine," and claims "there was much more serious correct reporting." Is that what she calls government restricting political speech? "Serious" and "correct"? An analysis that would make Hugo Chavez proud!

The Fairness Doctrine is a rule promulgated more than fifty years ago by the Federal Communications Commission. It required broadcast networks to provide "opposing viewpoints" when a controversial subject was discussed. The rule was based on a long-outdated rationale that the "scarcity" of broadcast spectra required the government to ensure that both sides of an issue were heard on the public airwaves. The rationale for the rule, which President Reagan rescinded in 1987, makes little sense in an era when we have an information glut—from television, the Internet, print, and radio. Oh, and there's that little matter of the First Amendment that protects political speech.

As talk radio flexed its muscles during the immigration debacle, the left-wing think tank Center for American Progress unveiled a "report" on the "structural imbalance of political talk radio."[11] The authors advocated reforming talk radio station ownership rules, increasing local accountability over licensing, and forcing commercial station owners to pay "fees" toward public interest programming if they misbehave. (Read: our guys failed miserably in the medium, so we need affirmative action in radio for liberal talk-show hosts.) It is worth pointing out that former Clinton White House aide John Podesta runs the Center. (He even let *The Laura Ingraham Show* broadcast there for a week in 2003!) The Center receives funding from billionaire socialist George Soros, who was also a contributor to the unsuccessful left-wing Air America radio network. The dearth of liberal talk shows was "the result of multiple structural problems in the U.S. regulatory system," the Center claimed. And to think I just thought Al Franken was a total on-air snore. At any rate, this report gave some impetus to a variety of open-minded and tolerant lefties on Capitol Hill to re-open a discussion of bringing back the Fairness Doctrine.

Thankfully, the effort is stalled—temporarily at least—due to the efforts of a few smart young turks in the House of Representatives. On the very day that the amnesty bill went down the tubes, Representative Mike Pence of Indiana (also a former radio talk-show host) introduced a measure that passed easily which prohibits the Federal Communications Commission from using federal funds to institute the Fairness Doctrine. A similar amendment in the Senate was rejected.

Never fear, Democrats will be back to muzzle talk radio in the future. By the way, the same folks who claim that "diverse viewpoints are being shut out" regularly refuse to come on my show to debate most issues—including the Fairness Doctrine. Brave souls.

With the uproar against illegal immigration that we saw in 2007, it's hard to see the Democrats getting very far with the Fairness Doctrine before the 2008 election. But if Hillary or Obama or some other warmed-over liberal gets into the White House—look out.

"Editing" the Internet

To no one's surprise, Hillary Clinton was unhappy about her husband's dalliances being reported on the Internet. In 1997, in a press conference where she announced a new White House initiative to advance greater government "cooperation" with the Internet, Hillary expressed concern about "a number of serious issues without any kind of an editing or gate-keeping function" on the Internet.[12]

The Clintons were perfectly happy when the "editing and gate-keeping functions" were performed by the likes of CBS and *Time* magazine, but there was now an unregulated and vast right-wing conspiracy that included not only magazines and books, but radio talk shows and the Internet. To be fair, the Web has made it easier for unsubstantiated and often false claims to circulate about public figures. The Wikipedia page about me, for example, regularly gets filled with lies or awful slurs (ditto for YouTube). We need to encourage and enforce accountability and responsibility, but you won't see me calling for government regulation. Hillary, on the other hand, has been gunning for government regulation of the Net for a decade.

It's not that far-fetched to consider government censorship of the Internet. Our government, after all, limited political speech with McCain-Feingold! In China, Internet surfers can't read Web sites about democracy or Tiananmen Square.[13] In Tunisia, the government has similar censorship rules limiting what their citizens can read, but that didn't keep the UN from holding its "World Summit on the Information Society" there.[14] While the final UN report did not advocate any UN regulation of the Net, the idea was floated.[15] The United States government is feeling diplomatic pressure to welcome more international "standards" for the Internet.

What would it mean if countries adopted global standards for the Internet? It would be bad news for individual liberty. Different countries have different thresholds for libel. Should an American Internet journalist or a blogger watch his words for fear that somebody in Saudi Arabia will read something he wrote that violates Saudi laws? The *Catechism of the Catholic Church* is online, and its teachings on homosexual behavior probably are illegal "hate speech" in Canada. If there were *any* global standards on publishing material on the Internet, the effect would probably be to restrict Americans' freedom of speech.

Of course some Internet regulation is necessary to protect our children. Most parents want the government's help. We should be smart enough in America to fashion laws that help smoke out child predators but that do not stifle political speech. In other words, stop the pervs but leave "Buckhead" alone.

McCain-Feingold and campaign finance laws also pose a real threat. In 2005, after a federal judge ruled that McCain-Feingold did *not* exempt the Internet, Federal Election Commission (FEC) chairman Bradley Smith warned that soon, the federal government would be regulating and restricting political blog posts or YouTube videos on the Internet just as it regulates radio and television ads.[16] Journalists currently are exempt from the McCain-Feingold campaign finance restrictions (so that their reporting can't be construed as political advertising), but the FEC could easily decide that bloggers don't count as journalists. Link to Tom Tancredo's campaign Web site and you could be making an illegal campaign contribution, or write a scorching blog entry against Rudy Giuliani just before a primary, and you could be breaking the law on political advertising.

Reporting Without a License

A cynic might think the old media love "campaign finance reform" so much because it almost always means regulating the political speech of everyone but the press. But who is *the press?* This question gets to the heart of potential threats to the new media.

Congress made some effort to define *the press* when the idea of a federal "shield law" came up in 2004 and 2005 as journalists went to jail for refusing to divulge their sources. A "shield law" (probably a good idea in the abstract) would protect journalists from being forced to reveal their confidential sources. But in order to limit this protection to journalists, the legislation had to define *journalist.* One bill required that you be paid for your reporting by a news organization in order to be protected.[17] So much for most bloggers or "citizen journalists." Many reporters would love to limit entry into their field, which is why the idea of licensing journalists still gets bandied about. It sounds far-fetched, but in Belgium, you can't call yourself press unless you have a license issued by the Ministry of the Interior. Rwanda also licenses journalists, as does Hugo Chavez's Venezuela.

In Paris, you'd better not film police brutality, a terrorist attack, or a mugging unless you qualify as a professional journalist. This law, passed in March 2007 and approved by France's Constitutional Council, prohibits anyone but professional journalists from recording acts of violence.[18] The measure is aimed at punishing thugs who tape their own beatdowns, but a similar law here would have made a criminal of the guy who taped the Rodney King beating or any of the amateurs who taped the jets crashing into the towers on September 11.

Returning *POWER TO THE PEOPLE*

If we want to break the elites' grip on America, we need to continue to chip away at their grip on information. We need to strengthen and defend the new media. This struggle starts by opposing all government efforts to restrict political speech on the radio and the Internet. Trying to quiet the other side (as the Fairness Doctrine effectively does) or using government might to force your voice into someone else's forum (as the Fairness Doctrine *explicitly* does) is un-American. As a conservative, I get upset every time I turn on the CBS *Evening News* or read the *New York Times*, but I don't call on the government to force them to be more balanced. We can't control the content of CBS, but we can all set up our own blog or Web site if we want. And we certainly don't have to watch the CBS *Evening News* or read the *New York Times*—or at least not in isolation. Thanks to the free market and the new media, we have a vast variety of choices, and we can actually find media outlets that truly are alternative—and that are honest, and entertaining, and informative. The market's invisible hand is the best tool for introducing balance into the media—not government regulation.

"Media reform" really means censorship (directed against conservatives) and "campaign finance reform" really amounts to the same thing. If you make a compelling video against Hillary Clinton's presidential campaign, and you post it on YouTube, should you be forced to fill out Federal Election Commission forms? If the FEC deems this ad is worth $10,000, are you making an illegal contribution? *No*, you are practicing your rights as protected by the First Amendment to the Constitution—and it's our job, and the job

NEW MEDIA'S WAR OF THE ROSIE!

》》》 Take a bow, people! New media and all of you who watch, read, and listen to us have chalked up significant victories over the years. One of the sweetest came in April 2007, when the dinosaur media (ABC) dumped Rosie O'Donnell as one of the co-hosts of its mid-morning show *The View*. (The story she spun about her departure was pathetic: "I have decided that we couldn't come to terms" and "[ABC] wanted me for three years." Yeah, right.) Thousands of you contacted ABC to complain about Rosie O'Donnell's lewd comments ("Eat me!") and anti-Catholic bigotry (singling out Catholic justices on the Supreme Court). Talk radio and blogs publicized her filthy slurs and ABC was caught flat-footed. Power to the People!

of the people we elect to Congress and the White House, to make sure that "reform" doesn't mean repealing the First Amendment.

》》》 Digital Pitchforks

The new media levels the playing field—and that means we need to get our players on the field and in the game. So get involved! Pro-lifers, evangelicals, free-marketers, and any conservatives wary of the Republican Party elite (and that should be all of us) ought to unite on the Web in 2008 (and beyond) and work to nominate good, conservative candidates in every district in the country. Does anyone really believe that the Republican National Committee (RNC) knows better than the people in Peoria what message and what candidate will best play in Peoria?

Too many of the top officials in the RNC are not in line with traditional conservative views on everything from immigration to trade disputes. It's time that we let the RNC know that it exists for us—not the other way around. We need to build online networks of people with the same basic principles and the same political goals. Once we rally behind the best candidates, we can make a difference with small cash contributions. One-third of President Bush's campaign contributions in 2004 came in sums of less than $200. A lot of people giving money can make a difference.

And if you have something important to say, say it. Become a blogger, but be a good one. Too many bloggers (including popular ones) use their platforms to pontificate and argue over things they know nothing about. Public debate and a wealth of opinions are great, but the best thing the new media can provide us with is *facts*. Are you a meteorologist? Help us parse the media's reporting on global warming. Are you a student at Duke? Tell us what your professors said about the bogus rape charges against the lacrosse team.

Whether you're an expert on an issue, an amateur connoisseur, or just the guy who happens to be on the ground where the story is taking place, become a citizen reporter, rather than a citizen pundit. Launch a blog about local neighborhood issues. Make it heavier on facts than on opinion. Make it civil in tone, and informative in substance. Many small-town papers lack local reporters who really know where the story is. Become that local reporter even if you don't work for the press.

But remember the pitfalls of the new media, and avoid them. First you have to actually unplug yourself from the Internet long enough to go to the meetings, talk to your neighbors, see the scene with your own eyes. If 80 percent of life is showing up, being on the Internet doesn't count as "showing up."

Second, you need to resist the temptation to play "gotcha" by broadcasting the tape of someone's misstep or posting a photo of the person on a bad hair day. (Exceptions allowed for Hillary coverage.) Our citizen journalists need to be responsible journalists.

On the state and national levels, you can become a fact-checker of the old media. The *New York Times* might report that the South Pole is getting warmer, but if you know where NASA keeps the temperature data online, you can look it up, crunch the numbers, and see if the *Times* is accurate or sloppy and misleading—and then get the word out via your blog. (The South Pole is *not* getting warmer, in case you were wondering.)[19]

The blogosphere worked wonders in debunking the Bush-National Guard and Lebanon-in-smoke media falsehoods; why not create permanent forums for such decentralized citizen fact-checking? Do you live in Boston and want to make the *Globe* a little more accountable? We could use a permanent *Globe*Watch with hundreds of local readers working independently and collaboratively to root out serious omissions, errors, and deceptions in the paper.

Do you have a digital camcorder or voice recorder? Record public school board meetings when they discuss the latest politically correct absurdities they want to drive down your kids' throats. Post the recordings on your blog and let other parents know. Take a camera with you to the pro-choice, antiwar, or pro-illegal immigration marches in your city. Often these groups know the media are usually friendly to their agendas and so they feel comfortable and often say shocking things. So at public events record them, take their pictures, and report the real story on your blog. Recording and disseminating audio, video, and snapshots used to require huge investments. Today, it requires only the same technology that allows you to share pictures of your kids with friends.

Technology can be dangerous. But it can also be liberating. And the Internet, if we seize the opportunity it provides, could be the greatest source of returning power to the people that we'll see in our lifetimes. We shouldn't miss it.

9

BLINDING US WITH SCIENCE

The doctors told pregnant Mrs. Hassick she had a choice. She could bring her child into the world with a club foot—subjecting him to ridicule, pain, and immense inconvenience—or she could abort little Derek. Seventeen years later, Derek Hassick's feet held up just fine as he marched in Washington as part of the thirty-fourth annual March for Life.[1]

Derek was lucky. Not only did his mother "choose" to give him life, but as it turned out, the prenatal diagnosis was wrong: he didn't have a club foot. Unfortunately, other parents facing the same situation would have chosen differently. In Britain, for instance (where such statistics are available), twenty British babies were aborted between 1996 and 2004 because they had a club foot.[2] In 2005, a British Crown Prosecutor refused to pursue charges against two doctors who performed a late-term abortion on a woman whose unborn child had a cleft lip and palate, even though (like club foot) this is a correctable condition.[3] So now imagine the lives and the talent that the world has lost because of the tens of millions of abortions carried out each year because the babies were different.

Sadly, this is not an area where we can feel good by comparing ourselves to the Europeans. According to a study done by one U.S. hospital, 86 percent of babies diagnosed in the womb with Down Syndrome were aborted.[4] Moreover, in 2003 nearly *one in three* of all American pregnancies ended in abortion,[5] and almost always because having a child would be inconvenient: only 4 percent of women who had abortions in 2004 cited physical health problems as the primary reason, while about 86 percent cited reasons such as "not ready for a child," "can't afford a baby," or "would interfere with education or career plans."[6] Wherever you stand on the issue of abortion, these facts should repulse you. The sad truth is that there is a terrible sickness that runs through our culture today: it's a sickness of selfishness, a culture that justifies the manipulating of human life and nature to ends that, under common morality—or even common sense—are hard to justify.

The culture tells us that if something can be done, it should be done, and that worrying about the moral consequences is theocratic obscurantism.

This is usually where the Science-Is-God folks start screaming "You're anti-science!" "You don't believe in progress!" "You're one of those weirdos who would deny your sick child life-saving treatment so that God can heal her!" That line of argument is silly. One can both believe in the wonders of science and rejoice in medical and scientific breakthroughs and also believe that we must take care not to throw out our humanity in the name of "scientific progress." Today too many people—many of whom have become disillusioned by or disconnected from a solid belief in God—have put all their faith in science. Scientists are granted special status, almost an infallibility of sorts, among those who believe that man—not God—is in control of what happens to the planet and its inhabitants. This humanist mindset necessarily holds that man is thus capable of curing, fixing, repairing, building, and creating anything he wants. The adherents of this brave new faith have powerful lobbies and have recruited influential supporters from academia, the media, and corporate America. It should surprise no one that with this power, they can compel us all to tithe on their behalf through huge government research grants and programs.

The sacrifice goes beyond money. We even offer human sacrifices to this new god of "science" when we allow men in white coats to clone embryos—and then destroy them by harvesting their stem cells. This science-trumps-all world view was at the heart of the Michael Bay film *The Island*, starring Ewan McGregor and Scarlett Johansson. Set in the near future, the movie depicts residents of an isolated compound who have been cloned as full-grown adults so that their organs and body parts can be harvested. It is the latest in futuristic cosmetic procedures. The rich elites on the outside of the compound abuse their bodies to any degree because they have the money to grow new ones from cloned versions of themselves inside the compound. These days this doesn't seem like such a wildly far-fetched possibility. In Missouri, clone-and-kill is now a constitutional right, and in California it is the state's most heavily subsidized industry. So at least two states in the Union are on the fast track to making science fiction a reality! Goodbye Botox, hello doppelganger!

FROM BIG SCREEN TO MAINSTREAM?

>>> In *Gattaca*, a 1997 film starring Ethan Hawke and Uma Thurman, we see a world of sterile, genetically enhanced designer babies, where the potential for disease and life expectancy is determined at birth. In this society, at the time of your birth, the state analyzes your DNA and mandates your occupation and place in life. Some humans are more useful to the society than others. Ethan Hawke's character is one of the last "natural" children, born with a heart condition. He lives as an ostracized member of society, and the plot involves his attempt to prove to others that every human life is valuable—and that a "natural" child (with heart defects and all) is perhaps even more valuable than those who were genetically engineered. Could this be in our future? If we are blinded by science, anything is possible.

The abuse of science goes far beyond the embryos. We turn to science to "improve" ourselves through billions spent on cosmetic surgery; not the sort of surgery that heals burn victims, but the sort of surgery that enhances busts and sucks the fat out from our bellies. While we may need to take better care of ourselves, we are created in God's image. Turning to drastic surgical augmentation or reduction edges us closer to playing Dr. Frankenstein with our own bodies.

"Science" has even taken the place of child-rearing. Is your kid too wild? Is he a boy? Then drug him. An estimated *one million* school children in Texas alone have been prescribed Ritalin.[7]

But why wait until he's six to redesign your child with drugs? Nowadays you can design your child genetically before he's born. Creating "designer babies" is a growing trend, but it usually means killing the ones who aren't up to snuff. That is, you make many little embryos in a petri dish, and with advanced genetic testing, determine which ones match your wishes for a child. The rest of the embryos are biowaste. Is this what IVF was supposed to lead to?

All of this genetic engineering should remind us of Winston Churchill's warning of "a new Dark Age made more sinister, and perhaps more protracted, by the lights of perverted science."[8] It should sound eerily similar to the ugliest parts of our recent past. But apparently we're rapidly forgetting what we should have learned from the terrible "scientific" atrocities of the last century, when Communism ("scientific socialism") tried to make a new man on class grounds and National Socialism tried to make a new man on racial grounds. Now some of us are apparently trying to make a new man on "pro-choice" grounds. But when man violates natural law—the natural order of creation, of our humanity, of our human nature, and of moral truths that we can all understand through reason—he violates himself. C. S. Lewis, who never saw designer babies, but who did witness Communism and Nazi Germany, put it best: "What we call Man's power over Nature turns out to be a power exercised by some men over other men with Nature as its instrument."[9]

Most scientific developments are profoundly good, and many have been empowering, such as the Internet. But there is also no reason why science should be off-limits from the free play of ideas, from questioning its moral direction when necessary, or from criticizing some of its presumptions. Unfortunately, science has become highly politicized, in large part because of its government funding. And one byproduct of that—to make sure the funding goes to where certain people think it should—is that scientific development has become a matter of elite "consensus" that laymen are not allowed to question.

We're told that because of a "scientific consensus," we need to hand over our lives, liberty, and tax dollars to the United Nations—or fry from global warming. We're told that if we provide billions in tax dollars for embryonic stem cell research, the crippled will walk and the blind will see—and we'll soon get over any moral qualms we have about treating human embryos as petri dish experiments. We're told that science will make physical disabilities a thing of the past, because if we can't cure disabled people, we can spot them in the womb and kill them. We would be cleansing the undesirables and handicapped from society before they take their first breath. This behavior fosters a culture of death, and as history shows us, it never stops with just the unborn. If this evil were able to bloom fully in our country, people with viruses or ailments similar to those of Franklin D. Roosevelt (polio) or Stephen Hawking (ALS) could be next on the chopping block. No one would be safe.

To question the validity of these scientific predictions, promises, bribes, or threats is to be regarded, at least by the elites, as not only ignorant, but dangerous. For example, *Boston Globe* columnist Ellen Goodman thought it fair to say that, "global warming deniers are now on a par with Holocaust deniers, though one denies the past and the other denies the present and future."[10] So much for free speech.

Cell-ing Out for the Fountain of Youth

> "If scientists are correct, stem cell research could result in a veritable fountain of youth by replacing diseased or damaged cells."
>
> —Senator Arlen Specter (R–PA)[11]

It has become conventional wisdom that stem cells harvested from embryos have the power to cure all that ails us—heart disease, Parkinson's, and muscular dystrophy. Heck, they can even make us look younger! (If only they could turn liberals into conservatives.)

Stem cells are human cells that have the potential to develop into many different types of tissue—kidney cells, brain cells, skin cells, and so on. Harvesting adult stem cells involves no ethical issues for obvious reasons. Taking stem cells from bone marrow doesn't kill us. But when an embryo is invaded for its cells, that embryo dies.

The liberal elite tell us to drop our "theocratic" ethical objections and provide federal and state funding for embryonic stem cell research without any restrictions. To do anything less would be uncompassionate and anti-progress. Ponce de Leon, according to legend, gave his life in search of the fountain of youth. Why shouldn't we sacrifice our scruples and tax dollars?

This utopian notion of a world where cures exist for all diseases and we all live to 150 is troubling at its core—and for reasons far beyond the monetary costs and any "religious objections." In our effort to strip away all the inconveniences of being human, we run the risk of wiping out the foundations of our humanity. Yes, we all want longer, healthier lives, but at what cost?

The embryonic stem cell agenda is a bold one. First, the stem cell promoters want no legal restrictions on the creation—through fertilization or cloning—and destruction of human embryos for the sake of research or treatment. Second, they want billions in federal and state dollars every year. And third, they don't want us to ask too many questions.

But we can't let biotech companies, opportunistic politicians, grant-hungry scientists, or gullible journalists shut us up. We need to ask questions. If we don't, we'll never get the whole story. For example, when Missouri voters passed a constitutional amendment in 2006 providing taxpayer funding for stem cell research (including cloning), the *St. Louis Post-Dispatch* described the measure (known as Amendment 2) as "the ballot proposal to protect embryonic stem cell research allowed under federal law."[12] They left out the cloning part, and left out the taxpayer funding part.

Such downright deception is part of nearly every campaign to expand stem cell research. *They* are the scientists, and so we're not supposed to ask questions—we're just supposed to hand over our money, thank them for working their magic, and wait patiently for the miracle cures their political patrons promise us. But by asking only a few questions, we can peel away many of the lies of the stem cell agenda.

⟩⟩⟩ Lie Number One: Embryonic Stem Cell Research Does Not Involve the Cloning of Human Beings

The first lie they tell us is that they're not talking about human cloning. They are. Both the Missouri amendment and a similar 2004 California initiative claimed to outlaw human cloning, as did a bill that passed the New Jersey legislature. In fact, these three measures all banned what is called "reproductive cloning," while providing government funding for cloning done for research or medical purposes—sometimes called "therapeutic cloning."

Here are the basics of cloning:

You start by taking a cell from a person—say you take a skin cell from Tiger Woods. Then, you remove the nucleus of the cell. The nucleus contains all of Tiger Woods's DNA, which is unique to him. The second step is to get your hands on an unfertilized human ovum—an egg purchased from a woman. The egg has its own nucleus, which you then remove, removing all of the egg-donor's genetic information. If you can place the nucleus of the skin cell into this denucleated egg and get the cells to begin dividing, you've got a very tiny version of Tiger Woods. Scientists use the term "somatic cell nuclear transfer" (SCNT) to describe the process. Now, maybe a second Tiger Woods would finally provide Tiger with some real competition on the PGA Tour, but you could easily imagine more unpleasant people to clone. Remember *The Boys from Brazil*? That was a political sci-fi thriller depicting a group of former Nazi scientists lead by Dr. Joseph Mengele (Gregory Peck), hiding in South America attempting to clone Adolf

Hitler. But the real point is not whether we clone good people or bad people, but that creating human duplicates for our own ends is simply wrong.

Most people agree that cloning is wrong. And that's why those promoting somatic cell nuclear transfer try to contend that SCNT is not cloning. But it is. The President's Commission on Bioethics unanimously agreed on this point: "The initial product of 'somatic cell nuclear transfer' is a living (one-celled) cloned human embryo."[13] While it was not the result of a sperm meeting an egg, this embryo would be no different from the human embryos in petri dishes created as part of in-vitro fertilization. If you implanted our previous example of a cloned embryo into a woman's uterus, it would start to grow, and nine months later she would give birth to a baby Tiger Woods.

In fact, SCNT follows exactly the same procedure used to make Dolly the sheep. (Speaking of sheep, I hope I'm not the only one who finds it disturbing that scientists now boast of having "created the world's first human-sheep chimera—which has the body of a sheep and half-human organs."[14] Does *The Island of Dr. Moreau* come to mind?) Still, measures to provide taxpayer funding for SCNT are actually "cloning bans," say the dinosaur media. How do they justify this seeming 180-degree distortion? To them, cloning is only "cloning," when the embryo is actually implanted in a uterus. Shockingly, in New Jersey, it is legal to implant the cloned embryo in a uterus—as long as you terminate it before birth.[15] That scenario doesn't count as cloning because the clone is killed when no longer useful.

This lie—refusing to call a clone a clone—is at the heart of the stem cell campaign. Along with a handful of conservative journalists, I worked on my radio show to educate the voters of Missouri about this issue during the 2006 campaign. The other side simply had a better organization, more money, and an earlier start.

〉〉〉 Lie Number Two: Conservatives Are Trying to Ban Stem Cell Research

According to the stem cell crowd, if we don't give them our money to conduct their research, we are "restricting" their research or even "banning" it. Let's set this straight: there is no national or state ban on the use of embryonic stem cells for research or treatment. Private medical facilities are free to pursue this controversial research. The debate is over whether the government should spend *taxpayer money* on it. As an analogy, religious high schools in the U.S. get no federal aid while public schools do—does this mean that Christian and Jewish education has been *banned*? No it doesn't, and limiting federal funding on embryonic stem cell research isn't "banning" the research.

But the sense of entitlement among scientists and those who feel they can do no wrong is so great, that if we're not fully funding everything scientists want to do, we're *restricting* them. You and I may *earn* the money, but it really belongs to the National Institutes of Health. President Bush, in August 2001, initiated federal funding of research using stem cells taken from human embryos. Those embryos had already been destroyed, he pointed out. But Bush would not allow federal funding for the creation and destruction of new embryos designed for stem cell research. Before Bush's decision there was *zero* federal funding of embryonic stem cell research. Nevertheless, the *Baltimore Sun's* front-page headline the day after Bush's announcement read: "Stem Cell Study Limited: President Decides to Restrict Federal Funding for Research."[16]

John Kerry went even further. During the 2004 campaign, he attacked Bush with this line: "At this very moment, some of the most pioneering cures and treatments are right at our fingertips. But because of the *stem cell ban*, they remain beyond our reach," [emphasis added].[17] Remember, research on human embryos and their stem cells was fully legal, and some of it was funded. If you don't fund *all* of it, or if you outlaw cloning, you are *banning* stem cell research, according to Kerry. That wasn't a slip of the tongue, either. Kerry referred to this *ban* four times in his August 7, 2004, radio address.

To his credit, in June 2007, President Bush vetoed another bill that would have provided federal funds to expand research using embryonic stem cells. The science-absolutists railed against him all over again.

))) Lie Number Three: Miracle Cures Are Just Around the Corner

The most despicable lie of the stem cell agenda is the promise of endless miracle cures. Remember Arlen Specter's fountain of youth comment? That was tame compared to what the Democrats have promised.

John Edwards reminded me of the snake-oil salesmen of old when he announced on the 2004 campaign trail: "If we do the work that we can do in this country, the work that we will do when John Kerry is president, people like Christopher Reeve are going to walk, get up out of that wheelchair and walk again."[18] Read that one again. He didn't say, that paralytics "might someday" walk again, or "can dream of walking again." John Edwards made a campaign promise that paralytics "are going to" walk if Kerry and Edwards were elected. Truth apparently is kryptonite to the Democrats.

A British scientist was candid about this approach. "One of the problems is that in order to persuade the public that we must do this work, we often go rather too far in promising what we might achieve.... I am not entirely convinced that embryonic stem cells will, in my lifetime, and possibly anybody's lifetime for that matter, be holding quite the promise that we desperately hope they will."[19] We could use some more of that candor on this side of the pond.

The key drivers in the stem cell agenda also hide their ulterior motives. Specifically, the people pushing hardest for taxpayer funding of stem cell research are the corporations that stand to make huge profits from such initiatives. The millions they spend running prime-time ads with Michael J. Fox tugging at your heartstrings are really a pretty small investment for the billions they get in return.

The pro-cloning side in Missouri spent $30 million in 2006.[20] At least 90 percent of that money came from one couple, James and Virginia Stowers.[21] Most newspapers described them as "cancer survivors" who run a "not-for-profit" medical institute. But in 2006, the Stowers Institute for Medical Research launched a for-profit company that would sell the Institute's discoveries to major biotech companies.[22] Thanks to the passage of Amendment 2, the Stowers Institute in Kansas City is in line to pocket billions of taxpayer dollars. Taxpayers pay for the research, and then Stowers' for-profit company patents the results and sells them for a profit. That part gets left out of most media accounts on the topic.

Even more serious than all this is what cloning and embryo farming will mean for humanity. Consider the words President Reagan's son Ron (a.k.a. "Non" Reagan) spoke at the 2004 Democratic National Convention. He described how scientists could clone you, take stem cells from your clone—thus killing it—which would provide you with a theoretically limitless supply of cells your body won't reject. "How'd you like to have your own personal biological repair kit standing by at the hospital? Sound like magic? Welcome to the future of medicine," he proclaimed.[23]

Creating another human being to be your "own personal biological repair kit" is, simply put, exploitation and slavery. If this is "the future of medicine," then we're in trouble. This dream of creating new humans to cure ourselves is exactly what C. S. Lewis warned about, "power exercised by some men over other men with Nature as its instrument."

Baby, You're Perfect!

"The right to choose" has for thirty years been a smokescreen for aborting unwanted children, but these days it is taking on a more literal meaning, along with the expression "family planning." It turns out the "right to choose" and family planning isn't just about how many children you have anymore. It's about how tall your children are, what sex, and certainly whether or not they have any disabilities. For now, the *tools* of this new family planning are the same, though—you abort the ones who don't match your wishes.

Creating "designer babies" is not a new idea. In China and India they've been killing newborn or *in utero* girls for decades.[24] But in the West, science is expanding what we can do to embryos and fetuses *in utero* and *in vitro*. What it amounts to is a form of "eugenics," a word created by Charles Darwin's cousin, an amateur scientist named Francis Galton who wanted to encourage bright and accomplished people to marry other bright and accomplished people, to marry younger and have more children in order to improve the human race. Eugenics, however, later moved (naturally, if unexpectedly) from such idealism to some of the worst horrors of the twentieth century.

Some of these horrors we have become numb to because they are so common. As noted earlier, it is perfectly legal today for women to abort babies for "eugenic" reasons, such as when the babies are diagnosed in the womb with some malady.

To justify their pro-choice stance on abortion, people often say— "This child's quality of life will be so diminished that it would be cruel to bring him into the world." Tell that to the thousands of couples in America waiting to adopt—couples who would open their hearts and homes to "special needs" infants.

Killing imperfect babies is not simply grounded in selfish barbarism, but in an actual philosophy articulated by leading academics and scientists. James Watson, one of the two men who discovered DNA, argued in 1973 that children born with serious genetic defects ought to be discarded in some cases. "If a child were not declared alive until three days after birth, then all parents could be allowed the choice...the doctor could allow the child to die, if the parents so choose, and save a lot of misery and suffering."[25]

All parents want their children to be healthy, and it's certainly fine and normal to hope your child is intelligent and attractive, too. But when we start saying that an "unwanted" child doesn't have a right to life and when we start manufacturing children to meet our specifications, we start playing God. Today's science-obsessed society tells us that it is not enough to want a baby of our own, but that we must endeavor to create a perfect one, precisely tailored to how we think the ideal baby should look, think, and behave. Talk about pressure.

Couples with fertility challenges deserve our empathy. They desperately want children. But when do we cross the line into dangerous moral terrain? Scandinavian Cryobank (motto: "Congratulations, it's a Viking!") promises you sperm from blond-haired, blue-eyed men—presumably named Sven.[26] But why take such chances with genetics when some companies allow you to pick out a sperm donor, an egg donor, and surrogate mother. All for one low price! The Abraham Center of Life provides exactly that service.

A reporter asked the Abraham Center's founder, Abigail Ryan, if she was making designer babies. "Designer babies? Yeah. Why not?" Ryan chuckled. "You know why I did it? Because I could."[27] This is our moral situation in the early twenty-first century: if science enables us to do something, we ought to do it. If such trends continue, in the future children will be picked out no differently than a new car or house, making human beings commodities with as many upgrades as you can afford.

The idea of designer children has its roots in eugenics, which reached its evil heights under the Nazi doctor Joseph Mengele. In the United States contraception crusader and eugenics enthusiast Margaret Sanger (whose American Birth Control League evolved into Planned Parenthood) called on the U.S. government to pay "all obviously unfit parents who allow themselves to be sterilized by harmless and scientific means."[28]

American eugenics didn't die with Sanger. Her ideas are now most prominently articulated by Princeton Professor Peter Singer, who has argued that killing a disabled newborn is morally fine. Singer predicts his worldview will triumph in the next generation:

> During the next 35 years, the traditional view of the sanctity of human life will collapse under pressure from scientific, technological, and demographic developments. By 2040, it may be that only a rump of hard-core, know-nothing religious fundamentalists will defend the view that every human life, from conception to death, is sacrosanct.[29]

Unsurprisingly, what counts as "diseased" changes depending on who makes these decisions. The Nazis targeted not only the mentally deficient or mentally ill, but Jews and homosexuals. For Margaret Sanger it was people with low IQs and black people. The common denominator was their dehumanization of anyone who became inconvenient.

Promoting Sex, Ignoring Consequences

The sexual revolution promised a generation that "free love" meant sex without consequences. Well, forty years and fifty new STDs later, not to mention more than 48 *million* abortions and a tripling of the percentage of families headed by single parents,[30] it's become clear that we haven't quite conquered nature enough to make sex consequence-free. But that doesn't keep us from trying.

The newest wonder of modern science that's supposed to set us free is the "morning after" pill, officially called levonorgestrel, but marketed as Plan B. Plan B is supposedly an "emergency contraceptive," but one of the ways it "prevents pregnancy," is by preventing an embryo from implanting in a woman's uterus. In other words, it "prevents" pregnancy by terminating a nascent life. Calling it a contraceptive is misleading. It's an abortion pill.

The Food and Drug Administration (FDA) approved Plan B in 1999, so anyone with a prescription could pick it up. That was not good enough for the pro-abortion crowd. When President Bush took office, Democrats demanded Plan B be made available over the counter, and they even blocked his nominee to head the FDA until he gave in to this demand. Now Hillary Clinton is leading the charge to provide federal funding for Plan B (oh yeah, the manufacturer's CEO is a Hillary campaign contributor). But that's not enough either.

Colorado governor Bill Ritter signed a bill in early 2007 that requires all hospitals to either provide Plan B for rape victims or to direct women to someone who will.[31] This presents a Catholic hospital with this choice: (a) violate the teachings of the Catholic Church by possibly inducing or aiding in an abortion or (b) become outlaws.

It all makes you wonder whether "Plan B" refers to a backup plan for failed or forgotten contraception or the pro-choice and medical community's realization that they have failed in their 1960s dream of liberating women through pills, and Norplant, and other high-tech contraception.

One measure of the failure of these chemical wonders is that sexually transmitted diseases have become more rampant and much more deadly, with women suffering more than heterosexual men. When the pill arrived in 1960, 5.3 percent of births were out of wedlock. In 2005, after more than thirty years of abortion on demand in all fifty states and of universal sex education in the public schools, what are the results? In 2005, 36.8 percent of American babies were born out of wedlock.[32] And this is not part of a baby-boom either. It's the reverse. The proportion of unmarried women having babies has skyrocketed, but fewer American women are having babies at all—another unintended consequence of the sexual revolution.

These statistics suggest that science has not delivered on its promise to prevent unwanted pregnancies—let alone to deliver human happiness. The evidence is the opposite. Our alleged scientific and moral progress (or really regress) has spawned a plague of sexual diseases, broken homes, and unhappiness. But we tell ourselves we'd never go back, because that would be against progress.

And science, of course, has the answer to STDs, too. The answer is more government money and more government mandates. The cause célèbre today is the drug Gardasil, a vaccine against human papillomavirus (HPV). HPV is a family of viruses, many types of which are sexually transmitted, and some types of which can cause cervical cancer. It's great that we now have a vaccine for it. But many politicians believe that if science makes a vaccine available, we all have an obligation to be vaccinated.

Many states and the District of Columbia are trying to provide taxpayer funding for the HPV vaccine—in some cases, funding for *all* sixth-grade girls, regardless of economic need. In Texas, Governor Rick Perry unilaterally ordered that all young women get vaccinated (thankfully the Texas legislature shot it down). Similar efforts in Alabama and Michigan have been scaled back drastically. The chief lobbyist for these subsidies and mandates of the vaccine? Merck, the pharmaceutical company that makes Gardasil. But even Merck has had to back off, as its lobbying looked a little too shameless, and as articles came out arguing that the vaccine hasn't been adequately tested, or arguing that money spent on mandates requiring it would be better spent on other health priorities.

Science is supposed to provide us with options, but the *mandatory* HPV vaccine is a good example of how government can use it to take away our power as parents, telling us, in essence: your daughter is going to be sexually promiscuous, maybe even before she's an adolescent, but with this vaccine you don't have to worry about it! Right.

The Cosmetic and Chemical Brave New World

Somehow the term self-improvement has gone from being about the virtues of fortitude, patience, and self-denial, to being about diet pills, cosmetic surgery, and injections.

"Actress" Pamela Anderson, with her new and improved body, should be an object of pity. Instead she's an international celebrity who has made millions on the results of her enhancement-reduction odyssey. Someone should come up with a list of Hollywood actresses and actors who haven't had some major cosmetic procedure. Poor Bruce Jenner looks like he was in a fire. Can someone tell these men that most of them look better with age!

Hollywood is addicted to surgical self-improvement. The plastic surgeons are the *real* celebrities in Tinseltown—they should have their own category at the Oscars. "The award for 'Best breast lift on an actress over 40' goes to—." And because we are addicted to celebrities, we too have become cosmetic surgery addicts. People actually go into plastic surgeons' offices and request Angelina Jolie's lips or Ben Affleck's chin. (I guess it could be worse, they could be asking for Ben's brain.) Many of us have no problem cutting, pulling, peeling, or injecting ourselves for an image.

Americans spent $1.3 billion on 3.3 million Botox procedures in 2005. We spent $1 billion on 200,924 nose jobs, including 45,945 for men. Liposuction brought in $750,000,000 with 455,489 procedures. That year, 364,610 women had their breasts augmented, while 160,531 had them reduced. Besides Botox, the most popular cosmetic procedure for men was laser hair removal, with 232,240 procedures. If that's one procedure per guy in 2005, that means one in every 500 men had laser hair removal in that one year. A final capper: 33,369 American *men* underwent cosmetic eyelid surgery in 2005. [33]

The American Society for Aesthetic Plastic Surgery estimates that in 2006, 11.5 million Americans had cosmetic procedures done. These are not cheap operations. A tummy tuck costs an average of $5,232 while a facelift will run you over $6,000. A collagen injection to get rid of wrinkles, on the other hand, is a bargain at $400. [34]

One popular new option for a new mother is the "Mommy Makeover," consisting of a tummy lift, breast implants, and a breast lift. One plastic surgeon explained it this way:

> In this day and age, women are giving birth later, returning to their careers sooner and have busier schedules than ever before. Many are finding cosmetic plastic surgery to be the answer to returning to a pre-pregnancy shape they are comfortable with. [35]

The plastic surgeons don't make anything on the old exercise-and-eat-right plan for weight loss.

But this Mommy Makeover only goes so far. (More delicate readers may want to skip the rest of this section.) While much of this might seem like no big deal—to each his own—our quest for perfection has taken a truly gross turn. The next step is Laser Vaginal Rejuvenation. It's supposed to restore a woman's intimate parts to the way they were before she had a baby—or before she had so many different partners, as the case may be. A *Washington Post* article reported about D.C. doctor Christopher A. Warner and his mentor David Matlock, who perform this operation. The *Post* noted that Warner's and Matlock's patients "frequently request 'a nice sleek look' similar to images seen in *Playboy* magazine and on some cable TV channels. 'Women tell us they want to look like they're eighteen again,' Matlock said." The doctors' pitch makes this surgery sound like the aesthetic companion to Plan B—for a few thousand dollars you can buy your virginity back.[36]

Yeah, right. Thomas Stovall, former president of the Society of Gynecologic Surgeons, calls this laser surgery "a rip-off" that does nothing to "re-virginize" the patient. (It does reduce her bank account, however!)

One Nation, under Medication

More disturbing than what we're doing to our outsides is what we're doing to our insides. About half of the country is on one sort of prescription or another, according to the Centers for Disease Control.[37] Some doctors will prescribe anti-depressants if you so much as report feeling a bit down. Whatever happened to having a case of the blues? It's now fixed by a little white pill. The abuse of prescription tranquilizers, painkillers, and even Viagra is becoming widespread. And it's particularly noxious when we allow our children to be abused with drugs, through misdiagnosed Attention-Deficit Hyperactive Disorder (ADHD).

It is arguably true that some children really do have chemical imbalances that seriously hinder their ability to concentrate. My brother and sister-in-law say their son (my nephew) benefited tremedously from Ritalin. But youthful rambunctiousness does not always need to be medicated away. University of California researchers report that the world used three times as much ADHD medication in 2003 as it did in 1993.[38] About 2.5 million American children and teenagers take Ritalin or the like for ADHD, this study found.[39] Does this represent some plague of ADHD?

No. It represents a plague of overmedication, according to someone who should know. Dr. Robert Spitzer is the man who originally identified ADHD and the related Attention Deficit Disorder (ADD) in the 1970s and 1980s. In March 2007 he said that as many as 30 percent of those diagnosed with ADHD or ADD don't really have the disorder—it seems they are just energetic youths.[40]

Makes you wonder if in today's world, Huck Finn and Tom Sawyer would be outside acting like boys or inside and doped up.

Overmedication to treat a supposed problem can kill, as Michael and Carolyn Riley tragically learned. The Massachusetts couple was charged with murder when their four-year-old daughter died from an overdose of pills that the family doctor had been prescribing for ADHD since their girl was two and a half years old.[41] The parents simply did not understand that these drugs—supposed to help their child—could be deadly. And ADHD drugs are not the only potentially lethal ones.

Painkillers are also the drug of choice for many of today's youth. A Columbia University study of college students nationwide found a tripling of the abuse of prescription drugs, such as OxyContin, Percocet, Vicodin, and similar drugs from 1993 to 2005.[42] In 2005, 2.1 million Americans abused painkillers, according to the National Survey on Drug Use and Health.[43] Most teenagers who illicitly took painkillers to get high said they chose their drug in part because they figured these pills were safe—after all, they usually are swiping from Dad's stash, so how bad can they be?

Girls are getting hooked on diet pills, which are supposed to be prescription-only, but are also available online. A CDC study in 2005 found 8 percent of high school girls had used diet pills without a doctor's advice in the past thirty days.[44] The obsession with body-image has been fueled by size zero celebrities who look like walking sticks on the red carpet. Girls want to look like Nicole Richie or Paris Hilton and will do anything—including popping pills—to get there.

Global ~~Warming, Cooling~~ . . . Whatever.

Of course, where science is making the most news these days is on the environment, especially among those who bow down before the altar of environmentalism. Today's environmentalism is not the one Republicans like Teddy Roosevelt espoused—conservationism and respect for nature—but the holier-than-thou environmentalism that evangelist Al Gore preaches from his pulpit.

These preachy environmentalists have a holy scripture you cannot question. They have high priests whose interpretations are infallible. Their sermons warn of hellfire, rising oceans, and plagues as punishment for our sins. But they also promise salvation if we'll just stop asking questions and start following their commandments (and tithing). They are the church of Apocalyptic Man-made Global Warming, and they embody the arrogance and presumption of modern science.

The global warming alarmists, like earlier environmental alarmists, like Marxists, and like all utopian movements throughout the ages, salivate at the idea of a threat to all mankind. If they can convince us that this threat—manmade carbon dioxide and other greenhouse gases heating up the planet—is really the greatest threat we face today, then it will be easier for them to grab the sort of government power they want. As icing on the cake, because this is a *global* problem, it requires *global* governmental solutions.

The exploitation of science is the central element in the global warming crusade. There are many good questions any curious American would ask: How much is the planet really heating up? Will the negative effects of this warming really outweigh the positive effects? How much does human activity really contribute, and how much of the warming is being caused by non-human factors? How much can these government policies really slow the warming, and how will these policies affect our liberty and our economy?

But these questions undermine the dogmatic vision of the Church of the Apocalyptic Manmade Global Warming. They are heresies, and must be met with scorn. If you question them, they'll call you a "flat-earther." They'll decry that you are attacking Al Gore the way Galileo was attacked. They'll call your questions "dangerous." You may even get death threats, as discussed in more detail below. "The science is settled" mantra is their favorite refrain, and so you, dear laymen, don't need to ask any questions.

But the science is far from settled. This is *climate* we're talking about—very few systems are more complex and less capable of experimentation than the climate. You don't trust the weatherman if he forecasts rain in three days, so why should you trust Al Gore when he forecasts twenty-foot floods in a decade? The answer is that you shouldn't.

It's simply not true that all scientists agree that man is causing a global warming that will be catastrophic. Sami Solanki, a scientist at the Max Planck Institute for Solar System Research, came up with a novel thesis: the Sun causes the heat. Solanki's studies found a near-perfect correlation between the Sun's irradiance and the planet's mean temperatures. While an increased greenhouse effect has certainly made some impact, he says, the Sun appears to be the prime determinant of the Earth's temperature. This idea is buttressed by observed warming on Jupiter, Mars, Pluto, and Neptune.

Timothy Ball, a Canadian scientist and former professor of climatology, questioned the Apocalyptic Manmade Global Warming thesis in a documentary titled *The Great Global Warming Swindle*. According to Ball, after the film's release, he received several death threats. The same nastiness is regularly spewed at the climate-change experts at the Competitive Enterprise Institute, who battle against government regulation of CO_2. They report being urged in hate-filled e-mails to gas themselves in their garages (someone should teach these angry greens the difference between Carbon *Mon*oxide and Carbon *Diox*ide). Richard Lindzen, who once served on the Intergovernmental Panel on Climate Change, explained that if heresy is not punished by death, it at least is paid back with excommunication: "Scientists who dissent from the alarmism have seen their funds disappear, their work derided, and themselves labeled as industry stooges," he said. "Consequently, lies about climate change gain credence even when they fly in the face of the science."[45]

Still, the refrain "we must act now" resonates with the dinosaur media: they advocate taxes on

HOW HOT IS HOT?

>>> Whoopsie. Scientists are now having to "re-do" their previous estimates of planetary temperatures over the ages. After drilling 1.2 miles through a glacier in Greenland, researchers now say that hundreds of thousands of years ago the earth was *warmer* than previously believed. (Scientists examined the oldest plant DNA ever uncovered.) Now they believe that between 116,000 and 130,000 years ago—the period between the last ice ages—the earth's temperatures were 9 degrees Fahrenheit *higher* than they are now. Hey Al, did the Abominable Snowman cause the global warming back then?

Source: "Oldest DNA Ever Recovered Shows Warmer Planet: Report," Breitbart.com, July 5, 2005.

carbon dioxide, which will dramatically increase our electricity and heating bills and the price we pay at the pump. Al Gore's Book of Revelation, *An Inconvenient Truth*, implores lawmakers to resurrect the Kyoto Protocol, which is a serious threat to our sovereignty. Al Gore's allies hope that if the global warming story is apocalyptic enough it might scare us into giving up more money and more power to our benevolent leaders, who will save us from the deluge. Remember, it's important that we give them money, but not that we ask questions.

Returning *POWER TO THE PEOPLE*

So, how do we battle the unrestrained cult of science? We can't exactly all go out and get Ph.D.s so that we can refute the elites on each point. But with common sense and simple morality (and the courage to speak out) we can undercut many of the arguments of those who abuse science. In 2006, after we started spreading the word that Missouri's Amendment 2 was really about cloning and killing, we made a real dent in the support for the measure, even as Michael J. Fox took to the airwaves on behalf of the cloners. An October 12 poll found 57 percent of likely voters said they would "definitely" support the measure and only 27 percent would "definitely" oppose. Eleven days later, after our big push, the definitely yes camp shrank to 45 percent and the definitely no counterparts grew to 36 percent.[46] In the end, the Amendment passed by only 50,000 votes out of 2 million cast, even though we were outspent by about $29 million to about $1 million.

We eroded support for this measure simply by taking the time to learn the basics of the science and explain them to people. The other side continued to tote around their Nobel laureates and scientists, but the people began to listen to our facts. If we had just a few more days, we might have sunk the measure.

We also need to demand that science be harnessed for *saving* life, not ending it or merely altering it. Medical science, when it's used properly, is a pro-life enterprise. Through the extraordinary medical research and application of our nation's doctors, hospital staff can now perform all sorts of medical miracles that can save young lives. And science is the best teaching tool we have. Just think about the increased availability and resolution of ultrasound imagery. When *Time* magazine publishes pictures of a twelve-week-old child in her mother's womb, and you can see her tiny little fingers, her mouth, and her eyes, it makes it that much harder to argue that a baby in a womb is not a baby worth loving.

We should use this science to make sure that women considering an abortion have a chance to see their *own* unborn child. Lawmakers in South Carolina have proposed a bill to require all abortion clinics to show an ultrasound to women considering abortion.[47] This measure has been met with outraged scorn from the "pro-choice" crowd who know exactly how this will affect a woman's choice. When we use it to reveal more about ourselves—instead of using it to cover up who we are—we usually will end up empowering ourselves.

Medical science also helped save the life of tiny Amillia Taylor, who may grow up to be a living rebuke to nearly every late-term abortion. Born at only twenty-two weeks of gestation, Amillia Taylor weighed only ten ounces at birth and was nine inches long.[48] She didn't have great chances, but her parents and the doctors never gave up. Today, she is home and healthy.

No duty is more incumbent upon us than protecting the sanctity of human life—not just in protesting abortion, but in protecting embryos and preventing cloning. And we can argue the science as well. There is no reason why we can't find moral alternatives to embryonic stem cell research. In fact, we have them. For instance, every new mother can donate stem cells from her newborn's umbilical cord. These cells provide great promise, and don't cost any lives. A new study from Wake Forest University in 2007 showed stem cells in amniotic fluid might be just as versatile as embryonic stem cells. And stem cells don't just come from infants. Adults have stem cells that can be safely extracted and used for experiments or developed into organ tissue.

The fact is people with a moral compass—that is, the American people—only need to know the facts to come up with the right answers. It's time we challenged the purveyors of pill-popping, environmental alarmism, and genetic-engineering on the facts and on the science—and reminded them that morality counts too.

Just because science makes something possible does not mean it should be done. Science is most amazing when informed by our conscience—not our convenience and vanity. It takes unshakable moral principles and usually devout religious beliefs to stand fast in the face of the dazzling promises and bold threats from modern science unleashed. We need to be ready to be the "rump of hard-core, know-nothing religious fundamentalists," Peter Singer derides for being willing to "defend the view that every human life, from conception to death, is sacrosanct." We need to stand up for man in the face of the behemoth of science unfettered by ethics.

10

TAKING THE REAL POWER TRIP

It was my first trip to the Holy Land, and true to form, I was running late. My producer and I were desperate to see the fabled Via Dolorosa: the well-trod path where it is believed Jesus carried his Cross on Good Friday nearly 2,000 years ago. Most visitors set aside half a day to visit the Stations of the Cross. Not us. We had only an hour to make our pilgrimage, hop in the car, and get to a studio across town for the start of the radio show.

An Irish priest, Father Eamon Kelly, who had recently moved to Jerusalem (he was a friend of a friend), volunteered to hold a private Mass for us and then escort us through the Stations. By the time we arrived in the Arab Quarter, it had become painfully obvious that Father Kelly was completely lost. We started searching the alleys and dashing down the serpentine streets for markers identifying the First Station (where Jesus was condemned to death). With the dense crowds and the time pressure, I started losing my patience and was ready to pack it in. "This is absurd," I thought, "we'll never find it." Then as I craned my head to find an exit, I suddenly found myself face to face with a plump, balding Arab man.

"Can I help you?" he asked.

"No," I said pushing past him, certain that he wanted me to purchase postcards or other crafts I didn't need from his shop in the marketplace.

"No, believe me," he insisted. "I don't want to sell you anything. I can help you." With my guard up, and I'm sure a knitted brow, I told him we were searching for the First Station of the Cross. "Follow me," he said. We walked behind this stranger through the throngs milling about the windy streets. We reached the hallowed spot situated in what is now a Muslim school. And without asking us if we needed an explanation of the site, our impromptu guide began to explain the spiritual significance of the First Station. This kind Muslim man knew more about this part of my faith than I did. I told him that, and we had a good laugh.

We found ourselves doing "speed stations." Sprinting to the second marker, we got our briefing, said a quick prayer, and then were off to the third station. At each stop my new Muslim friend spoke with a reverent appreciation of these places connected to Christ's Passion. He knew the history of each site, the points of interest, and even the biblical references. Had he been wearing brown, he could have passed for St. Francis. When we reached the Third Station,

I turned to ask him a question, but he was gone. I never had the chance to say thank you or get his e-mail address.

Later that evening, after my show, with the bustle of the day behind me, I was thinking of my impromptu tour guide. Amidst the chaos and distrust in that part of the world, grace was still present—and he showed it to me. The kindness of this stranger made me feel hopeful about what is possible. After seeing many depressing reminders of the Arab-Israeli conflict during our trip, I saw the beauty of that small gesture. When we allow ourselves a calm moment of reflection, we start to notice these little gifts from God sprinkled throughout the day. In this ten-minute exchange with my Arab guide, I was reminded that God never abandons us. In this case, He actually showed me the way! Today all of us could use some Divine direction, and a little heavenly backup wouldn't hurt either.

Power to Do What?

If you've gotten this far in the book, you know well the extent to which political and cultural forces can eat away at the values we hold most dear. You now know the concrete steps you can take to avoid ceding your power to people and organizations determined to impose their worldview on you and yours. Securing our borders, strengthening our families, and rebuilding our school curricula are all going to require a sustained commitment of time and effort. But there may be moments when you may ask, why bother? What is the point of all of this? Power to what end?

Unlike the Far Left radicals who never really meant it when they said "Power to the People," the power I've described is not power over others—it's the power to live our lives and raise our families in the manner we believe is best. It really boils down to liberty. After life, it is our primary American right, a right that so many brave Americans died defending. The Founding Fathers didn't dream up the idea of liberty, they merely reaffirmed it as a natural right given to all men by God. But with this awesome right, this awesome power, comes responsibility—a word we hear little of today.

Lord Acton wrote that liberty is not "the power to do what we like, but the right of being able to do what we ought."[1] This is a critical point. Our Framers understood that liberty must be directed, restrained, and given a noble purpose to last. The guardsman of liberty was always morality, informed by religious practice. Yes, I said *religious practice*.

In the late eighteenth century, no serious person was debating whether faith and virtue were instrumental to the future of the Republic. As Samuel Adams, one of the signers of our Declaration of Independence wrote:

> A general dissolution of Principles and Manners will more surely overthrow the Liberties of America than the whole Force of the common enemy. While the people are virtuous they cannot be subdued; but once they lose their virtue they will be ready to surrender their liberties to the first external or internal invader.... If virtue and knowledge are diffused among the people, they will never be enslaved. This will be their great security.[2]

Adams's point is that liberty depends on virtue, and virtue in turn depends on religious practice. (I can almost hear Bill Maher throwing a "separation of church and state" hissy fit right now.)

The practice of religion is not some curiosity that should be relegated to the ghettos of the culture, but a primary activity that needs to be championed. Good citizenship requires a commitment to virtue and morality—and with apologies to the spirituality-by-any-means crowd—I don't know another way to acquire them than by religious means. The father of our country reminded us of this in his farewell address way back in 1796:

> Of all the dispositions and habits which lead to political prosperity, *Religion and morality are indispensable supports....* And let us with caution indulge the supposition, that morality can be maintained without religion. Whatever may be conceded to the influence of refined education on minds of particular structure, reason and experience both forbid us to expect that National morality can prevail in exclusion of religious principle.[3] (Emphasis added.)

Washington could not have been clearer—religious practice that encourages moral behavior is a prerequisite for the survival of our political system. Let's get real. God created us, and we are expected to act in ways that are pleasing to Him. Only by preserving our religious values will we be able to make the right choices, and take full advantage of freedom's promise. My friend Ina likes to say, "Laura, God has given us rules for a reason—and we'd all be a lot happier if we tried a little harder to follow them." Ina is a smart woman.

Many of the problems in our society today—our cultural breakdown, vulnerability to terror, family dissolution, declining schools—were not created overnight, nor will they be resolved overnight. During our day-to-day battles there will be inevitable setbacks and disappointments. I have to admit, there are moments when I wonder whether some of these causes are lost forever. Yet speaking as someone who has had her share of challenges over the last few years, I know we must do everything we can to replace doubt and cynicism with faith. We must have confidence that whatever the outcome in any of our own personal, political, or cultural struggles, our loving God is still there waiting for us to "come home." We run the race, hope to win, but are comforted to know that as long as we return to God's will, we cannot lose.

Hoorays for Hollywood! Boos for God!

Aside from Peeps and dyed eggs there is a perennial tradition that you can be assured will resurrect itself each Easter. No, it is not Peter Rabbit or the White House Easter Egg Roll. It's the media elites' religious target practice, timed each year to coincide with the Christian and Jewish high holy days.

During the Easter season of 2003 Dan Brown's *Da Vinci Code* set the tone that would color seasons to come. Brown's heretical fantasy revealed a supposed plot by the Church to suppress the true story of Jesus: basically that He married Mary Magdalene, had a few kids, and retired to the south of France. This was Jesus loosed from his divinity with a weakness for the girls—just the type of Savior the elites could welcome to the Hamptons without alienating the Clintons. *Fast Times at Jerusalem High*!

For those who say Dan Brown's "Jesus takes a bride" conspiracy is "just fiction" and that people shouldn't be offended by "a work of fiction"—may I suggest that you inform *Dateline NBC*, and for that matter, filmmaker James Cameron of that little fact. In April 2006 *Dateline* featured a straight-faced "report" on *The Jesus Papers*, a book by Michael Baigent—the guy who co-authored an absurdly reasoned and baseless hit on Christianity titled, *Holy Blood, Holy Grail*. Baigent was actually one of Dan Brown's muses. As expected, Baigent was trotted out by NBC as a Jesus expert who happily announced that Jesus was not born of a virgin, was not divine, was not celibate, and, incidentally, fathered a child. When asked to substantiate his charge that Jesus's tomb was empty because the Lord was off frolicking in Galilee with Mary Magdalene, Baigent responded, "Unfortunately, in this case, there are no facts." Still, NBC had no problem giving this faith-hater a platform to spread his idiocy.

In the lead-up to Easter 2007, Academy Award winner James Cameron and Simcha Jacobovici (whom I'll deal with later) announced that they had made a stunning archeological discovery. They claimed to have found the tomb of Jesus and his family. That's right. Jesus, his Mother, his supposed "wife" Mary Magdalene, their alleged offspring, Judah, and some guy named Matthew were all supposedly buried in the same crypt beneath an apartment house outside of Israel. Were Amelia Earhart and Jimmy Hoffa entombed there as well?

Let's put aside the fact that there is a long-venerated historical and archeologically verifiable tomb of Jesus located within the Church of the Holy Sepulchre, or the fact that no Jewish or Christian archeologist in the Holy Land would vouch for the Cameron/Jacobovici claims. Their Discovery Channel documentary, *The Last Tomb of Jesus* announced that the odds were 600-to-1 in favor of the claim that the tomb was Jesus's family plot based on the statistical likelihood of these biblical names appearing on a collection of ossuaries (bone boxes), in the same crypt. When you don't have hard evidence, I guess a good statistician will do. (Even the statistician eventually tried to soft-pedal his involvement in this sham.)

The documentary made the absurd claim that Mary Magdalene may have been Jesus's wife and the lead apostle at Christianity's founding. (Grrrrl power in 33 AD!) They even ran DNA tests on remains in the boxes, which revealed (gasp!) that the occupants of the Mary Magdalene box and the Jesus box could not have been siblings. I still don't understand how this proves that they had to be married—but maybe I'm over-thinking this.

The Last Tomb of Jesus would become one of Discovery Channel's most hyped and most watched programs of the year, despite the fact that this "greatest archeological discovery in history" had twenty-six years ago been unearthed, investigated, and dismissed by the Israeli Antiquities Authority as just another old tomb. I guess discoveries can be repeated again and again at the Discovery Channel. Maybe Geraldo can reopen Al Capone's vault for Discovery next season.

All this raises the question—what was Discovery thinking? Were its execs merely trying to capitalize on the *DaVinci Code*'s success for ratings? Or does Discovery delight in poking Christianity in the eye just in time for Holy Week? By the way, experts now say that the names scrawled on the sides of the ossuaries may not be those that James Cameron and Simcha Jacobovici believe they see. Which, by the way, is no shock to Jacobovici—he's been to this carnival before.

In his 2003 Discovery Channel documentary entitled, *James: Brother of Jesus*, Jacobovici insisted that James—not Jesus—was the real leader of the early Church. To substantiate the claim he produced (surprise, surprise) an ossuary with the name "James, son of Joseph, brother of Jesus" carved upon it. The ossuary was later declared a hoax by the Israeli government and the owner is still battling fraud charges in the Israeli courts. Will the Discovery Channel "discover" the concept of retraction? Not likely. Calumnies against Christianity don't need to be rectified. Just for fun, imagine if James Cameron or Simcha Jacobovici produced a documentary making the case that Muhammad's brother or main squeeze was the true leader of Islam? Not that you have to worry about such a documentary ever being made, because if it ever hit the screen, Cameron & Co. would be hiding in an ossuary until the fatwa was lifted (which would probably not be for at least six hundred years, when you consider that al Qaeda is still seeking revenge for the Reconquista of southern Spain).

Easter 2007 also provided us with a bitter treat that could have been called the Willy Wonka blasphemy. A New York artist named Cosimo Cavallaro created an anatomically correct, two-hundred-pound chocolate Jesus confection called "My Sweet Lord." (Cute.) Cavallaro announced on CNN that this display was a "sweet, delicious, tasteful" celebration of the body of Christ and that he wanted visitors "to taste and feel what they're looking at in their mouth."[4] One of my listeners joked that Cavallaro should have dipped himself in chocolate—boiling if possible! Pressure from the Catholic League eventually derailed the exhibit. But would this guy dare to sculpt an edible, nude Martin Luther King, Jr.? Or John F. Kennedy? Or a wee Mahmoud Ahmadinejad fashioned from a couple of Hershey's Kisses? One hopes that good taste would prohibit those displays, but Jesus continues to be fair game for these pathetic artistic frauds.

Whether trumpeting the innocence of Christ's betrayer in *The Gospel of Judas* or displaying filthy depictions of the Savior in art galleries (remember "Piss Christ"?), liberals tell us they are just being open-minded, and exercising their First Amendment rights. What they are really being is purposely destructive, both to the faith of millions, and to the republic itself. With each sacrilegious sideswipe, they spit on the core faith of believers all over America. Their goal is to erode the foundations of religious belief. This is by design. If they can rattle our belief in the existence or claims of Christ, and undermine the veracity of the entire Judeo-Christian canon, they can stifle the values that spring from them, and lead us further down the path of cultural confusion, darkness, and despair.

The Godless Delusion

The pop assault on religious values has intensified in recent years. A string of atheistic bestsellers from Sam Harris's *The End of Faith*, to Richard Dawkins's *The God Delusion* have crept into the American consciousness and ironically found their way beneath many a Christmas tree.

For all the liberal cries for tolerance, where are the voices demanding tolerance from Dawkins? His hatred for religion is deep-seated and vicious. Even *Publisher's Weekly* said in its review of *The God Delusion*: "For a scientist who criticizes religion for its intolerance, Dawkins has written a surprisingly intolerant book, full of scorn for religion and those who believe." Professor Dawkins strains to drive a wedge between science and faith, but more often collapses into ad hominem attacks. So God in the Old Testament is "psychotic" and "an evil monster," St. Thomas Aquinas's proofs of God's existence are "fatuous," and Mother Teresa is "sanctimoniously hypocritical." (Why does every atheist feel obliged to beat up on Mother Teresa? I mean I could understand Torquemada or Ted Haggard, but Mother Teresa?!)

Naturally, the dinosaur media has lauded Dawkins, who confirms their belief that there is no Being more supreme than the *New York Times* Editorial Board. Christopher Hitchens's *God Is Not Great* hit number one on the *New York Times* bestseller list in June 2007. The popularity of such atheistic tomes demonstrates that some people will go to any length to find justifications for their non-belief so they can go on to live reckless lives free of the "shackles of religion." As G. K. Chesterton once said: "Atheism is the most daring of all dogmas, for it is the assertion of a universal negative." Nothing "fatuous," "psychotic," or "sanctimoniously hypocritical" in that reasoning now, is there?

Revealing his true agenda, Sam Harris predicted, "At some point there is going to be enough pressure that it is just going to be too embarrassing to believe in God."[5] Nice try, Sam. But what we are really embarrassed about is you.

Though these atheists have little to support their dogmatic non-belief, they are convinced that by keeping the pagan "pressure" on, you will either be shamed into joining their ranks or will at least hide your faith. But before you throw God out with the test tube, you should look closely at their claims and realize that though we cannot prove the existence of God, nor can they prove His non-existence. And don't forget, there are many reasonable arguments that vouch in God's favor. As Dr. Francis Collins, the renowned scientist, director of the Human Genome project, and a Christian, has written:

... [R]eason alone cannot prove the existence of God. Faith
is reason plus revelation, and the revelation part requires
one to think with the spirit as well as with the mind. You
have to hear the music, not just read the notes on the
page.... I have found there is a wonderful harmony in the
complementary truths of science and faith. The God of the
Bible is also the God of the genome. God can be found in the
cathedral or in the laboratory.[6]

On my radio show, I have actively sought out guests who head
up atheist groups. I do not pretend to be a religion "expert" or
even to know my faith as well as I should, but one of my priest
friends likes to remind me, "one must know the basic tenets of
one's faith in order to defend it from scorn, ridicule, and attack."
Debating atheists with facts and a healthy dose of satire sharpens
my own spiritual thinking—though their comments test my
patience. One of these occasions occurred in early January 2007. I
had seen an article in *Newsweek* about something called "The
Blasphemy Challenge." Basically, the point is to encourage young
people to renounce God publicly, and thus risk eternal damnation.
It tempts the young to stand up to the Almighty and demonstrate
that they're not "afraid of God." (Their shocking ignorance of
Christianity surfaces again, given that Jesus repeatedly tells His
apostles in Holy Scripture to "Be not afraid.")

So we booked Brian Sapient on my show, one of the co-founders
of this atheist recruitment farce. Here's an excerpt of the interview:

> **Laura:** So what you're trying to do here is to get people
> to put their souls on the line ... but you don't believe in a
> soul. So what are people putting on the line?
>
> **Brian:** Showing people that you are not scared of what
> we are led to believe. We should be scared of—obviously we
> are a predominantly Christian society—so they are scared of

Yahweh's hell. We are so un-scared that we would commit ourselves to a hell we don't believe exists.

Laura: What informs your value system?

Brian: Reason, logical thought.

Laura: But where did that come from?

Brian: Your brain.

Laura: But where did that come from?

Brian: The biological process...evolution...and you know.... Would you propose that it came from a God somehow?

At this point I wanted to give up or blow up.

Laura: I believe love comes from God. But you think that love comes from evolution?

Brian: Well, actually, I think love does come from reason.... I think moral codes came well before religion does. I don't think we need religion to be good people. If we did atheists—you know—would be locked up.

Laura: Why do we have Good Samaritans? Why shouldn't it be every man for himself? Why should we have Christian missionaries right now working in Africa in places where the UN won't even go?

Brian: To some extent I think it *is* every man for himself. But inherent in that is that we need other people in order to look out for yourself—

Laura: No, you're not going to get away with that on my show. The missionary or volunteer doesn't need to be there. They don't have to be there. They are there for something greater than themselves.

Brian: You don't want to bring up missionaries in Africa to me.... That's a sore subject. They are actually doing a horrible injustice to the people there.... They are spreading

AIDS worse than had they come in there and taught how to use a condom.

Laura: What would have happened if all of us had listened to God's commands?

Brian: We would have killed each other off by now.

Thou shalt not lose one's patience with ignorant misfit twenty-somethings who spent too much time in atheist chat rooms. After the segment was over I reminded myself that while I was never exactly an agnostic, or an atheist like Brian, I was spiritually uninformed for many years. There is always hope. We need to keep engaging with the Brians out there, as frustrating as it may be. One listener e-mailed me, asking that I tell Brian: "Whether you like it or not, thousands of people across the country are out there praying for you!"

That probably really ticked him off.

The members of Team Atheist continue to load the cannons. The recently released book *The Jesus Dynasty*, by James Tabor advances the charming idea that Jesus was neither the Son of God nor the son of Joseph, but was the offspring of a Roman soldier named Pantera.[7] At least he's original.

Bill Maher is also part of the Lynch God Squad. The comedian who claims he is "spreading the anti-gospel" (no arguments there) has a plan to "Borat" people of faith. Just as Sacha Baron Cohen lampooned Americans by preying on their good will and gullibility and editing them within an inch of their prejudices, so Bill Maher will attempt to portray religious people as idiots—and if I had to guess, bigoted ones. His documentary, called *A Spiritual Journey* will feature Maher "interviewing various religious figures in order to question his own skepticism."[8] I'll bet. You can look forward to seeing groundbreaking depictions of Evangelicals as a bunch of zealous yahoos and Catholic priests as pedophiles. With the recent success of films like *Jesus Camp* and *Deliver Us from Evil*, Maher

LAME LINES OF THE NON-BELIEVERS

))) "I keep my faith open and just try to practice the Golden Rule."

))) "As long as you're a good person, faith doesn't matter."

))) "I'm a spiritual person, but I'm not religious."

))) "I practice a non-judgmental faith."

))) "Religion has retarded the development of civilization."

))) "Religion causes war."

will likely end up with an Oscar nomination for his efforts.

These shameless atheistic attacks, and the routine mockery of religion, are done to further marginalize faithful voices from the public square. The hope of the crusading atheists is to make religious people and their ideas appear goofy, out of touch, freakish, and unreasonable. Suddenly, morality and virtue, the very things the founders built into the American experiment, is considered mawkish and elbowed aside. John Adams understood that "our constitution is made only for a moral and religious people. It is wholly inadequate to the government of any other."[9] Considering the hostility to religion and morality in today's America, we'd better convene a new constitutional congress.

Faith Substitutes— Taste Great! Less Filling!

There is a spiritual yearning in the human heart. It is a part of our basic wiring. All of us want to be connected to God and to the supernatural world that we believe is out there. Traditional religions make demands upon us and insist that there are requirements to being a child of God; mainly, living as He would have us live. For many people today, these requirements are a bridge too far.

They want the experience of faith, but are unwilling to pay the admission price. So they try to satisfy their supernatural appetite void with spiritual junk food. These faith substitutes can take a variety of forms and have become an American cottage industry.

Some place rocks on their chakras, strike a few yoga positions, and try to channel the dead to feel spiritual. Others consult their horoscopes, in hopes that the stars will show them the way. There are runes, tarot cards, palm readers, and all manner of New Age quick fixes to get your faux spiritual groove on. Whatever the new trend—Buddhist chanting while barbecuing, yoga with your dog, etc.—it'll find a platform on *Good Morning America*, *Oprah*, or *Ellen*.

We saw this play out in early 2007 with the Oprah Winfrey-created literary sensation—Rhonda Byrne's bestselling DVD and book *The Secret*. One thing shouldn't be secret—the Byrne book is the latest in a long line of empty spiritual promises. The "Secret"? Think positively! Project "happy" and you'll get happy! It's essentially Norman Vincent Peale's *The Power of Positive Thinking* without God. Byrne tries to boost her credibility by telling readers that this "Secret" was used by Beethoven, Plato, and Einstein. (Conveniently, none are around to protest the misappropriation of their good names.) Major bookstore chains gave *The Secret* its own display case for can't miss revelations such as the truth behind "The Law of Attraction." (If you believe in something strongly enough, it will come your way! "You are the most powerful magnet in the universe...so as you think a thought you are also attracting like thoughts to you.") There might be something to this theory after all. Byrne believed that a sucker was born every minute and she found every last one of them.

It isn't feeding the homeless, or restoring peace to the planet that Byrne has her eye on; it's feeding your whims. If you want that new Porsche, see yourself in it, and bam! It's yours. Want that hot babe at the pool? Just believe strongly enough and presto! You've got a model on your arm for the night. The goal of Byrne's "Secret" is not at all spiritual, but entirely material. It's all about getting stuff in the here and now, and grabbing all you can. Eternity is for suckers.

The history of *The Secret* reveals that behind every successful pop psychology book, there's a major huckster. Rhonda Byrne was an Australian television producer mourning the death of her father when she came across a book written in 1910 titled *The Science of Getting Rich*. She claims this was her first brush with "The Secret." Later she approached Esther and Jerry Hicks, a carny couple who had been traveling the country selling *The Law of Attraction* to audiences for more than two decades. The Hicks charge people $195 a ticket to hear Esther channel the voice of "Abraham." That's right, dear old Esther channels a few spirits and plays Carnac for the crowd. The Hicksses' sideshow act and their wacky philosophy became the backbone of Byrne's documentary, *The Secret*. Then trouble arose. Though she could be heard on the film, Esther Hicks did not much appreciate that she never appeared on camera and was not the center of attention. After a protracted contract dispute over credit and revenue, Rhonda Byrne edited the Hicksses out of the film, and shot a new version without them. *The Secret* DVD (the original and the new and improved) has gone on to sell more than one *million* copies.

Deceptive philosophies like *The Secret* spread like wildfire because they make no significant demands on the practitioners and urge no change of heart. These faux faith alternatives promise great things, but ultimately deliver adherents over to material emptiness and falsehoods. C. S. Lewis put it best: "The Christian and the Materialist hold different beliefs about the universe. They can't both be right. The one who is wrong will act in a way which simply doesn't fit the real universe. Consequently, with the best will in the world, he will be helping his fellow creatures to their destruction."[10]

Separation of Church and Brain

For those immune to the allures of dime-store faith replacements like *The Secret*, the elites have opened up another offensive against religion. They are trying to sue God right out of the public square. Faith is fine—just keep it to yourself, please. The anti-religion elites do this, of course, in the name of the defending the Constitution. An 1802 letter from Thomas Jefferson to the Danbury Baptists in which he refers to the "wall of separation of church and state" is the only Holy Scripture for groups such as the ACLU, People for the American Way, and Americans United for the Separation of Church and State. Contrary to what these groups argue, Jefferson was not suggesting that the government quarantine religious practice so as not to infect a broader population. Jefferson was underscoring the religious liberty of the American people—the liberty to practice their religion free of government coercion and interference. But the letter has been totally misused and misinterpreted, and in the process so has the establishment clause of the Constitution.

If the Anti-God Mob were honest with us and themselves, they would admit that they're most comfortable operating in a religion-free zone. How else to explain the fact that each Christmas our court dockets sparkle and shine with cases challenging the constitutionality of publicly displayed Christmas trees, Nativity scenes, and Menorahs. Christmas carols, mentions of Santa, and (God forbid) the term "Merry Christmas" are now on the judicial endangered species list. The hilarious Jackie Mason and Raoul Felder, Jewish guys writing in a Catholic periodical, said of this madness: "It is significant that the

> # WHY I LIKE IKE
>
>))) "Without God, there could be no form of government nor American way of life. Recognition of the Supreme Being is the first—and most basic—expression of Americanism."[11]
>
> **—Dwight D. Eisenhower**

ACLU's position is that pornography is protected under the Constitution, while the Christmas tree is not. So, if this bunch were successful, the only way you could see a Christmas tree is if you visit a porn shop that had one.... The point is, of course, if Christmas is abolished from public display, can the fate of Chanukah and the myriad of other Jewish holidays be far behind?"[12]

Not content to secularize religious holidays, the Pagan Jihad also includes fatwas against America's religious heritage. In 2004, the ACLU bullied Los Angeles County into removing a teeny cross from the city's official seal. In ACLU-land, the cross constituted an "impermissible endorsement of Christianity." Even though the cross had been part of the seal for almost fifty years, and represented the obvious historical and religious roots of the City of the Angels, the county agreed to remove the symbol, replacing it with a Spanish mission and a few American Indians.[13]

Now nothing is sacred, not even memorials to our dead veterans. A federal lawsuit was recently filed to remove a cross planted in honor of World War I veterans at Sunrise Rock in the Mojave Desert. Who could be offended by such a thing in the middle of the Mojave Desert? The atheist scorpions?

War memorials have become a routine target for the religion haters, and perhaps no struggle has been as hard fought or as protracted as the one waged over the Mount Soledad Memorial in San Diego. Starting in 1989, courts repeatedly ruled the cross unconstitutional in a variety of legal challenges. But the city of San Diego and conservatives pushed back. In 2006, President Bush signed a bill transferring ownership of the memorial from the city to the federal government. Thanks to the tenacity of the people the memorial has survived.

This is certainly not the last stand of the godless gaggle, and we should vigilantly oppose them whenever and wherever they attempt to dismantle the religious and cultural heritage of America.

REAGAN'S REVOLUTION

))) "To those who would crush religious freedom, our message is
plain: you may jail your believers. You may close their
churches, confiscate their Bibles, and harass their rabbis and priests, but you
will never destroy the love of God and freedom that burns in their hearts. They
will triumph over you."[14]

—Ronald Reagan

Things aren't any easier for God at our nation's universities either.
At Virginia's College of William and Mary in late 2006, the college
president Gene Nichol announced his decision to remove a brass
cross from the altar of the Wren chapel so that it would "welcome
students of all faiths" or even those of no faith.

Following President Nichol's logic he should have removed the
altar, razed the entire building, and built a multicultural arts center
and gift shop in its place. Oh, and did I forget the food court? If it
even vaguely reminds the college community of Christianity, it
must be suspect.

The public reaction to the removal of the cross was swift and
intense. Talk shows across the country buzzed with the cross con-
troversy. Petitions bearing more than a thousand names were
submitted to the Board of Visitors demanding that the cross be
returned to the altar. Alumni and students protested. One longtime
donor to the college was so outraged by the cross flap, he rescinded
a $12 million donation in disgust. Money talks, as they say, and
this got the attention of the college. Within a week, the college had
a surprise announcement. The good news: the brass cross would be
returned to the chapel. The bad news: it would be nowhere near the
altar and would be placed under glass.

This outcome is symbolic of what the secularists consider an appropriate religious display—make it a museum piece and hermetically seal it, in hopes that the image will have less impact on passerbys. (Sort of like an Aztec exhibit at the Met.)

Query: how is an environment hospitable only to atheists, agnostics, and hemp-wearing pantheists *welcoming* to the overwhelming majority of Americans? I would not feel welcome in the Wren chapel—a chapel that has to hide its Christian identity because of political correctness. What about *my* feelings?

Enough is enough. We must stand firm and not let this expunging of our religious heritage continue. The human heart cries out for visual images of goodness, tangible reinforcement of what we believe and why. Our Constitution protects our right to display these images wherever we like, including public spaces. Symbols of faith are part of our American experience and important reminders of our higher calling. Without them how can we credibly pass on to our children a sense of morality, and an appreciation of our Judeo-Christian heritage? But maybe that's the point. The elites on the far left don't really want us to pass our values on to our children or to anyone else for that matter.

These external symbols of our belief are not irrelevant because they contribute to the wider culture. These outward expressions affect the internal ones—and lead directly to our greatest power as a people. As citizens, our most important acts are intimately linked

> # GIVE 'EM HEAVEN HARRY
>
>))) "The fundamental basis of this nation's laws was given to Moses on the Mount. The fundamental basis of our Bill of Rights comes from [biblical] teachings. . . . If we don't have the proper fundamental moral background, we will finally wind up with a totalitarian government which does not believe in rights for anybody except the state."[15]
>
> **—Harry Truman**

to the moral decisions we make in our daily lives, and the example we set for others. Our personal example and the practice of faith is contagious and will profoundly shape the future—a future that begins in the heart and soul of each of us.

When Faith Hits Home

Looking back at my life, I realize that I never really felt "God's tap on my shoulder" until almost ten years ago, when my mother was diagnosed with lung cancer.

One night I was helping my mother into bed. She couldn't walk well at that point, and the rounds of chemotherapy had wasted her small five-foot frame to skin and bones. She needed her pillows arranged *just so* in order to sleep more than an hour or two. I do not know what compelled me, but I opened up a Bible we had in the house and just started reading to her from the New Testament. In the fog and sadness of that night I do not recall the passages I read, but I hope they spoke to my mother as she drifted away from me. During those long days and nights of her illness, many friends called. Some told me they were praying for her or asked to pray with me on the telephone. I have to admit, I thought that was a bit odd—praying, especially with others, was not something I normally did—but I gladly welcomed any and all prayers.

She died a few months later, in May 1999, with my entire family gathered around the bed we had set up for her in the living room. My tough, funny, hardworking mother fought until the end. She would always say to me, "Laura, I did the best that I could," invariably adding, "someday you'll understand." She did do her best, and in time I would understand.

I remember sitting in the Glastonbury funeral home with my brother Jimmy and his wife Stephanie, filling out forms for her burial. Choosing her burial clothes, writing her obituary, choosing the casket, reserving the limousine to carry her to the cemetery—somehow in the dazed numbness, it all got done. I felt alone and broken.

Initially, I tried to fill her absence in my life with people and things that made me even more unhappy. I was hosting a daily television show for MSNBC and not really enjoying it. I was making one bad personal decision after another. It was a miserable time. About three months after my mother's death, I realized I hadn't cried since her funeral. This sense of detachment was not "normal." For a time I buried myself in work and speeches in a lame attempt to do an end-run around the grief.

This only made matters worse.

Years after my mother died, when I finally let myself remember her, I began to appreciate all she had given me. For a time it was simply too painful to recall what she did for my brothers and me—how she did without so we could have nice clothes or a used car; how she worked at Willie's Steakhouse into her seventies "until they let all the old gals go" (the tip money helped pay our college tuition). My mother lived her life for her children. She spent so little money on herself, that during high school, I remember begging her to buy a new purse to replace the ratty, old, black leather one that she had lugged around for years. Back then I was embarrassed. Today I consider that old purse a treasure. Looking back as an adult in the middle of my life, I now appreciate what a beautiful gift my mother gave my brothers and me by always putting her needs and desires second, and ours first. In the aftermath of her passing, I gradually began to sense God's presence in my life. This was my mother's final gift to me.

* * * * *

I cannot remember exactly when we stopped attending church regularly but I think I was around eleven or so. The Pilgrim Baptist

Church in Glastonbury, Connecticut, was a conservative family church filled with cheerful, outgoing people. I went to Sunday school (hated it), summer Bible camp (ditto), and church picnics (liked the sports and games). To this day, I remember how on my way out the door after church every week Pastor Howard Wood would shake my small hand with a big smile on his face. "Ann, you have a special girl here!" he would say to my mother. I felt like I was ten feet tall.

My dad stopped going to church first, and then I think my mother just slowly fell away from it. She had been raised Catholic and was taught by nuns in a Polish school in Willamantic, Connecticut. She never told me why she left the Church and I did not ask. That generation (she was born in 1920) didn't dwell on such personal matters. They were too busy working hard, raising their families, trying to make ends meet. I often wonder what she would think about my becoming a Catholic. She's smiling, I think.

I remember saying "Now I lay me down to sleep" bedtime prayers when I was really young and saying grace during holiday meals, but other than that, God was not really part of our conversation at home. Maybe that explains why it took me so long to start becoming spiritually curious.

Listeners who have heard me mention my conversion to the Catholic faith often ask—"what made you do it?" I usually say something funny like, "I'm half-Polish, so it was a John Paul II thing!" But the only real answer I have (at least thus far in my spiritual journey) is the Holy Spirit came to me. My conversion began with heartfelt conversations I had with Pat Cipollone, an old friend who would eventually become my godfather. I did what most curious God-seekers do—I read the Bible, reflected on the Gospels, and really focused on praying. I found myself praying all the time—while brushing my teeth, on the treadmill, on the drive to the studio.

I remember when I walked into the rectory of St. Patrick's Church in Washington to meet with Monsignor Peter Vaghi for the first time. Pat had suggested I chat with him. On the outside I was a cool cat. On the inside, I was freaking out. But after our first half-hour meeting, I felt like I had known him for years. I was totally comfortable opening up to him, and by the time I walked out the door I realized that something profound was happening to me.

Monsignor Vaghi and I would continue to meet each week at St. Patrick's and during those sessions I slowly learned to forgive myself and others. Mother Angelica, the spunky media mogul, once said: "Forgiveness means, 'to give.' It means to give before your neighbor does." I learned that with forgiveness, it's always better if we make the first move.

At the Easter Vigil in 2003, I was baptized by Monsignor Vaghi (I had no baptismal record), was confirmed, and received my first Holy Communion. I chose "Caroline," my mother's middle name, as my communion name. I was walking on air that night. For the first time, for as long as I could remember, I felt like I was finally "home." It was the strangest thing—this faith thing. How could this have happened to me? The person who used to make Catholic jokes in junior high school! The person who walked into her first meeting with a priest and said, "Great to meet you, but there is no way in hell that I'm going to become a Catholic!" God has a sense of humor, doesn't He?

Faith is a great support during good times, but in the dark moments of my bout with cancer in 2005, it was my rock. From the moment I was diagnosed, amazing things began happening to me. Yes, that's right—*amazing* things. I remember a cell phone conversation I had with my godfather as I drove myself to the studio in early May. It was four days after my second operation and my entire right breast was swollen, my armpit was bulging with lymphatic fluid, and I just broke down. "I can't go on the air," I wailed.

"Laura, you're going to be fine. Everybody is praying for you," Pat insisted. "Ya gotta psych yourself up here! I know this stuff that has happened to you is really lousy, but remember, it's all spit-balls off a battleship!" I understood why he had the reputation as

ETERNAL THOUGHTS

》》 "We have no right to decide where we should be placed, or to have preconceived ideas as to what God is preparing us to do. God engineers everything; and wherever He places us, our one supreme goal should be to pour out our lives in wholehearted devotion to Him in that particular work."[16]

—Oswald Chambers

》》 "Don't live as if this life will continue forever. It won't. Live instead with eternity in view."[17]

—Billy Graham

》》 "Not enough of us use our talents and our positions in testimony to God's goodness."[18]

—Ronald Reagan

one of the top litigators in Washington legal circles—he could give one heck of a closing argument. The pep talk was exactly what I needed. He reminded me that everyone has trials—it's how we deal with them that matters. During commercial breaks I said little prayers, and I think they worked. When our closing theme music played in the final hour of my show that day, I sat back in my chair and exhaled a quiet "thank you" to God for helping me keep it together. From that point on, I knew I was going to make it.

Cancer was a gift from God. Yes, I know that sounds weird but it's true. During my struggle, my faith was never stronger. Sure, I had plenty of low moments, but I felt that God was giving me the strength to get through it. I thanked Him for helping me catch the cancer early, and for all that He had given me. My family and true friends rose to the occasion. My own trials reminded me to pray for all those people across the country in hospitals and nursing homes who felt frightened and alone.

I had always heard that suffering could bring you closer to God. Now I believe it. In the midst of my battle with cancer, I began to understand the redemptive power of suffering and the unexpected peace found on the other side of the cross. It is a mystery, and one that I don't pretend to fully comprehend, but in my weakness I discovered a great power that sustained me—great because it was not mine. It was God's. The pain shook me from my comfort zone and forced me to see beyond myself—to see the world as it truly is. I now know that this was part of God's plan for me. Though it isn't always comfortable, He has a plan for each of us, and for our nation. We are placed here for a brief time to do God's will, to serve others, and to strive to advance the common good. I don't always live up to this, but this I now know.

No Greater Love

Like the other millions of Americans in the fight against cancer, I was drafted unwillingly. I fought for my own survival—nothing really valiant in that.

Americans who have volunteered to serve their country are the ones who are really courageous, because they fight not only for themselves but for all of us. They put themselves on the line for the cause of freedom.

In the spring of 2005, I met one of these young heroes at Walter Reed Army Medical Center—nineteen-year-old Marine Corporal Kade Hinkhouse. His Humvee had been hit months earlier by an IED, leaving a gaping hole in the right side of his skull, taking his right leg, and paralyzing the left side of his body. His brain injury left his speech impaired but he still managed to convey more wisdom about the situation in Iraq (how important it is "that we get the job done") than most people I've interviewed on Capitol Hill.

A year later, Kade came by my studio after eighteen months in recovery. He was on his way home to Colorado—his hair had grown back, he was fitted with a high-tech prosthesis, and he had regained much of the movement in his left arm. He was in a great mood, focused on his plans to become a history teacher. How can any of us really be in a bad mood about stupid little things when young men like Kade can project such a wonderful upbeat attitude after suffering so much? He'll be a great teacher.

Whenever I start to feel down about something happening in my own life, I snap myself out of it by thinking about all of our injured troops convalescing in military hospitals here and abroad. I have nothing to complain about and everything to be grateful for. As I travel the country and the world, the example of our American military never fails to astound me. They demonstrate an amazing selflessness and more often than not, incredible faith.

I believe patriotism is best defined by sacrifice. To defend ourselves and the liberty we hold dear, we must be willing to sacrifice something. It may not mean putting yourself on the front-lines in Iraq, but if you love this country, surely you can skip the mid-day venti Mochaccino and contribute seven bucks to a veterans' fund. Whether we are talking about raising a child or defending the homeland, love is shown in sacrifice.

Stop and think about it for a minute. What makes people offer their lives for another or for their country? You could argue that anyone would give her life to protect her children or family. But to offer one's life for strangers, for an idea, for a belief—that takes real faith. And people still do it every day.

The practice of faith and its expression has the power to change our behavior and society at large. How many of us will ever forget the images of New York firefighters—so many of them Catholic—carrying their heavy hoses and equipment, entering the Trade Center Towers when everyone else was running out? We wonder if we would be able to muster the same courage—the same sense of self-sacrifice. In most Catholic churches you'll find images of Jesus nailed to the cross. It isn't that we don't believe Jesus rose from the dead (we do). The crucifix is a reminder that our redemption was won in Christ's sacrifice, and that pain and suffering, even death, are not the end for us. On some deep level, I'm sure those police officers, firefighters, and rescue workers who rushed into the chaos and destruction on September 11, were inspired by the image and example of Christ's sacrifice. They lived their faith that day. What did Jesus say? "Greater love than this no man hath, that a man lay down his life for his friends." (John 15:13)

In a letter written during the Vietnam War, Lieutenant Ray Stubbe, a young navy chaplain, noted that we tend to derive the greatest spiritual benefit when we "face the loss of all the trivia of modern day society."[19] He chronicled the harsh experience of his Marines and then added: "You would be amazed at the faith expressed here. There are evidences of genuine and deep prayer life, of reading and knowing the Bible backwards and forwards, of sacrificial concern for others." *Sacrificial concern*—this is not a phrase we hear enough about today, outside of the great contributions of our military to the cause of freedom and security. Yet this is the animating spirit that made martyrs of the holy and compelled a great generation to face powerful foes in Europe and the Pacific. We must seek to cultivate a sense of sacrificial concern in the republic. This basic virtue will ensure the strength of America and her goodness.

Like many around the world, I was deeply struck last April by the horror of what happened on the campus of Virginia Tech. Yet as we tried to make sense of the sheer evil of the slaughter of thirty-two innocents, we also learned about the heroic nature of one man's sacrifice. Liviu Librescu, a seventy-six-year-old Holocaust survivor, told his students to flee as he threw his own body in front of the classroom door as the killer approached. He saved the lives of his entire class, but lost his own. This story touched people around the world.

Sacrificial concern needn't be dramatic to be effective. You don't have to patrol a street in Ramadi to show sacrificial concern for others. When I was sick I met countless people who generously put my well-being ahead of their immediate needs. I called them my angels. Some of those who came to my aid weren't even close friends. They were friends of friends who themselves had survived breast cancer—like Nancy Stevenson. She became my telephone buddy, gave me some wigs, and from day one told me I would be fine. "Keep moving forward and don't get freaked out by all the chemo side effects they list in those cancer books. As a matter of fact, throw out *all* the cancer books," she laughed.

Around the time when I was trying to decide whether to subject myself to a brutal regimen of chemotherapy or just radiation and hormone therapy, I drove out to Virginia to a picnic at my friend Ann's house. I didn't want to go, didn't want to answer questions about what was happening, but forced myself to be social. I was getting worried about living alone during the ordeal that was before me and wondered whether I would have enough energy to take care of myself. On the patio I saw Dan and Sandy Casey, a married couple whom I knew only casually. They asked how I was doing and I told them what my concerns were. "Well, then, meet your new family!" said Sandy. "We have an extra bedroom and we know the drill with cancer." She explained that her sixteen-year-old son Michael had battled cancer and that they'd be happy to adopt me until I was well enough to be on my own. She gave me her card and wrote a funny note on it: "Welcome to your new family!" I thanked God once again.

It turned out that I didn't need to take Dan and Sandy up on their kind invitation because a friend from my old law firm, Katie, offered to move into my house during the toughest months of chemotherapy. She rearranged her entire life to help me and I will never forget that. An old friend of mine from my MSNBC days, Felicia called me out of the blue: "Laura, I just heard about what happened, and I'm coming down there tomorrow." She lived in New York, and I hadn't seen her in at least five years, yet she showed up on my doorstep the next day with a bag of gifts and a huge smile. She insisted that she buy me expensive 1,000-count Italian sheets for my bed—"Sweetheart, this is the time to treat yourself!" she laughed.

My greatest moment of joy during this period was when my friends Pat and Becky, a few weeks into my illness, asked me to be godmother to their daughter, who was due in the early summer. Sofia was born on the day I started chemotherapy.

My brothers and friends took turns joining me during my four three-hour sessions in the chemo room. My pal Patty—a mother of two young boys—made three out of four! She joked about sneaking in margaritas. Yes, the angels were everywhere—too many to mention here. (See acknowledgments.)

LOVE IN ACTION

》》》 "Do ordinary things with extraordinary love: little things like caring for the sick and the homeless, the lonely and the unwanted, washing and cleaning for them. You must give what will cost you something. This then is giving not just what you can live without, but what you can't live without, or don't want to live without....Then your gift becomes a sacrifice, which will have value before God. Any sacrifice is useful if it is done out of love. This giving until it hurts—this sacrifice—is what I call love in action."[20]

—**Mother Teresa**

During my breast cancer "adventure," I received hundreds of e-mails from people whose lives had been touched by cancer. They shared their stories—their heartaches and their triumphs. A number of women who heard me urge listeners to do their annual physicals and self-exams, e-mailed to thank me. They had discovered that they, too, had breast cancer, and most had thankfully caught it early. As much as I wished that I hadn't become a member of the cancer club, I saw that there was a purpose to my illness. People who were facing their own health crises, have told me that I helped them. At first I really didn't understand how I was much help to anybody during this period. But later I understood that just by dragging myself to that studio everyday, and by being open about what I was experiencing, similarly afflicted people were comforted. My listeners laughed and cried right along with me. In retrospect I am convinced this helped my recovery. The encouraging words from so many people I knew and so many I will never meet kept me going—sacrificial concern in action.

This giving of self is what it will take to recapture what we have lost in America. People marvel at how debased and crass our culture is. They puzzle over how we got here. We got here because too many of us stopped giving a damn. We became obsessed with the next pay grade, the bigger house, and the next vacation. Too many of us lost our sense of purpose, our faith, our belief in the innate goodness of America, and our concern for our fellow man.

The elementary school children who box care packages for our troops, the volunteers for Habitat for Humanity (yes, Jimmy Carter deserves credit), the college students who spent their springs breaks helping the victims of Hurricane Katrina, the candy-stripers at our retirement homes—these are the people who deserve the media attention in our country. These are the nation's battalions of home-based heroes. We must recognize them as such if we are to build a national movement of sacrifice.

Returning *Real POWER TO THE PEOPLE*

It is not enough for us to defend American soil or to maintain a thriving economy. It will all be in vain if we fail to nurture and refresh America's soul. And that is only possible through individual belief demonstrated through action.

If we lose faith in God, it will be very difficult to keep faith with our duty to defend America—from without and within. The Founding Fathers clearly understood this. Only five months after the signing of the Declaration, at a time when the ravages of war and a poor harvest threatened the country, Congress set aside December 11, 1776, as a Day of Fasting and Repentance. They implored "Almighty God (for) forgiveness of the many sins prevailing among all ranks....."[21] Can you imagine Nancy Pelosi co-sponsoring a bill like that on the House floor today? (Although I realize the concept of pork-barrel Washington fasting is a bit of a stretch.)

Then at the start of the Revolutionary War, when General George Washington was leading little more than a ragtag army against the premiere fighting force in the world, he demanded that his men refrain from profanity, maintain "exemplary lives," and "attend carefully [to] religious exercises."[22] He went so far as to order the officer of each regiment to lead prayer for the men in their respective companies.

If we wish to be a moral people dedicated to preserving liberty and true freedom, then we must find a way to avoid the tempting snares littering the cultural landscape. This demands the same resolve Washington's men had. The stakes are just as high.

This is no time for relativism, no time to drop our guard and permit our values to be trampled under foot. This is when we must fly our colors of faith proudly. The example of Pope John Paul II and Ronald Reagan should urge us on. These two men, through determined action and a rock solid faith, buried Soviet communism. They had a clear moral vision that stirred the hearts of people the world over. Their words and prayers reshaped the culture, stunned the naysayers, and liberated millions of people. Could the fall of the Soviet Union have occurred without faith? Highly doubtful. Reagan believed that he was fulfilling God's will in standing up to the Soviets and obviously John Paul II did as well. Do we have that same faith today to beat back the new threats to our country, our culture, and our way of life? If we find unity in faith, there is no challenge—internal or external—that can overwhelm us.

No, I am not advocating some sort of theocracy. I think we are all in agreement that religious creeds should *not* be the law of the land in America. The only theocracies in existence today, are of the radical Islamic variety. And do we really want our own version of Saudi Arabia's Ministry of the Propagation of Virtue and the Prevention of Vice roaming the streets, searching for morality offenders? (If Paris, Britney, Lindsay, and the Three-Six Mafia come to mind, maybe it's best not to answer that question.) We con-

> # GOD AND THE GIPPER
>
> ❱❱❱ "For the West, for America, the time has come to dare to show to the world that our civilized ideas, our traditions, our values, are not—like the ideology of and war machine of totalitarian societies—just a façade of strength. It is time for the world to know that our intellectual and spiritual values are rooted in the source of all strength, a belief in a Supreme Being, and a law higher than our own."[23]
>
> **—Ronald Reagan**

servatives want government out of religion; we don't want religious leaders to become our government. At the same time this does not mean that religion should be absent from public life or shoved to the sidelines when we confront moral or ethical issues. When we go beyond paying mere lip service to our faith, and actually live it, we win and America wins.

The commonsense ideas and creative strategies I have presented throughout this book are indispensable for our growth as a people and a nation. Yet without faith to sustain us through good times and bad, without our belief in the Almighty to renew our sense of purpose, all our efforts will be stillborn. The culture, politics, the media, everything around us is a reflection of not just our national soul—but our individual souls as well. Each moral choice we make reverberates into the lives of those around us and throughout the world.

Whether the next generation will enjoy those God-given rights of Life, Liberty, and the Pursuit of Happiness hinges on our choices— the personal moral choices we make today and throughout our lives. Only by being rooted in faith and following our individual consciences will we have the clarity to recognize what is true in order to resist the false promises of the in-crowd. Only then can we summon the moral resolve necessary to rescue our culture, our country, and future generations.

This is true power. This is eternal power available to all of us— rich and poor, Democrat and Republican, black, white, yellow, and brown. It is the power that no individual, institution, or outside force can take away from us.

After all, God Almighty is the ultimate super power.

ACKNOWLEDGMENTS

Two years ago, the last thing on my mind was writing another book, or going on another book tour. At the time, I was wrapping up five months of treatment for breast cancer and beaten down pretty bad. Like millions of my fellow cancer conquerors I was just taking one day at a time, hoping that God wanted me around for a while longer. The people who helped me see that year of challenges into a time of personal, physical, and spiritual renewal are those who made *Power to the People* possible.

My father and my three brothers always reminded me that I wasn't alone. Curtis, Jimmy, and my sister-in-law Stephanie flew in to help turn chemotherapy sessions into causes for celebration. Brooks kept me going with beautiful classical music. The memory of my mother—always a fighter—was a constant source of strength.

My friend Katie Sexton turned her own life upside down to help make sure I got out the door every morning. The Cipollones provided a fun, happy place to call my second home. My godfather Pat Cipollone was a reservoir of wisdom and advice, and managed to make me laugh even at oncology appointments. His wife Becky,

with her infinite kindness, urged me to use this trial as an opportunity to get closer to God. I still smile when I think of their girls
and boys rubbing my peach-fuzz head, or taking my wig off to
model it themselves.

During this time, countless friends, listeners, and total strangers
reminded me that God's blessing are all around us. My old college
pal Wendy Long was a reassuring hands-on presence since the day I
was diagnosed. Chuck and Ina Carlsen were their usual generous,
loving selves. The always upbeat Patty Coleman won the attendance
award in the chemo room. Danielle and David Frum made sure that
I always had dinner plans and a refreshing pool to swim in. My
friend of twenty years Melinda Sidak always kept the laughs coming. My "little sister" Lia Macko never let me forget that I was
going to be okay. Jill Sorensen flew in from California to join the
boost-Laura brigade. Patricia DeSanctis, Bob Brauneis, Mona
Charen, Kate and Jim O'Beirne, Jim and Cheryl Keller, Clarence and
Ginny Thomas, Peggy Noonan, Edd and Nina Hendee, Kate
Brokaw, Dan and Jan Patrick, the Scalia family, Ann Corkery,
Randy Wallace, Todd Mack, Jim Hirsen, Mel Gibson, Wesley Neal,
Rich Schulte, Ken and Alice Starr, Msgrs. Peter Vaghi and Charles
Antonicelli, Alex and Jennifer Azar, and too many others stepped up
to give of themselves in ways big and small that I will never forget.

The fact that I hadn't seen her in years didn't stop my old
MSNBC friend Felicia Taylor from showing up with the latest in
fashionable head covering. (We went from the chemo room to Rio
in six months!) My almost-sister-in-law Julie Taubman introduced
me to the best minds in cancer treatment and insisted that I celebrate my hair falling out with a trip to her home on Long Island.
Joe Robert made sure that I had medical consultations with the
National Institutes of Health. Rob and Cheri Arkley welcomed me
to their home in California.

Drs. Russell Bridges and James Ramey were both godsends. Drs.
William Grace, Marc Lipmann, and my personal oncologist Fred

Smith helped me navigate the confusing world of cancer treatment. My surgeon Kathy Alley made the scary stuff seem less so. I thank God for Dr. Adam Brufsky, who was listening to my show when I announced my illness, and who allays my fears when I call in a panic about some new pain. Nurses who work in oncology are amazing people, too—and somehow the ones who worked for Fred always made me laugh, even when my veins kept collapsing.

Power to the People would not have been possible without regular input from my friend Stephen Vaughn, who is (almost) always right on the big issues. From day one, he was there to offer suggestions and cheer me on.

Then there's Raymond. Raymond Arroyo, more than anyone, helped me by providing intellectual guidance, editing help, and a constant stream of one-liners. "It was a dream in my head," but now it's a book.

New friends Phil and Rachel Lerman regularly remind me that Democrats make good friends, too.

I owe thanks to Marji Ross, the president of Regnery Publishing, who pushed me to take the writing plunge again; Harry Crocker and Tim Carney, who helped shepherd this project through with careful editing and research help; Kate Frantz, who had the unenviable task of deciphering my last-minute edits; and Patricia Jackson for organizing the *Power to the People* tour across America.

My producers Matt Fox, A.J. Rice, and Joe Vollono, and intern Brad Feldman all helped out and put up with me through this project. Rebecca Hagelin provided great family anecdotes. This book, like my radio show, is a team effort, and I have a great team. Thanks also to everyone at Talk Radio Network and its president Mark Masters. And of course, my listeners—my extended family— make it fun to sit behind the microphone every day. Thank you.

God has given me a second chance. I hope I am worthy of it.

NOTES

CHAPTER ONE: POWER TO THE FAMILY

1. Phillip Longman, "The Return of Patriarchy," *Foreign Policy* (March/April 2006).
2. Ibid.
3. Ibid. (emphasis added).
4. Ibid.
5. Ibid.
6. Ibid.
7. Ibid.
8. Press release, "Child Care Linked to Assertive, Noncompliant, and Aggressive Behaviors," National Institutes of Health, National Institute of Child Health and Human Development, July 16, 2003.
9. "The State of Our Unions: the Social Health of Marriage in America, 2006." A report from the National Marriage Project, Rutgers University. Http:/marriage.rutgers.edu.
10. David Brooks, "Mosh Pit Meets Sandbox," *New York Times*, February 25, 2007.
11. Ibid.

12. Judith Warner, "Hot Tots, and Moms Hot to Trot," *New York Times*, March 17, 2007.

13. Ibid.

14. Ibid.

15. See http://www.hbo.com/biglove/ (last visited March 24, 2007).

16. David Blankenhorn, *The Future of Marriage* (New York: Encounter Books, March 14, 2007).

17. William J. Doherty, et al., "Why Marriage Matters: Twenty-One Conclusions from the Social Sciences," Institute for American Values, 2002.

18. Tim Leslie, "The Case Against Same Sex Marriage," *Crisis Magazine* 22, no. 1 (January, 2004): 28-31.

19. David Blankenhorn, "Defining Marriage Down," *Weekly Standard*, Vol. 12 Issue 28, April 2, 2007.

20. Pope John Paul II, "World Message of Peace," 2005.

21. Cheryl Wetzen, "Youths Fear Decay of Family," *Washington Times*, April 27, 2007.

22. "Convention on the Rights of the Child," UNICEF, http://www.unicef.org/crc.

23. "Convention on the Rights of the Child," Part I, Article 13.

24. Ibid.

25. "Key Points on the Alternative Minimum Tax," Urban-Brookings Tax Policy Center, (January 21, 2004). Available at http://www.brookings.edu (last visited April 14, 2007).

26. Ibid.

27. Sheen said this on the television show *Entertainment Tonight* in February, 1996 according to Arlene Vigoda, "Marriage Doesn't a-Peele," *USA Today*, February 20, 1996.

28. Charlene Wear Simmons, Ph.D., "State Grounds for Divorce: A Brief History,"California Research Bureau, California State Library. Http://www.library.ca.gov/CRB/98/04/stateground.pdf.

29. Ibid.

30. Elizabeth Schoenfeld, "Drumbeats for Divorce Reform," *Policy Review* (May and June 1996), available at http://www.hoover.org/publications/policyreview/3583026.html (last visited April 25, 2007).

31. Ibid.

32. "State Grounds for Divorce: A Brief History"

33. "The State of our Unions: The Social Health of Marriage in America, 2006."

34. Leah Ward Sears "The Case for Strengthening Marriage" *Washington Post*, October 30, 2006, A17.

CHAPTER TWO: DON'T FENCE ME IN...BUT PLEASE FENCE THEM OUT

1. Theodore Roosevelt, to the president of the American Defense Society, January 3, 1919; last message, read at meeting in New York, January 5, 1919, Mem. Ed. XXIV, 554; Bishop II, 474.

2. Ibid.

3. Michelle Malkin, "Welcome to Reconquista," www.michelle-malkin.com/archives/004848.htm.

4. In Feburary 2007, a spokesman for the Smithfield Packing Co., in Tar Heel, North Carolina, reported that hundreds of workers began failing to show up for work after the company started a process to verify the Social Security numbers used by 500 to 600 workers. Associated Press, Feburary 19, 2007.

5. President Theodore Roosevelt, "Letter," *Kansas City Star*, December 1, 1917.

6. Karin Brulliard, "Latino Groups Lobby for More Rights," *Washington Post*, February 6, 2007.

7. Ibid.

8. Edward Wyatt, "From the 'Dog Whisperer,' a Howl of Triumph," *New York Times*, May 23, 2006.

9. Karl Rove, "Keynote Address, Hillsdale College's Churchill Dinner," Washington, D.C., December 4, 2006.

10. Howard Pankratz, "Gomez-Garcia Gets the Max: 80 Years," *Denver Post*, October 26, 2006.

11. Thomas J. Lueck and Colin Moynihan, "Man Held Without Bail in Murder of Actress," *New York Times*, November 7, 2006.

12. Press Release, "One Man Arrested for Rape," Shreveport (La.) Police Department, October 2, 2006.

13. Familysecuritymatters.org.

14. "Information on Certain Illegal Aliens Arrested in the United States," U.S. Government Accountability Office, May 9, 2005, available at http://www.gao.gov/new.items/d05646r.pdf.

15. Heather Mac Donald, "The Illegal-Alien Crime Wave," *City Journal*, Winter 2004. Available online at: http://www.city-journal.org/html/14_1_the_illegal_alien.html.

16. Patrick McGreevy and Richard Winton, "L.A. Police Immigrant Policy Faces Another Test," *Los Angeles Times*, April 11, 2007.

17. Heather Mac Donald, "The Illegal-Alien Crime Wave," *City Journal*, Winter 2004. Available online at: http://www.city-journal.org/html/14_1_the_illegal_alien.html.

18. Yolanda Woodlee, "The Hunt for Work Fosters Tension," *Washington Post*, January 26, 2007.

19. Selim Algar, "Outcry over Immigrant Pickup Spot in Southampton," *New York Post*, March 12, 2007.

20. President George W. Bush, "A Nation of Immigrants and Laws," May 15, 2006.

21. Liza Porteus, "States Grapple with In-State Tuition for Illegal Immigrants," FOXNews.com, March 6, 2006.

22. Richard Lapper, "US Migrant Workers Send Home $62.3 bn," *Financial Times*, March 15, 2007.

23. Joel Mowbray, "Open Door for Saudi Terrorists," *National Review*, July 1, 2002.

24. "The 2006 Elections: State by State; West," *New York Times*, November 9, 2006.

25. President George W. Bush, Signing Ceremony, Homeland Security Appropriations Act, October 18, 2006.

CHAPTER THREE: PROTECTING THE PEOPLE

1. Second debate between Al Gore and George Bush, October 11, 2000. Available online at: http://www.debates.org/pages/ trans2000b.html.

2. Condoleezza Rice, "Campaign 2000: Promoting the National Interest," *Foreign Affairs*, January/February 2000.

3. Ibid.

4. This exact quotation comes from the president's press conference on December 15, 2003. He has delivered variations of the line numerous times.

5. George W. Bush, Press Conference of the President, December 13, 2003, http://www.whitehouse.gov/news/releases/2003/12/ 20031215-3.html.

6. "Saddam Hussein's Defiance of the United Nations Resolutions," Policies and Initiatives, The White House, http://www. whitehouse.gov/infocus/iraq/decade/sect2.html.

7. See "The Index of Global Philanthropy, 2006," The Hudson Institute. Available at: http://gpr.hudson.org/files/publications/ GlobalPhilanthropy.pdf.

8. Thom Shanker and David Cloud, "Military Wants More Civilians to Help in Iraq," *New York Times*, February 7, 2007.

9. "Iran Responsible for 1983 Marine Barracks Bombing, Judge Rules," CNN.com, May 30, 2003. Available at: http://www. cnn.com/2003/LAW/05/30/iran.barracks.bombing/.

10. See the Department of State web page on the embassy bombing: http://usinfo.state.gov/is/international_security/terrorism/ embassy_bombings.html.

11. See the Department of State web page on the U. S. S. *Cole* attack: http://usinfo.state.gov/is/international_security/ terrorism/uss_cole.html.

12. "Last World Trade Center Bombing Conspirator Sentenced," CNN.com, April 3, 1998, available at: http://www.cnn.com/ US/9804/03/wtc.bombing/.

13. Quoted from "Osama bin Laden vs. the U.S.: Edicts and Statements," PBS *Frontline*: http://www.pbs.org/wgbh/pages/ frontline/shows/binladen/who/edicts.html.

14. March, 1997 CNN interview with Peter Arnett, as quoted on PBS *Frontline*'s website: http://www.pbs.org/wgbh/pages/front-line/shows/binladen/who/edicts.html.

15. Dave Clark, "Iraq's Shiites Gather for Massive Pro-Hezbollah March," Agence France Presse, August 3, 2006.

16. You can see a translated version of this poll at: http://little-greenfootballs.com/weblog/?entry=22524_Al_Jazeera_ Arabic_Poll-_49.9%25_Support_Osama_Bin_Laden&only.

17. "Attitudes to Living in Britain—A Survey of Muslim Opinion," http://www.imaginate.uk.com/MCC01_SURVEY/Site% 20Download.pdf.

18. "The Great Divide: How Westernerns and Muslims View Each Other," Pew Global Attitudes Project, June 22, 2006. Http:// pewglobal.org/reports/display.php?ReportID=253.

19. Pew Global Attitudes Project, "The Great Divide: How Westerners and Muslims View Each Other," released June 22, 2006.

20. Irwan Firdaus, "Iran's President Says Not Afraid of Attack by the United States," Associated Press Worldstream, May 12, 2006.

21. Porter Goss, "Testimony Before the Senate Armed Services Committee," March 17, 2005.

22. Raphael Minder, et al., "Cheney Questions Chinese Ambitions," *Financial Times*, February 24/25, 2006.

23. Amit Chanda, "EC Chief Sends Tough Message to China on Human Rights and Economy, while General Invokes Nuclear Threat," World Markets Analysis, July 15, 2005.

24. Danny Gittings, "General Zhu Goes Ballistic," *Wall Street Journal*, July 18, 2005.

25. Quoted in Bill Gertz, "China Warns U.S. of Missile Strike; American Ships Heighten Taiwan Tension," *Washington Times*, February 29, 2000.

26. Paula DeSutter, testimony before a hearing of the U.S.-China Economic and Security Review Commission, September 14, 2006.

27. Shirley A. Kan, "China and Proliferation of Weapons of Mass Destruction and Missiles: Policy Issues," Congressional Research Service, December 11, 2006.

28. Alfred de Montesquiou, "Chinese President Pushes Sudan on Darfur," Associated Press, February 2, 2007. Http://www.boston.com/news/world/africa/articles/2007/02/02/chinese_president_hu_jintao_visits_sudan/

29. Peter Goodman, "China Invests Heavily in Sudan's Oil Industry," *Washington Post*, December 23, 2004.

30. Daniel T. Griswold, "Peace on Earth? Try Free Trade Among Men," The Cato Institute, December 28, 2005. Http://www.cato.org/pub_display.php?pub_id=5344.

31. Sebastian Mallaby, "China Plays the Cold War Card in Sudan," *Washington Post*, February 7, 2006.

32. Murray Waas, "Clinton administration failed to monitor China's use of missile-technology exports," http://www.salon.com/news/1998/05/29newsa.html.

33. Shirley A. Kan, "China: Possible Missile Technology Transfers from U.S. Satellite Export Policy—Actions and Chronology," Congressional Research Service, September 5, 2001.

34. Audra Ang, "China Confirms Test of Space Weapon but Denies New Arms Race," *Wilmington Star*, January 24, 2007.

35. See Dr, Lyle Goldstein and Bill Murray,"From Humble Origins: China's Submarine Force Comes of Age," *Undersea Warfare*, Winter 2004.

36. See "Attacking Terrorist Networks at Home and Abroad," The White House, available at: http://www.whitehouse.gov/homeland/progress/attacking.html.

37. Transcript of Press Conference Announcing Florida Terrorism Indictments, Department of Justice, June 23, 2006.

38. Dan Eggen, FBI Agents Still Lacking Arabic Skills, *Washington Post*, October 11, 2006, A01.

39. "Budget, Historical Tables," Budget of the United States Government, (2004), Washington, 45-52.

40. Jim Talent, "More: The Crying Need For a Bigger U.S. Military," *National Review*, March 5, 2007, 30.

41. October 7, 2001, available at: http://archives.cnn.com/2001/WORLD/asiapcf/central/10/07/ret.binladen.transcript/index.html.

42. February 23, 1998, available at: http://www.fas.org/irp/world/para/docs/980223-fatwa.htm.

43. August 1996, available at: http://www.pbs.org/newshour/terrorism/international/fatwa_1996.html.

44. FBI Transcript, Testimony of FBI Director Robert S. Mueller, III, before the Senate Committee on Intelligence of the United States Senate, February 16, 2005.

45. President Ronald Reagan, "Address to the Nation," March 23, 1983.

46. Quoted in: Kiron Skinner, "Reagan's Plan," *Hoover Digest*, 1999, No. 4.
47. President Ronald Reagan, "Speech to the House of Commons," June 8, 1992, available at: http://www.fordham.edu/halsall/mod/1982reagan1.html.

CHAPTER FOUR: JUDGE FOR YOURSELF

1. "President Nominates Harriet Miers as Supreme Court Justice," Press Release, the White House, October 3, 2005
2. Ibid.
3. See the October 2005 archive from the "David Frum" blog at National Review Online, available at: http://frum.nationalreview.com/archives/?q=MjAwNTEw.
4. Charles Krauthammer, "Withdraw this Nominee," *Washington Post*, October 7, 2005.
5. The Editors, "Start Over," National Review Online, October 14, 2005. Available at: http://www.nationalreview.com/editorial/editors200510141544.asp; and William Kristol, "What is to Be Done ... About the Harriet Miers Nomination," *Weekly Standard*, October 17, 2005.
6. "White House Defends Talk of Miers' Religion," CNN.com, October 12, 2005, available at: http://www.cnn.com/2005/POLITICS/10/12/miers.religion/index.html.
7. Special Report with Brit Hume, FOX News Channel, roundtable discussion, October 5, 2005.
8. Harriet Miers, Speech to the Executive Women of Dallas (1993).
9. 5 U.S. 137
10. *Palm Beach County Canvassing Board v. Katherine Harris, Supreme Court of Florida*, November 21, 2000.
11. *Planned Parenthood v. Casey*, June 29, 1992, 505 U.S. 833.
12. Quoted in: Jack Backlin, "Alive and Kicking—A Commentary," September 19, 2005, Slate.

13. Abraham Lincoln, First Inaugural Address, March 4, 1861.

14. Nancy Pelosi, press conference, Washington, D.C., June 30, 2005.

15. *Federalist* 78.

16. *Montoy v. Kansas*, Decision and Order, Remedy, The District Court of Shawnee County, Kansas, Division Six.

17. *Charlie Rose Show*, PBS, October September 26, 2006.

18. 410 U.S. 113.

19. Abortion statistics are available at the Alan Guttmacher Institute's website, www.guttmacher.org.

20. Edward Lazarus, "Liberals, Don't Make Her an Icon," *Washington Post*, July 10, 2003.

21. Alan Dershowitz, *Supreme Injustice: How the High Court Hijacked Election 2000* (London, U.K.: Oxford University Press, 2001), 194.

22. "One of the most curious things about Roe is that, behind its own verbal smokescreen, the substantive judgment on which it rests is nowhere to be found." Laurence Tribe, "The Supreme Court, 1972 Term—Foreword: Toward a Model of Roles in the Due Process of Life and Law," *Harvard Law Review* 1, 7 (1973). Senator Sam Brownback of Kansas cited Ginsberg during the Alito hearings. He quoted her as writing in the North Carolina Law Review in 1985: "*Roe*, I believe, would have been more acceptable as a judicial decision if it had not gone beyond a ruling on the extreme statute before the court. . . . Heavy-handed judicial intervention was difficult to justify and appears to have provoked, not resolved, conflict."

23. These polls and others are available at: http://www.pollingreport.com/abortion.htm.

24. 410 U.S. 179.

25. 530 U.S. 914.

26. Editorial, "Denying the Right to Choose," *New York Times*, April 19, 2007.

27. Editorial, "A U-turn on abortion," *Los Angeles Times*, April 19, 2007.

28. Mark Sherman, "Court Backs Ban on Specific Procedure," Associated Press, April 18, 2007.

29. Center for Responsive Politics, www.Opensecrets.com.

30. 514 U.S. 779.

31. Ibid, Thomas, J., dissenting.

32. This was the language used by Justice William O. Douglas to find a right to privacy in the Constitution that is not there. He wrote in *Griswold v. Connecticut* (1965) that "The foregoing cases suggest that specific guarantees in the Bill of Rights have penumbras, formed by emanations from those guarantees that help give them life and substance. Various guarantees create zones of privacy." This is the language that has allowed the Court do whatever it has wanted to do, because it can always find hidden rights in various unseen "penumbras and emanations."

33. For a brief argument against the idea of birthright citizenship, see: John C. Eastman, "Born in the USA? Rethinking Birthright Citizenship in the Wake of 9/11," testimony before the U.S. House of Representatives, Committee on the Judiciary, Subcommittee on Immigration, Border Security and Claims, September 29, 2005.

34. 542 U.S. 507.

35. Ibid., Scalia, J., dissenting.

36. Available at: http://www.supremecourtus.gov/opinions/05pdf/05-184.pdf.

37. Public Law 109-148 [H.R. 2863, Title X, "Detainee Treatment Act of 2005."]

38. U.S. Constitution, Article I, Section 9.

39. 403 U.S. 602.

40. 505 U.S. 577.

41. 545 U.S. 844.

42. 545 U.S. 677.

43. *Epperson v. Arkansas*, 393 U.S. 97 (1968).

44. Sandra Day O'Connor, remarks before the Southern Center for International Studies, October 28, 2003.

45. 536 U.S. 304.

46. Bureau of Democracy, Human Rights and Labor, Country Report on Human Rights Practices, China, U.S. Department of State. Http://www.state.gov/g/drl/rls/hrrpt/2006/78771.htm.

47. *Roper v. Simmons* 543 U.S. 551.

48. Ibid, Brief of amici curiae President James Earl Carter, Jr. and others (Nobel Peace Prize Laureates) in Support of Respondent, 3.

49. *Roper v. Simmons.*

50. *Grutter v. Bollinger*, 539 U.S. 306.

51. Ruth Bader Ginsburg, " 'A decent Respect to the Opinions of [Human]kind': The Value of a Comparative Perspective in Constitutional Adjudication," Constitutional Court of South Africa, February 7, 2006. Available at http://www.supreme-courtus.gov/publicinfo/speeches/sp_02-07b-06.html.

52. *Grutter v. Bollinger*, 539 U.S. 306 (2003), Ginsburg, J. concurring.

53. 539 U.S. 558.

54. Quoted in: Robert S. Sargent Jr., "The Relevance to Our Constitution of Foreign Law," *Enter Stage Right*, January 31, 2005.

55. McConnell v. Federal Election Commission, 540 U.S. 93, Thomas, J., dissenting.

56. Ibid., Scalia, J., dissenting.

57. *Wisconsin Right to Life v. FEC.* Decided June 25, 2007.

58. 545 U.S. 469.

CHAPTER FIVE: KEEPING IT LOCAL

1. *Texas v. White*, 74 U.S. 700 (1868).

2. For a catalog of recent Supreme Court cases on the death penalty, many of them dealing with Texas, see the Death Penalty Information Center's webpage on the Supreme Court: http://www.deathpenaltyinfo.org/article.php?did=248&scid=38.

3. Alexis de Tocqueville, *Democracy in America*.

4. U.S. Census Bureau, "State Government Tax Collections: 2006," available online at: http:www.census.gov (last visited April 26, 2007).

5. Historical Tables, Budget of the U.S. Government: Fiscal Year 2008.

6. Michael Powell and Michelle Garcia, "Pa. City Puts Illegal Immigrants on Notice," *Washington Post*, August 22, 2006.

7. "Legislative Action Since Kelo," Castle Coalition, January 16, 2007.

8. U.S. Census Bureau, "States Ranked by Total Taxes and Per Capita Amount: 2004" (Revised March 2006), http://www.census.gov/govs/statetax/04staxrank.html.

9. See: http://www.innovations.harvard.edu/awards.html?id=3838.

10. V. Dion Haynes, "Bonuses, Relaxed Rules Proposed," *Washington Post*, June 6, 2006.

11. Jacques Chirac's opening remarks at the 6th Conference of the United Nations Framework Convention on Climate Change at The Hague, November 2000.

12. As quoted in: Peter Henlein, "Climate Panel Recommends Global Temperature Ceiling, Carbon Tax," Voice of America, February 28, 2007.

13. For a comparison of pre-industrial and current greenhouse gas concentrations, see: T.J. Blasing and Karmen Smith, "Recent Greenhouse Gas Concentrations," July 2006, Oak Ridge National Laboratory, Carbon Dioxide Information Analysis Center.

14. Elizabeth Bryant, "Turmoil and Bitterness After the 'Non,'" United Press International, May 29, 2005.

15. "EU Chief Barroso to Host Summit on Troubled Constitution in Portugal," *International Herald Tribune*, April 25, 2007.

16. Ibid.

17. See the OECD's website on taxation, at: http://www.oecd.org/topic/0,2686,en_2649_37427_1_1_1_1_37427,00.html and see the Center for Freedom and Prosperity's Coalition for Tax Competition website: http://www.freedomandprosperity.org/.

18. See "CFP Hails Death of EU Savings Tax Directive," press release, Center for Freedom and Prosperity, July 24, 2002.

19. Associated Press, "Utah Snubs Federal No Child Left Behind Act," MSNBC.com, May 2, 2005, http://www.msnbc.msn.com/id/7713931/.

20. Education Trust Statement, "Utah Must Confront Inequities in Public Education," March 1, 2005.

CHAPTER SIX: CULTURE SHOCK

1. D. Parvaz, "Nudity, Sex Articles in Abercrombie & Fitch 'magalog' Draw Fire, *Seattle Post-Intelligencer*, December 3, 2003.

2. "Children as Young as Six Suffering from Anorexia," *Daily Mail*, March 26, 2007.

3. David Cay Johnston, "Indications of a Slowdown in Sex Entertainment Trade," *New York Times*, January 4, 2007.

4. Ibid.

5. Ibid.

6. Matthew Miller, "The (Porn) Player," *Forbes*, July 4, 2005, 124.

7. "My Bare Lady," FoxReality.com, About the Show.

8. Transcript, *Larry King Live*, November 29, 2005.

9. David Clay Johnston, "Is Live Sex On-Demand Coming to Hotel TVs?," *New York Times*, January 17, 2007.

10. Ibid.

11. Kathleen Deveny with Raina Kelley, "Girls Gone Bad," *Newsweek*, cover story, February 12, 2007.

12. Ibid.

13. "Sexualization of Girls Is Linked to Common Mental Health Problems in Girls and Women—Eating Disorders, Low Self-Esteem, and Depression," APA Press Release, February 19, 2007.

14. "Report, Task Force on the Sexualization of Girls," American Psychological Association, February 19, 2007.

15. Lev Grossman, "Tila Tequila," *Time*, December 16, 2006.

16. Ibid.

17. Ibid.

18. "MySpace Generation," The Urban Post, Http://www.theurbanpost.com/article.php?id=8.

19. Press Release, "New Research Reveals Risky Internet Behavior Among Teens, But There Are Encouraging Signs of Improvement with Increased Involvement of Parents and Guardians," National Center for Missing and Exploited Children, May 10, 2007.

20. Brandon Leonard, "Teens Tackle Online Predators," *Washington Times*, June 28, 2007.

21. Sara Rimer, "For Girls, It's Be Yourself, and Be Perfect, Too," *New York Times*, April 1, 2007.

22. Out-of-wedlock births to girls ages 15-20 are falling, according to the Centers for Disease Control: http://www.cdc.gov/nchs/data/hus/hus06.pdf#010; Teen pregnancy rates are also falling. See: http://www.cdc.gov/nchs/products/pubs/pubd/hestats/teenpreg1990-2002/teenpreg1990-2002.htm.

23. L.D. Johnston et al., "Teen drug use continues down in 2006, particularly among older teens; but use of prescription-type drugs remains high," University of Michigan News and Infor-

mation Services, December 21, 2006. Available online at: www.monitoringthefuture.org.

24. J.C. Abma et al., "Teenagers in the United States: Sexual Activity Contraceptive Use, and Childbearing, 2002," Vital Health Statistics, December 2004.

25. David Clay Johnston, "Is Live Sex On-Demand Coming to Hotel TVs?," *New York Times*, January 17, 2007.

26. Kimberly Palmer, "The Anti-Britney: The New Look," *U.S. News & World Report*, April 15, 2007.

CHAPTER SEVEN: SCHOOL'S OUT...OF CONTROL

1. Four years later, when I was already working for the Reagan administration, all parties settled the suit under seal.

2. Organization for Economic Cooperation and Development, Programme for International Student Assessment, 2003, data available at http://pisacountry.acer.edu.au/.

3. Http://nces.ed.gov/nationsreportcard/pdf/main2005/2007468_2.pdf.

4. See, for example. "Increasing the Odds: How Good Policies Can Yield Better Teachers," National Council on Teacher Quality, available at http://www.nctq.org/nctq/images/nctq_io.pdf.

5. Goldhaber, D.D., & Brewer, D.J. (2000). "Does teacher certification matter? High school teacher certification status and student achievement," *Educational Evaluation and Policy Analysis*, 22, 129-145.

6. Arthur Levine, "Educating School Teachers," The Education Schools Project, September, 2006. Available at http://www. edschools.org/pdf/Educating_Teachers_Report.pdf

7. Http://nces.ed.gov/nationsreportcard/pdf/main2005/2007468_2.pdf.

8. 2006-2007 NEA Resolutions, resolution F-9, available at: http://www.nea.org/annualmeeting/raaction/images/resolutions2006-2007.pdf.
9. Steven G. Rivkin et al., "Teachers, Schools, and Academic Achievement," Econometrica, March 2005.
10. NEA Resolutions, F-16.
11. Daniel de Vise, "Clauses and Commas Make a Comeback," *Washington Post*, October 23, 2006.
12. "The Vent," *Atlanta Journal-Constitution*, March 28, 2007.
13. Candy Dawson Boyd, et al., *Social Studies People and Places*, 2005, Scott Foresman, 2005.
14. Http://nymag.com/listings/attraction/jacob-k-javits-convention-center/.
15. Diane Ravitch, Testimony before the Senate Committee on Health, Education, Labor, and Pensions, September 24, 2003.
16. David Francis, "Concerns Raised Over Alexandria Sex Education Curriculum Guide," *Washington Examiner*, January 12, 2007.
17. Jonathan Saltzman, "Judge Dismisses Lexington Suit Over School Lesson Involving Same-Sex Couples," *Boston Globe*, February 23, 2007.
18. Memorandum and Order, Parker v. Hurley, United States District Court, District of Massachusetts, Feburary 23, 2007, available at http://pacer.mad.uscourts.gov/dc/cgi-bin/recentops.pl?filename=wolf/pdf/parker%20opinion%20mlw.pdf.
19. Marjorie King, "Queering the Schools," *City Journal*, Spring, 2006.
20. Ibid.
21. Ibid.
22. Hillary D. Rodham, Commencement Speech, Wellesley College, May 31, 1969. Available at http://www.wellesley.edu/PublicAffairs/Commencement/1969/053169hillary.html.

23. Daniel Klein, "Ideology of Faculty in the Social Sciences and Humanities," http://lsb.scu.edu/~dklein/survey/KleinPresentationOnIdeologyofFaculty.pdf.

24. David Horowitz and Eli Lehrer, "Political Bias in the Administrations and Faculties of 32 Elite Colleges and Universities," Center for the Study of Popular Culture, http://www.frontpagemag.com/Content/read.asp?ID=55.

25. Michael Berube, *What's Liberal About the Liberal Arts: Classroom Politics and "Bias" in Higher Education* (New York: W.W. Norton & Co, 2006).

26. Dana Cloud, "UT Professor on Terrorism," September 13, 2001, available at http://www.progressiveaustin.org/danaclou.htm.

27. Ibid.

28. Quoted in: Jay Nordlinger, "The Luxury of a Movie Star, the Democrats' Odd Glee, Decapitating Margaret, &c.," National Review Online, July 8, 2002.

29. Lisa Black, "Gay Awareness Panel Roils School," *Chicago Tribune*, March 8, 2007.

30. "Parents in Dark on Gay Class," *Washington Times*, March 16, 2007.

31. National Center for Education Statistics, Department of Education.

32. Michele Norris, "New Orleans Students Describe Coping After Katrina," National Public Radio, "All Things Considered," March 1, 2006.

33. Nichole Stricker, "Volunteers Claim Enough Support to Oppose School Choice," *Salt Lake Tribune*, April 9, 2007.

CHAPTER EIGHT: THE REVENGE OF THE "LOUD FOLKS"

1. "Verizon Drops Pop Singer from Ads," Jeff Leeds, *New York Times*, May 10, 2007.

2. "Rated PG with No Dirty Dancing," Kelefa Sanneh, *New York Times*, May 21, 2007.

3. Available at: http://www.cbsnews.com/stories/2004/09/08/60II/main641984.shtml.

4. Available at: http://www.freerepublic.com/focus/f-news/1210662/replies?c=47.

5. Http://littlegreenfootballs.com/weblog/?entry=12551_One_More_CBS_Document_Example&only.

6. Charles Johnson's catalogue of the "Fauxtography Scandal" is available at: http://littlegreenfootballs.com/weblog/?entry=22391_Fauxtography_Updates&only. Michelle Malkin's coverage is here: http://michellemalkin.com/archives/2006_08.htm.

7. Matthew Currier Burden, *The Blog of War*, (New York: Simon and Schuster, 2006).

8. These reports are all collected in: John E. O'Neill and Jerome R. Corsi, *Unfit for Command*, (Washington, D.C.: Regnery, 2004).

9. Michael Dobbs, "Swift Boat Accounts Incomplete," *Washington Post*, August 22, 2004; "Connections and Contradictions," *New York Times*, August 19, 2004.

10. "Statistics," Sentry PC, Http://www.sentrypc.com/statistics.htm.

11. "The Structural Imbalance of Political Talk Radio," Center for American Progress, June 20, 2007. Available at http://www.aclu.org/freespeech/internet/onlinefreespeech.html.

12. "Transcript of the First Lady's Press Briefing on Millennium Project Part 5 of 6," U.S. Newswire, February 11, 1998.

13. One summary of Chinese Internet censorship is "People's Republic of China: Controls tighten as Internet activism grows," Amnesty International, http://web.amnesty.org/library/Index/ENGASA170012004.

14. Tunisian Internet censorship is covered in: "False Freedom: Online Censorship in the Middle East and North Africa," Human Rights Watch. http://hrw.org/reports/2005/mena1105/.

15. See the comments of Senator Norm Coleman at "Let the UN Govern the Internet?" Heritage Foundation, November 17, 2005. http://www.heritage.org/press/events/ev111705c.cfm.

16. Declan McCullagh, "The Coming Crackdown on Blogging," CINet News.com, March 3, 2005, http://news.com.com/ The + coming + crackdown + on + blogging/2008-1028_3- 5597079.html.

17. Gilbert Cranberg, "Proposed Shield Law Comes Close to Government Licensing of Reporters," Nieman Watchdog, August 8, 2006. Http://www.niemanwatchdog.org/index.cfm?fuseaction=background.view&backgroundid=00113.

18. Peter Sayer, "France Bans Citizen Journalists from Reporting Violence," IDG News Service, http://www.macworld.com/ news/2007/03/06/franceban/index.php?lsrc=mwrss.

19. Check out the surface temperature analysis at http://data.giss. nasa.gov/cgi-bin/gistemp/gistemp_station.py?id= 700890090008&data_set=1&num_neighbors=1.

CHAPTER NINE: BLINDING US WITH SCIENCE

1. Josh Drobnyk, "Allentown Students Join March Against Roe v. Wade," *The Morning Call of Allentown*, January 23, 2007.

2. "Babies Aborted for not Being Perfect," *Daily Mail*, March 30, 2005.

3. Joanna Jepson, "Murder, Even 'In Good Faith', Is Still Murder," *Telegraph*, March 20, 2005.

4. Caruso TM, Westgate MN, Holmes LB, "Impact of prenatal screening on the birth status of fetuses with Down syndrome at an urban hospital, 1972–1994," *Genetics in Medicine* 1998; 1:22–8.

5. These statistics are available at: http://www.nrlc.org/abortion/ facts/abortionstats2.html.

6. These statistics are available from the Alan Guttmacher Institute. See "Reasons U.S. Women Have Abortions: Quantitative and Qualitative Perspectives," Perspectives on Sexual and Reproductive Health, 2005. Available at: http://www. guttmacher.org/pubs/journals/3711005.pdf.

7. Ryan D. Pittman, "Ritalin Prescriptions on the Rise," *Daily Texan*, November 2, 2000.

8. Quoted in David Cannadine, ed., *Blood, Toil, Tears and Sweat: The Speeches of Winston Churchill* (Boston: Houghton Mifflin, 1989), 130–31.

9. C.S. Lewis, *Abolition of Man* (San Francisco: Harper, 2001).

10. Ellen Goodman, "No Change in Political Climate," *Boston Globe*, February 9, 2007.

11. Arlen Specter on the Senate floor, March 16, 2005, Congressional Record, 2764.

12. Jo Mannies, "Fox Visit Shows How Stem Cells are Tangled up with Senate Race," *St. Louis Post-Dispatch*, October 5, 2006.

13. "Human Cloning and Human Dignity: An Ethical Inquiry," The President's Council on Bioethics, July 2002, Chapter 3. Available at http://www.bioethics.gov/reports/cloningreport/ terminology.html.

14. Claudia Joseph, "Now Scientists Create a Sheep That's 15% Human," *The Mail*, March 27, 2007.

15. Robert D. Novak, "Christopher Reeve Republicans," *Chicago Sun-Times*, February 5, 2003.

16. Karen Hosler, "Stem Cell Study Limited; President Decides to Restrict Federal Funding for Research," *Baltimore Sun*, August 10, 2001.

17. Senator John Kerry, "Democratic Response to the President's Weekly Radio Address," August 7, 2004.

18. Quoted in, Jay Ambrose, "Democrats Offer 'False Hope' with Stem Cell Promises," Scripps Howard News Service, October 13, 2004.

19. Paul Long, "State Law Respects Life, Science," *Detroit Free Press*, February 10, 2006.

20. "Detailed Summary of Committee Disclosure Report," Mo. Coalition for Lifesaving Cures, available at: http://www.mec. mo.gov/CampaignFinanceReports/CFFilerHTML/ ReportMenu/SummaryCDSum.asp.

21. "Detailed Summary of Committee Disclosure Report," Mo. Coalition for Lifesaving Cures, available at: http://www.mec. mo.gov/CampaignFinanceReports/CFFilerHTML/ReportMenu/ SummaryCD1.asp?CDRCP_id=16697&MECID=C051219& MyYear=2006&Com=MO%20COALITION%20FOR%20 LIFESAVING%20CURES.

22. Jason Gertzen, "Bringing the Biomed World to KC's Door," *Kansas City Star*, March 18, 2007.

23. Ron Reagan, speech at Democratic National Convention, July 27, 2004, available at: http://politicalgateway.com/news/read. html?id=535.

24. See the U.S. State Department 2006 Country Reports on Human Rights for India and the People's Republic of China. Available at http://www.state.gov/g/drl/rls/hrrpt/2006.

25. Jamie Talan, "Classic Nordic Traits Top Sell," *Times Union* (Albany, New York), June 5, 2005.

26. Ibid.

27. James Watson, "Children from the Laboratory," *Prism*, May 1973.

28. Margaret Sanger, "The Function of Sterilization," *The Birth Control Review*, October 1926, 299.

29. Peter Singer, "The Sanctity of Life," *Foreign Policy*, September 1, 2005.

30. For abortion statistics, see: http://www.nrlc.org/abortion/facts/ abortionstats.html; For single parent statistics, see: http:// www.ofm.wa.gov/trends/tables/fig204.asp.

31. April M. Washington, "Emergency Contraception Measure Becomes Law," *Rocky Mountain News*, March 16, 2007.

32. "Percentage of Births to Unmarried Women," Child Trends Data Bank, available at http://www.childtrendsdatabank.org/indicators/75UnmarriedBirths.cfm.

33. Matthew Herper, "Fastest-Growing Plastic Surgeries," Forbes.com, May 15, 2006.

34. Source: American Society for Aesthetic Plastic Surgery, available at http://cosmeticplasticsurgerystatistics.com/statistics.html.

35. Jennifer Harper, "Moms Opt for Nip/Tuck," March 23, 2007, *Washington Times*.

36. Sandra G. Boodman, "Cosmetic Surgery's New Frontier," *Washington Post*, March 6, 2007.

37. *Health United States*, 2004, Centers for Disease Control.

38. Richard M. Scheffler, et. al., "The Global Market for ADHD Medications," *Health Affairs*, March/April 2007.

39. "Mental Health in the United States: Prevalence of Diagnosis and Medication Treatment for Attention-Deficit/Hyperactivity Disorder, United States, 2003," Centers for Disease Control, September 2, 2005.

40. Jenny Hope, "The Great ADHD Myth," *Daily Mail*, March 9, 2007.

41. Maria Cramer and Raja Mishra, "Girl Fed Fatal Overdoses, Court Told," *Boston Globe*, February 7, 2007.

42. "Wasting the Best and Brightest," The National Center on Addiction and Substance Abuse at Columbia University, March 2007.

43. Available at http://www.oas.samhsa.gov/NSDUH/2k5NSDUH/2k5results.htm.

44. See: http://www.cdc.gov/omh/Highlights/2006/HSept06YRBSS.htm.

45. Richard Lindzen, "Climate of Fear," Wall Street Journal, April 12, 2006.

46. Survey USA poll, October 21 to October 23, 2004., available at http://www.surveyusa.com/client/PollReportEmail.aspx?g= 078e65d9-7cd0-4f86-bf71-adcc760b51f2.

47. "Abortion Ultrasound Bill Advances in S.C." CBS/AP, March 21, 2007. Available at http://www.cbsnews.com/stories/2007/ 03/21/national/main2593092.shtml.

48. Pat Wingert, "The Baby Who's Not Supposed to Be Alive," *Newsweek*, February 23, 2007.

CHAPTER TEN: TAKING THE REAL POWER TRIP

1. Lord Acton, J.Rufus Fears, ed., *Essays in Religion, Politics, and Morality; Selected Writings of Lord Acton* (Indianapolis: Liberty Classic, 1988.

2. *The Writings of Samuel Adams*, ed., Harry Alonzo Cushing (G. P. Putman's Sons, 1908), Vol. 4, 124.

3. George Washington, "Farewell Address," in W.B. Allen, ed., *George Washington: A Collection* (Indianapolis: Liberty Classics, 1988), 521-522.

4. *Anderson Cooper 360°*, CNN, March 30, 2007.

5. Gary Wolf, "The Church of the Non-Believers," *Wired*, November 2006.

6. Dr. Francis Collins, "Collins: Why This Scientist Believes In God," CNN.Com, April 6, 2007.

7. Marianne Meed Ward, "Chocolate's too hot," *The Toronto Sun*, April 8, 2007.

8. Ian Mohr, "Maher mapping 'Journey'," *Variety*, June 7, 2006.

9. John Adams, "Letter to the Officers of the First Brigade of the 3rd Div. of the Militia of Massachusetts," October 11, 1798.

10. *C.S Lewis Reading and Meditations*, Walter Hooper, ed. 1992, Harper Collins San Francisco.

11. President Dwight D. Eisenhower, June 14, 1954, as the words "under God" were added to the Pledge of Allegiance.

12. Jackie Mason and Raoul Felder, "Christmas, Let It Be," *Catalyst* Jan-Feb 2007.

13. John Antczak, "ACLU Demands Removal of Cross from Los Angeles County Seal," Associated Press, September 9, 2004.

14. President Ronald Reagan, "Remarks at the Annual Convention of the National Religious Broadcasters," January 31, 1983.

15. President Harry Truman, in Alan Sears and Craig Oston, *The ACLU vs. America* (Nashville, TN: Broadman and Holman Publishers, 2005), 143.

16. Oswald Chambers, *My Utmost for His Highest* (Grand Rapids, MI: Discovery House Publishers, 1992).

17. Billy Graham, *Hope for Each Day* (Nashville, TN: Countryman, 2002), 191.

18. President Ronald Reagan, in Paul Kengor, *God and Ronald Reagan* (New York: HarperCollins, 2004), 165.

19. Andrew Carroll, "Why We Pray," *Wall Street Journal*, March 9, 2007.

20. Mother Teresa, *A Simple Path* (New York: Ballantine Books, 1995), 99.

21. Michael Novak, *On Two Wings* (San Francisco: Encounter Books, 2002), 18.

22. Gen. George Washington, General Order, July 9, 1776, quoted in *A Brief History of the U.S. Army Chaplain Corps*, available at: http://www.usachcs.army.mil/HISTORY/Brief/TitlePage.htm.

23. President Ronald Reagan, "Remarks at Notre Dame," May 17, 1981.

INDEX

A

ABC, 13–15, 169

Abercrombie & Fitch (A&F), 163–64

abortion, 4, 38, 128; Constitution, U.S. and, 107, 112, 113; Democrats and, 114; *Doe v. Bolton* and, 112, 124; local control and, 156; "morning after" pill and, 272–73; partial-birth, 104–5, 113; physical health problems and, 257–58; *Roe v. Wade* and, 111–14, 124, 139; science and, 257–58, 269–70, 282; Supreme Court, U.S. and, 7, 104–5, 107, 108, 111–14, 124, 139

Abraham Center of Life, 271

Abramoff, Jack, 65

Access Hollywood, 174, 175

ACLU. *See* American Civil Liberties Union

Acton, Lord, 288

Adams, John, 298

Adams, Samuel, 288

ADD. *See* Attention Deficit Disorder

ADHD. *See* Attention Deficit Hyperactive Disorder

adult entertainment industry, 169–74; empowerment and, 171–72; family and, 172; Internet and, 169, 170; media and, 171. *See also* pornography

advertising, sex in, 161–64

affirmative action: Constitution, U.S. and, 131; international law and, 124; Supreme Court, U.S. and, 124, 131

Afghanistan, 116, 123

African Americans, family and, 33

AFT. *See* American Federation of Teachers

Aguilar, David, 58

Aguilera, Christina, 177

Ahmadinejad, Mahmoud, 83, 84, 293

Akon, 168, 182, 235–38, 242

Aldrete-Davila, Osbaldo, 53–54
Alito, Samuel, 102, 104, 105, 113, 130
al Jazeera, 82
Alliance for the Separation of School and State, 225
Almihdhar, Khalid, 56, 59
al Qaeda, 58, 61, 80, 83, 89, 96, 214, 292
Alternative Minimum Tax (AMT), 34
Amazing Grace, 185
America: defense of, 6, 316–18; God, belief in and, 316–18; Israel and, 82; jihad against, 80–83; Muslims in, 83, 90; national security and, 6; religion in, 10–11; religious heritage of, 118–22, 302; trade with China of, 86–89
American Birth Control League, 271
American Civil Liberties Union (ACLU), 90; America's Judeo-Christian moral heritage and, 121; church and state, separation of and, 301; God, belief in and, 10; illegal immigration and, 63; political speech and, 126; pornography and, 302; prayer in schools and, 119; sex education and, 207
American Civil Rights Institute, 131
American Council of Trustees and Alumni, 210
American Federation of Teachers (AFT), 199, 200
American Pie, 170, 182
American Psychological Association (APA), 25, 176, 177
American Society for Aesthetic Plastic Surgery, 275

Americans United for the Separation of Church and State, 301
amnesty. *See* illegal immigration
AMT. *See* Alternative Minimum Tax
Anderson, Pamela, 274
Angelica, Mother, 308
APA. *See* American Psychological Association
Apocalyptic Manmade Global Warming, 278, 279, 280
Aquinas, St. Thomas, 294
Aristotle, 210
Army Wives, 22
Arpaio, Joseph, 51, 143
Associated Press, 50, 114
Atkins v. Virginia, 123
Atlanta Journal-Constitution, 202
Attention Deficit Disorder (ADD), 277
Attention Deficit Hyperactive Disorder (ADHD), 277
Austen, Jane, 211
AVN Media Network, 169

B
babble.com, 24
The Bachelor, 180–81
Baigent, Michael, 290
Ball, Timothy, 280
Baltimore Sun, 266
Bank of America, 59
Barletta, Lou, 143
Barnes, Fred, 104
Bates, Stephen, 79
Bay, Michael, 259
Beethoven, Ludwig von, 299
Bennett, Bill, 143
Berube, Michael, 212
Bible, 295, 312
Big Brother, 180

Big Love, 28
Big Oak Boys' Ranch, 39–40
Big Oak Girls' Ranch, 39–40
Bilbray, Brian, 65
Bill of Rights, 140, 304
bin Laden, Osama, 80, 81–83, 86, 94, 117
"Bipartisan Campaign Finance Reform Act." *See* McCain-Feingold campaign law (2001)
birth control. *See* contraception
Black and Blue (Quindlen), 22
Blackburn, Marsha, 64
BlackFive, 240
Blackmun, Harry, 111
Blades of Glory, 171
Blair, Charlotte, 57
Blair, Tony, 93–94
Blankenhorn, David, 28
blogging, 237; conservatives and, 8; fact checking and, 238–42; Iraq war and, 240–41; media, liberal monopoly of and, 238–42; Supreme Court nominations and, 105
The Blog of War (Burden), 240
Bloomberg, Michael, 55
Bombeck, Erma, 24–25
border control. *See* illegal immigration
Border Patrol, U.S., 41, 47
Bork, Robert, 103, 105, 129–30
Boston Globe, 255, 262
Boxer, Barbara, 80
The Boys from Brazil, 264–65
Bozell, Brent, 194
Brandeis, Louis, 141
Brewer, Dominic, 200
Breyer, Stephen, 120–21

Britain: London subway bombing (2005) in, 82; Muslims in, 79, 82; War on Terror and, 82
Broaddrick, Juanita, 233
Brooks, David, 24
Brothers & Sisters, 14–15
The Brothers Karamazov (Dostoevsky), 17
Brown, Dan, 290
Brown, Janice Rogers, 102
Brown University, 210, 212, 226
Bryant, Bear, 39–40
Buchanan, Pat, 43, 179
Burden, Matthew, 240
Burger, Warren, 119
Burress, Phil, 193–94
Bush, George H. W., 102
Bush, George W., 18, 97; campaign finance reform and, 126, 131; Communist China and, 84, 86; education and, 149; embryonic stem cell research and, 266, 267; foreign policy and, 74, 77, 78–79; illegal immigration and, 45–48, 50, 52, 55, 68, 246; National Guard memo and, 238–39; No Child Left Behind Act and, 149, 220–21; pornography and, 188; Supreme Court nominations of, 101–5, 128; taxation and, 153; war memorials and, 302; War on Terror and, 117
Bush v. Gore, 111
Byrne, Rhonda, 299–300

C

cable television: media, Left monopoly on and, 7–8; Supreme Court nominations and, 105; tabloidization of news on, 164

CAIR. *See* Council on American-Islamic Relations

Calderon, Felipe, 48

California: divorce in, 36; illegal immigration and, 50, 52, 63, 142

California, University of, 31

California, University of, Berkeley, 211

California Proposition 187, 142

California Proposition 209, 131

Cameron, James, 290–92

campaign finance reform: Constitution, U.S. and, 131; McCain-Feingold campaign law (2001), 125, 126, 131, 250; Supreme Court, U.S. and, 125, 131

capital punishment. *See* death penalty

Capus, Steve, 234

Carter, Jimmy, 91, 123, 203, 314

Carter, Rosalynn, 204–5

Caruso, David, 179

Castro, Fidel, 84

Catholic Church: Ingraham, Laura and, 307–8; "morning after" pill and, 272–73

Catholic League, 293

Cato Institute, 60, 87

Cavallaro, Cosimo, 292–93

Cavuto, Neil, 172

CBS, 52, 169

CBS Evening News, 42

CBS News, 231–32

CDC. *See* Centers for Disease Control

celebrity obsession, 158–59, 174–78

censorship, 161

Center for American Progress, 248

Center for Cultural Reporting and Criticism (NYU), 30

Center for Trade Policy Studies (Cato Institute), 87

Centers for Disease Control (CDC), 276, 278

Central Intelligence Agency (CIA), 91

Chambers, Oswald, 309

Charlie Rose show, 109

Chavez, Cesar, 205, 251

Chavez, Hugo, 84

Chavez, Linda, 45

Cheney, Dick, 84, 86

Cheney, Lynne, 220

Chesterton, G. K., 294

Chicago, University of, 226

Chicago Tribune, 219

Child Online Protection Act, 188

children: day care, effects of on, 23; divorce and, 36; environmentalism and, 16; family and, 27–32, 33; feminists and, 23; government protection of, 188–90; health care and, 16; immigration laws and, 16; Left and, 16, 18; marriage and, 28–30; over-medication of, 276–78; parents, influence of on, 40; science and, 260; society and, 32; taxation and, 16

China, 91, 99, 123; American trade with, 86–89; as global superpower, 6, 89; nuclear weapons and, 85; space, militarizing and, 88; threat of, 84–86

Chirac, Jacques, 150, 152

Churchill, Ward, 212–13, 216

Churchill, Winston, 261

CIA. *See* Central Intelligence Agency

Cipollone, Pat, 307

The Citadel, 226

Citibank, 59

Citizens for Community Values, 193–94

City Journal, 209

civil rights movement, 141

Clark, Laura, 204

Clayman, Gregory, 174

Cleanhotels.com, 193–94

CLEAR Act, 55

Clinton, Bill, 212; China and, 86, 88; foreign policy and, 74, 75–76; military and, 91; sex scandals of, 192, 233, 249; welfare and, 146

Clinton, Hillary Rodham, 128, 170, 190, 249; family and, 31–32; Kyoto Protocol and, 151; "morning after" pill and, 272; universities, decline of and, 210

cloning, 4; Dolly the sheep and, 265; embryonic stem cell research and, 263, 264–65, 268, 281; reproductive, 264; SCNT and, 264–65; therapeutic, 264

Close, Sandy, 31

Cloud, Dana, 213–14

ClubJenna, 171

CNBC, 172

CNN, 112, 164, 173, 212, 231, 292

Cohen, Sacha Baron, 297

Cold War, 84, 98, 316–17

Cole, USS, 80

Cole, William, 196–97

College of William and Mary, 303

College Republicans, 215

colleges. *See* universities

Collins, Francis, 294–95

Commerce Department, U.S., 88

Communism, 261

Communist China. *See* China

Communist Party of China, 87

Compean, Jose, 53–54

Competitive Enterprise Institute, 280

Concerned Women for America, 176, 219

Congressional Research Service, 85, 88

Connerly, Ward, 131, 228

conservatism, conservatives: blogging and, 8; Bush, George W., Supreme Court nominations and, 101, 103; embryonic stem cell research and, 266–67; family and, 19; foreign policy and, 75; hate speech and, 214–16; media, new and, 7–8; Supreme Court, U.S. and, 104, 105; talk radio and, 8; at universities, 214–16

Constitution, U.S.: abortion and, 107, 112, 113; affirmative action and, 131; America's Judeo-Christian moral heritage and, 121; Bill of Rights, 140, 304; campaign finance reform and, 131; Establishment Clause of, 118–22, 301; faithfulness to, 102, 103, 106, 129; Fifth Amendment, 145; First Amendment, 118–22; Founding Fathers and, 102, 107, 154; Fourteenth Amendment, 139; local control and, 140; originalism and, 102; "penumbras and emanations" of, 116; pornography and, 302; prayer in schools and, 122; property rights and, 127; religion and, 301, 304; Supreme Court, U.S. and, 104, 106–8, 109, 111, 122–25, 137; Takings Clause of, 145; Tenth Amendment, 135, 137, 140, 154–55; term limits and, 114, 115–16 contraception, 38; "morning after" pill and, 272–73

Convention on the Elimination of All Forms of Discrimination Against Women (1979), 124

Convention on the Rights of the Child, 32

Cooper Union, 226

Corsi, Jerome, 241

cosmetic surgery: empowerment and, 9; "Mommy Makeover" and, 275–76; science and, 260, 274–76; vanity and, 9

CosmoGirl!, 166–67

Cosmopolitan, 165

Council on American-Islamic Relations (CAIR), 90, 95

Couric, Katie, 158

Covenant Keepers, 39

crime, illegal immigration and, 5, 47, 50, 51–53, 65

Cronkite, Walter, 233–34

Croyle, John, 39–40

Cryobank, 270–71

C-SPAN, 136

D

Dads.org (St. Joseph Covenant Keepers), 39

DailyKos, 241

Dallas, University of, 226

Dalton, Jenny, 25

Daniels, Stormy, 171

Dartmouth College, 195–97, 210, 226–27

Dartmouth Review, 196, 197

Darwin, Charles, 269

Dateline NBC, 179, 290

Da Vinci Code (Brown), 290

Dawkins, Richard, 293–94

Dean, Howard, 6, 97

death penalty: federalism and, 144; international law and, 123; Supreme Court, U.S. and, 123, 139

Declaration of Independence, 3–4, 122, 316

"Declaration of War Against the Americans Who Occupy [Saudi Arabia]" (bin Laden), 81

DeGeneres, Ellen, 180

Deliver Us from Evil, 297

democracy, 78; Iraq and, 79, 97; military and spread of, 74; states and, 141, 146–47; Supreme Court, U.S. and, 111–16

Democratic Party, Democrats: abortion and, 114; education and, 224; embryonic stem cell research and, 267; illegal immigration and, 45, 46, 52, 63; Iraq war and, 79–80; media, new and, 241; "morning after" pill and, 272; national security and, 80, 97, 98; Supreme Court nominations and, 105; talk radio and, 8, 247–49; taxation and family and, 34–35

Dershowitz, Alan, 111

"designer babies," 9, 260–61, 269–72

"Design for the Little Darlings" (Dalton), 25

Desperate Housewives, 21, 22

DeSutter, Paula A., 85

Deutsch, Donny, 172

Discovery Channel, 291–92

Disney, 185

diversity: cultural, 139; education and, 6, 203, 207; ideological, 6;

political correctness and, 134; universities and, 210, 211–14

divorce, 29, 29–30; children, welfare of and, 36; Hollywood and, 35–36; "no-fault," 36–37; serial, 35–36. *See also* marriage

Dobson, James, 103

Doe v. Bolton, 112, 124

Dole, Bob, 154–55

A Doll's House (Ibsen), 21

Donohue, Bill, 194

Dostoevsky, Fyodor, 17

Dre, Dr., 168

Drudge Report, 241

drugs: celebrity obsession and, 177; illegal immigration and, 53–54

Dukes of Hazzard, 163

E

East Timor, 76

eating disorders, 177

ebonics, 202–3

education: charter school programs and, 147, 224; classical, 202, 211, 212; Democrats and, 224; diversity and, 6, 203, 207; ebonics and, 202–3; empowerment and, 197–98; government and, 219–21; home-schooling and, 221, 221–22, 223; illegal immigration and, 46, 59, 64, 65; illiberal, 215; liberal, 198, 212; local control and, 143–44, 146–47, 156; moral, 222; No Child Left Behind Act and, 141, 149, 156, 220–21; parenting and, 225; political correctness and, 6; power to the people and, 6, 199, 216–29; sex, 163, 206–9; teachers' unions and, 147; virtue and,

198; vouchers and, 146–47, 224. *See also* public schools; universities

Education Trust, 156

Edwards, John, 128, 267

Egypt, 82, 94

Eichmann, Adolf, 213

Eight Is Enough, 13–15

Einstein, Albert, 299

Eisenhower, Dwight D., 301

Elfman, Jenna, 14–15

Ellen, 299

embryonic stem cell research, 4; cloning and, 263, 264–65, 268, 281; conservatives and, 266–67; Democrats and, 267; government funding for, 263, 268; media and, 265; miracle cures and, 267–69; objections to, 263; science and, 259, 282–83; scientific consensus and, 262–63

Eminem, 168

employment, illegal immigration and, 55–57, 64, 67

empowerment: adult entertainment industry and, 171–72; "anything goes" mentality and, 4; cosmetic surgery and, 9; education and, 197–98; family and, 5, 16, 19; science and, 261. *See also* power to the people

The End of Faith (Harris), 293

environmentalism, environmentalists: anti-population growth and, 15; children and, 16; global warming and, 150–51, 278–81; illegal immigration and, 65

ESPN, 169

Establishment Clause, 118–22, 301

E! Television, 173, 177

ethics, science and, 9
EU. *See* European Union
eugenics, 269–71
European Commission, 152
European High Court on Human Rights, 124
European Union (EU), 18, 151–52
euthanasia, 4

F

Facebook, 178–79, 182, 242
family: adult entertainment industry and, 172; African Americans and, 33; alternative forms of, 28–30; anti-child bias and, 19–20; anti-population growth and, 15; "anything goes" mentality and, 28; attack on, 5, 20–23; children and, 27–32, 33; complementarity and, 29; conservatives and, 19; culture and, 5, 37; definition of, 27–28; empowerment and, 5, 16, 19; fathers and, 33; feminism and, 18, 19; God and, 31; government and, 5, 19, 31–37; health care and, 19, 37–39; individualism and, 5, 18; John Paul II and, 31; large vs. small, 13–15, 15–19, 19–20; parenting and, 23–27; power to the people and, 5, 37–39; society and, 20; taxation and, 34–35; on television, 14–15, 21–22, 28; traditional, 5, 27–32, 33–34, 37
Family Law Act of 1969, 36
Family Life Today, 39
Family Ties, 21
fashion industry, 191–92
fathers: adult entertainment industry and, 172; family and, 33; on television, 23

FBI. *See* Federal Bureau of Investigation
FCC. *See* Federal Communications Commission
FDA. *See* Food and Drug Administration
Fear Factor, 180
FEC. *See* Federal Election Commission
Federal Bureau of Investigation (FBI), 91
Federal Communications Commission (FCC), 247, 248
Federal Election Commission (FEC), 250
Federal Highway Trust Fund, 148
federalism: death penalty and, 144; liberal, 137; local control and, 136–38, 142–45; Supreme Court, U.S. and, 114, 144–45
Federalist Papers, 137–38, 139, 148
Federal Marriage Amendment, 155
Federation for American Immigration Reform, 64
Feinstein, Dianne, 247
Felder, Raoul, 301–2
feminism, feminists: children and, 18, 23; family and, 18, 19
Fergie, 167
Ferrell, Will, 171
FHM, 167, 168
Field, Sally, 14
Fifth Amendment, 145
50 Cent, 169, 177, 202
Financial Times, 25, 60
First Amendment, 161, 213; campaign finance reform and, 125, 126; political speech and, 125; pornography and, 188, 189; religion and, 118–22

"The Fiscal Cost of Low-Skill Households to the U.S. Taxpayer" (Heritage Foundation), 46
Fishbein, Paul, 169–70
Flockhart, Calista, 14
Florida Supreme Court, 107
Flynt, Larry, 170, 173
Focus on the Family, 103
Food and Drug Administration (FDA), 272
Forbes, 171
Foreign Affairs, 75
foreign policy: Bush, George W. and, 74, 77, 78–79; Clinton, Bill and, 74, 75–76; conservatives and, 75; democracy, spread of and, 74, 78; diplomacy and, 76; Hollywood and, 74; humanitarianism and, 6, 74, 76, 77–78, 79; national security and, 6, 74–80, 97; nation-building and, 6, 75, 78
Foreign Policy magazine, 18
Founding Fathers: Constitution, U.S. and, 102, 107, 154; God, belief in and, 12, 316; government and, 134, 137; liberals and, 138–39; liberty and, 4, 288; local control and, 140–41; political speech and, 125; representation and, 135–36; Supreme Court, U.S. and, 7, 108; term limits and, 114
Fourteenth Amendment, 139, 155
Fox, Michael J., 268, 281
FOX News Channel, 52, 164, 172
Framers. *See* Founding Fathers
Francis, Joe, 172
Franken, Al, 248
freedom: family and, 20; Founding Fathers and, 4, 288; meaning of, 4; morality and, 288; power to the people and, 287–89; of speech, 125–27, 213; virtue and, 4, 288
French Revolution, 125
Fritz, Marshall, 225
Frum, David, 103
The Future of Marriage (Blankenhorn), 28
FX, 180

G
Galilei, Galileo, 279
gang activity, 47, 53
GAO. *See* General Accounting Office
Gattaca, 260
Gay, Lesbian, Straight Education Network (GLSEN), 208–9
gay marriage, 109, 128, 155, 206–7
Geffen Records, 169
General Accounting Office (GAO), 52
Geneva Conventions, 118
Genius Jones, 25
Georgia Division of Family and Children Services, 36
Georgia Tech, 215, 227–28
Giffords, Gabby, 65
Gilchrist, Jim, 214–15
Ginsburg, Ruth Bader, 104–5, 112, 124
The Girls Next Door, 173
Giuliani, Rudy, 251
global warming, 150, 262, 278–81
GLSEN. *See* Gay, Lesbian, Straight Education Network
God: belief in, 10–11, 182; family and, 31; Founding Fathers and, 12; liberal assault on, 290–93, 293–98; marriage and, 28, 29;

God (continued)
  proofs of existence of, 294–95;
  science as, 258–59; suffering and,
  310; unalienable rights and, 4
The God Delusion (Dawkins),
  293–94
God Is Not Great (Hitchens), 294
The Golden Girls, 22
Goldhaber, Dan, 200
Gomez, Raul, 51
Gonzalez, Alfredo Rodriguez, 51
Gonzalez, Sigifredo, 58
Gonzalez v. Carhart, 113–14
Goodman, Ellen, 262
Good Morning America, 299
"Good Riddance to the Family"
  (Stacy), 30
Gore, Al, 74, 150, 151, 278, 279,
  281
The Gospel of Judas, 293
Goss, Porter, 83
government: children, protection of
  and, 188–90; education and,
  219–21; embryonic stem cell
  research and, 263; family and, 5,
  31–37; Founding Fathers and,
  134; illegal immigration and,
  42–43, 53–55; local control and,
  134–35; marriage and, 28, 31;
  national security and, 73–74; parenting and, 31–32, 32–34;
  pornography and, 188–90; religious practice and, 301; representation and, 134–36; science and,
  261; welfare and, 32–33
GQ, 167
The Graduate, 26
Graf, Randy, 65
Graham, Billy, 309

Graham, Lindsey, 45–46, 62, 64,
  245
Grant, Hugh, 175
Great Depression, 141
Greatest Generations Foundation,
  191
The Great Global Warming Swindle,
  280
Griswold, Daniel, 60, 87
Guardian (UK), 79

H
Habitat for Humanity, 314
Hagel, Chuck, 64
Hagelin, Rebecca, 37
Hajj, Adnan, 239–40
Hamas, 83
Hamdan, Salim Ahmed, 117–18
Hamdan v. Rumsfeld, 118
Hamdi, Yaser Esam, 116–17
Hamilton, Alexander, 108, 204
Hanjour, Hani, 56, 59
Hansen, Chris, 179
Hanson, Victor Davis, 61
Hard Copy, 174
Harris, Sam, 293, 294
Hart, Betsy, 185–86
Harvard University, 210
Hassick, Derek, 257–58
Haverford College, 212
Hawking, Stephen, 18, 262
Hayworth, J. D., 64–65
HBO, 28, 173
health care: children and, 16; family
  and, 19, 37–39; illegal immigra-
  tion and, 47, 61, 65
Hefner, Hugh, 170, 172–73
Helms, Jesse, 154
Help Save Manassas, 63
Heritage Foundation, 46, 92

Herman, Pee Wee, 175
Heyward, Andrew, 232
Hezbollah, 83, 239
Hicks, Esther and Jerry, 299
Hill, Anita, 129
Hilton, Paris, 10, 163, 164, 175, 176, 220, 278, 317
Hinkhouse, Kade, 310–11
"hipster parenting," 24–25
Hitchens, Christopher, 294
Hitler, Adolf, 213, 264–65
Holloway, Natalee, 164
Hollywood, 140; cosmetic surgery and, 274–75; divorce and, 35–36; foreign policy and, 74; Iraq war and, 96; morality and, 203
Holmes, Oliver Wendell, 107
Holocaust, 204, 262
Holy Blood, Holy Grail (Baigent), 290
Home Invasion (Hagelin), 37
Horowitz, David, 212, 227–28
Hotair.com, 240, 244
House of Representatives, U.S., representation in, 135, 136
How to Make Love Like a Porn Star (Jameson), 171
HPV (human papillomavirus) vaccine, 273–74
Hughes Electronics, 88
Hu Jintao, 86
Human Events Online, 241
Human Genome project, 294–95
humanitarianism, 6, 74, 76, 77–78, 79
Human Rights Campaign, 207
Huntsman, Jon, 156
Hurricane Katrina, 314
Hussein, Saddam, 76, 77, 78, 94, 163

Hustler magazine, 170, 173
Huxley, Aldous, 9
Hyde, Henry, 154

I

Ibsen, Henrik, 21, 27
illegal immigration: Americanization and, 43–44; amnesty and, 45–46, 48, 52, 64, 243–44; border control and, 5, 41–43, 48; Bush, George W. and, 45–48, 50, 52, 55, 68; businesses and, 59–60, 64; "Catch and Release" treatment and, 47; citizenship and, 47–49; "comprehensive immigration reform" and, 45–47, 48, 50–51, 52, 62, 64, 243–46; costs of, 46–47, 50, 61, 64, 65; crime and, 5, 47, 50, 51–53, 65; Democrats and, 45, 46, 52, 63; deportation and, 48; drug smuggling and, 42, 53–54; education and, 46, 59, 61, 64, 65; employment and, 55–57, 64, 67; environment and, 65; gang activity and, 47, 53; government and, 42–43; guest-worker plan and, 46, 48; health care and, 47, 61, 65; immigration laws, enforcement of and, 5, 42–43, 53–55, 64–66, 66–68; Iraq war and, 65; language and, 5, 43, 44, 46, 61, 69; local control and, 62–64, 142–43; "Matricula Consular" identification and, 59, 64; media and, 50, 64; national security and, 57–59, 74; Operation Gatekeeper and, 42–43; "path to citizenship" and, 48, 49; people and, 45, 49–50; power to the people

illegal immigration (continued)
  and, 5, 61–69; prisons and, 52,
  61; Republicans and, 45, 46, 65,
  245–46; "sanctuary" policies
  and, 52–53, 54, 65; September 11
  and, 46, 56, 59, 60; Supreme
  Court, U.S. and, 109; terrorism
  and, 58–59; visa system and, 59,
  60–61
Imaginary Heroes, 21
Imperial Beach, Cali., 42, 43
Imus, Don, 161, 190
An Inconvenient Truth (Gore), 281
individualism, family and, 5, 18
Indonesia, 82, 83
Ingraham, Laura: cancer battle of,
  157–58,   308–10,   313–15;
  Catholicism, conversion to of,
  307–8; at Dartmouth College,
  195–97; death of mother of,
  305–6; Holy Land trip of,
  285–87; as political analyst,
  231–34; Sapient, Brian, interview
  of by, 295–97; September 11 and,
  71–73
Intercollegiate Studies Institute (ISI),
  226
Intergovernmental Panel on Climate
  Change (IPCC), 150, 280
Internal Revenue Service (IRS), 35
International Criminal Court, 154
international law: affirmative action
  and, 124; death penalty and, 123;
  Left and, 124; Supreme Court,
  U.S. and, 111, 122–25
Internet: adult entertainment industry and, 169, 170; celebrity and,
  178–79; dangers of, 242–43; government regulation of, 249–51;
  media, Left monopoly on and,
  7–8; popular culture, battling

and, 187; pornography and, 187,
  243; science and, 261; social networking sites on, 178–79, 242;
  Supreme Court nominations and,
  105; voyeurism and, 242–43
Interscope, 169
Iran, 10; nuclear program in, 83, 85,
  86; Syria and, 83
Iran hostage crisis (1979), 80, 83
Iraq: democracy in, 97; insurgency
  in, 83, 96
Iraq war: democracy and, 79;
  Democrats and, 79–80; Holly-
  wood and, 96; illegal immigration
  and, 65; media and, 79, 96; mili-
  tary and, 78; Republicans and,
  79–80; winning, 96
IRS. *See* Internal Revenue Service
ISI. *See* Intercollegiate Studies Insti-
  tute
*The ISI Guide to All-American Col-
  leges*, 226
Islamic jihadists, 80–83
The Island, 259
Israel, 81, 82, 83, 89, 94
Israeli Antiquities Authority, 291
It Takes a Parent (Hart), 185

J
Jacobovici, Simcha, 290–92
James: Brother of Jesus (Discovery
  Channel), 292
Jameson, Jenna, 171
Jefferson, Thomas, 204, 301
Jenner, Bruce, 274
Jesus Camp, 297
Jesus Christ, 11; Cavallaro, Cosimo
  and, 292–93; *Da Vinci Code*
  (Brown) and, 290; sacrifice and
  love and, 312; tomb of, 291–92
The Jesus Dynasty (Tabor), 297

The Jesus Papers (Baigent), 290
Jiang, Kat, 181
John Paul II, 307; Cold War and,
316–17; family and, 31
Johnson, Charles, 239
Johnson, Scott, 238
Jordan, 82, 94
judiciary. *See* Supreme Court, U.S.
Justice Department, U.S., 52

K
Kaine, Tim, 49
Keisler, Peter, 189
Kelly, Eamon, 285
Kelo, Suzette, 127
Kelo v. New London, 108, 127, 130,
144–45
Kennedy, Anthony, 102, 107
Kennedy, Bobby and Ethel, 15
Kennedy, Edward (Ted), 19–20, 80,
221; illegal immigration and,
246; Supreme Court nominations
and, 128, 129
Kennedy, John F., 203, 293
Kennedy, Rose, 15
Kenya embassy bombing (1998), 80
Kerry, John, 18, 241, 266–67
Khan, A. Q., 85
Khidekel, Marina, 166–67
Kim Jong-il, 84
King, Martin Luther, Jr., 293
King, Rodney, 251
Kinsella, Sarah, 192
Klein, Daniel, 211
Klein, Jon, 234
Knox, Sasha, 171
Krauthammer, Charles, 103
Kron, Daniel, 25
Krugman, Paul, 227
Kuwait, 76

Kyl, John, 62, 244, 246
Kyoto Protocol, 150–51, 154, 281

L
The Language Police (Ravitch), 205
LAPD. *See* Los Angeles Police
Department
Larry King Live, 173
The Last Tomb of Jesus (Discovery
Channel), 291–92
The Laura Ingraham Show, 8
Lawrence v. Texas, 124
Lazarus, Ed, 111
Leary, Denis, 180
Lee v. Weisman, 119
Left: as anti-religious, 10; children
and, 16, 18; culture, American
and, 3; empowerment and, 2–3;
foreign policy and, 74; interna-
tional law and, 124; media
monopoly of, 7–8; national secu-
rity and, 74; political correctness
and, 3; power to the people and,
2–3, 287–88; Supreme Court
nominations and, 128–29; terrorism and, 94. *See also* liberals
Lehrer, Eli, 212
Lemon v. Kurtzman, 119
Lennon, John, 2
Lethal Vows, 22
Letourneau, Mary Kay, 164
Levine, Arthur, 200
Lewinsky, Monica, 192
Lewis, C. S., 261, 268–69, 299
liberalism: decline of, 3; Republicans
and, 3; secular, 18; university faculties and, 211–14
liberals: Founding Fathers and,
138–39; local control and,
138–40, 144; media and, 234–35;

liberals (continued)
popular culture and, 160–61; talk radio and, 161; universities and, 211. *See also* Left
Librescu, Liviu, 312–13
Life Goes On, 21
Lifetime, 21–22
Limbaugh, Rush, 8
Lincoln, Abraham, 108, 118
Lindh, John Walker, 116
Lindzen, Richard, 280
Little Green Footballs, 238, 239
local control: abortion and, 156; civil rights movement and, 141; education and, 143–44, 146–47, 156; federalism and, 136–38, 142–45; Founding Fathers and, 140–41; government and, 134–35; highway system and, 148–49; illegal immigration and, 62–64, 142–43; liberals and, 138–40, 144; national sovereignty and, 149–52, 154; No Child Left Behind Act and, 141, 149, 156; power to the people and, 8, 134, 153–56; public schools and, 143–44, 153–54; religious displays and, 156; states and, 133–34; voting with your feet and, 145–46; welfare and, 154
Lockheed Martin, 88
Lohan, Lindsay, 175, 176, 317
London subway bombing (2005), 82
Loral Space Technologies, 88
The Lord of the Rings (Tolkien), 153
Los Angeles Police Department (LAPD), 54–55
Los Angeles Times, 50, 114, 172
Lott, Trent, 62
love, sacrifice and, 310–15
Lowe, Rob, 175

Loy, James, 58
Ludacris, 169
Luttig, J. Michael, 102

M

McCain, John, 131, 245; campaign finance reform and, 125; illegal immigration and, 62, 246
McCain-Feingold campaign law (2001), 125, 131, 250
McConnell v. FEC, 125
McCreary County v. ACLU, 120
Mac Donald, Heather, 54
Macko, Lia, 233
Madison, James, 137–38, 140, 148
Madonna, 177
Maher, Bill, 173, 288, 297–98
Malhotra, Ruth, 215, 227
Malkin, Michelle, 237, 240
Mallaby, Sebastian, 87
Malvo, Lee Boyd, 73
Manhattan Institute, 54, 209
Marbury v. Madison, 106, 125
marriage: children, welfare of and, 28–30; complementarity and, 29; family and, 29; gay, 109, 128, 155, 206–7; God and, 28, 29; government and, 28, 31; as oppressive, 21; as public institution, 28–29; redefining, 30; sanctity of, 36; society and, 30–31; states' rights and, 155; twenty-first-century, 30. *See also* divorce
Married with Children, 21
Mary Magdalene, 290, 291
Mason, Jackie, 301–2
Massachusetts: gay marriage in, 109; taxation in, 145–46
Massachusetts Institute of Technology (MIT), 212

Massachusetts Teachers Association, 207
Matlock, David, 276
Maxim, 167, 168
Mayer, John, 40
media: adult entertainment industry and, 171; as anti-religious, 10–11; cable television, 105; culture and, 9–10; dinosaur, 50, 96, 235, 253, 265, 280–81, 294; embryonic stem cell research and, 265; illegal immigration and, 50, 64; Iraq war and, 79, 96; journalist, definition of and, 251–52; liberal monopoly of, 234–35; print, 165–68; reform of, 252–53; religion, assault on by, 294; sex and, 9, 160–65, 165–69, 176–77; Supreme Court nominations and, 102, 105; talk radio, 105. *See also* media, new
media, new: blogging, 8, 105, 237, 238–42; cable television, 7–8, 164; conservatives and, 7–8; Democrats and, 241; fact-checking and, 254–55; Internet, 7–8, 105, 170, 178–79, 187, 242–43, 249–51, 261; media, liberal monopoly of and, 234–35; pitfalls of, 254; power to the people and, 7–8, 252–55; Supreme Court nominations and, 105; talk radio, 7–8
men: adult entertainment industry and, 172; as fathers, 23, 33, 172; objectification of, 164; on television, 22–23
Mengele, Joseph, 264–65, 271
Men's Health, 167
Merkel, Angela, 152
Mexico, 42, 48, 58
Mexifornia, 61

Meyers, Lisa, 233
Mezer, Gazi Ibrahim Abu, 58–59
Michigan, University of, 124
Miers, Harriet Ellan, 130, 242; Supreme Court nomination of, 101–5
military: Clinton, Bill and, 91; democracy, spread of and, 74; expansion of, 91–92; federal spending on, 91–92; humanitarian missions and, 6, 74, 76; Iraq war and, 78; national security and, 6, 77, 91–92, 97; nation-building and, 6, 75; sacrifice and, 310–11
Millan, Cesar, 50
Miller, Arthur, 21
Ministry of the Propagation of Virtue and the Prevention of Vice (Saudi Arabia), 317
Minutemen, 66, 214
MIT. *See* Massachusetts Institute of Technology
Mitchell, Harry, 65
morality: citizenship and, 288; Hollywood and, 203; liberty and, 288; science and, 9
Moran, Jim, 115
"morning after" pill, 272–73
mothers: sexualization of girls and, 26; single, 29–30
Motion Picture Association of America, 186
movies, 183–85, 186–87
Moyers, Bill, 8
Moynihan, Daniel Patrick, 32–33
Moynihan Report, 33
Mrs. Warren's Profession (Shaw), 21
MSNBC, 164, 232–33
Mueller, Robert, 95
Muhammad, John Allen, 73

Murray, Justin, 192
music: popular culture, battling and, 183; rap, 168–69, 235–38
Muslims: in America, 83, 90; in Britain, 79, 82; in France, 82; in Spain, 82
My Bare Lady, 171
MySpace, 178–79, 182, 242, 243

N

NAEP. *See* National Assessment of Educational Progress
NARAL, 128
National Assessment of Educational Progress (NAEP), 198
National Center for Missing and Exploited Children, 178–79
National Coalition Against Censorship, 213
National Council of La Raza, 44, 245
National Council of Teachers of English, 202
National Education Association (NEA), 199, 200, 201, 202, 224
National Endowment for the Humanities, 220
National Enquirer, 158
National Institute of Child Health and Human Development, 23
National Institutes of Health, 266
National Journal, 65
National Organization for Women (NOW), 11
National Review, 7, 103, 245
national security: border enforcement and, 74; counter-terrorism and, 90–91; Democrats and, 80, 97, 98; enemies, knowing our and, 80–86; foreign policy and, 6,
74–80, 97; government and, 73–74; illegal immigration and, 57–59; military and, 6, 77, 91–92, 97; national unity and, 96–97; political correctness and, 95; power to the people and, 6, 89–99; Republicans and, 80, 97, 98; September 11 and, 71–73, 78; terrorism and, 71–74
National Security Agency (NSA), 91
National Socialism, 261
national sovereignty, 138; defending, 149–52; Kyoto Protocol and, 281; local control and, 149–52, 154; Supreme Court, U.S. and, 111, 122–25
National Survey on Drug Use and Health, 277
Nazism, Nazis, 45, 271–72
NBC, 169
NCLB. *See* No Child Left Behind Act
NEA. *See* National Education Association
Nelson, Lauren, 179
New America Media, 31
Newdow, Michael, 121–22
Newsweek, 176, 295
New York magazine, 205
New York Police Department (NYPD), 55
New York Post, 57
New York Sun, 215
New York Times, 7, 8, 26, 50, 52, 78, 114, 169, 171, 174, 181, 226, 233, 237, 294
New York University, 30
Nguyen, Tila (Tila Tequila), 178
Nice Treaty, 151
Nichol, Gene, 303

Nip/Tuck, 180

Nixon, Richard, 102

No Child Left Behind Act (NCLB), 141, 156, 220–21

North Korea, 84, 85, 91, 99

North Shore Student Advocacy, 219

Northwestern University, 212

Norwood, Charlie, 55

NOW. *See* National Organization for Women

NSA. *See* National Security Agency

nuclear weapons: China and, 85; Iran and, 83, 85, 86; Pakistan and, 85, 86

Nwangaza, Efia, 2

NYPD. *See* New York Police Department

NYPD Blue, 179

O

Obama, Barack, 128, 190

Oberlin College, 210, 212

O'Connor, Sandra Day, 107, 113; campaign finance reform and, 125; Imperial Judiciary and, 109–10; international law and, 122; retirement of, 101; War on Terror and, 117

O'Donnell, Rosie, 8, 253

OECD. *See* Organization for Economic Cooperation and Development

Olsen, Mary-Kate, 177

O'Neill, Eugene, 21, 27

O'Neill, John, 241

Operation Gatekeeper, 42

Oprah Winfrey Show, 299

O'Reilly, Michael, 65

The O'Reilly Factor, 171

Organization for Economic Cooperation and Development (OECD), 152–53, 198

O'Sullivan, John, 51

OTMs (Other Than Mexicans), 57, 58

Outside, 167

Owen, Priscilla, 102

Owens, Bill, 213, 231

P

Pace, Peter, 96

Padilla, Jose, 95

Pakistan, 82, 85, 86

Parade, 165–66

parenting: coolness and, 26–27; culture and, 16; education and, 217–19, 225; family and, 23–27; government and, 31–32, 32–34; "hipster," 24–25; importance of, 40; "new urban," 24–25; permissive, 9; "PlayStation," 24, 185–86; popular culture, battling and, 182–84, 185–87; sex education and, 207–8; sexualization of girls and, 25–26; single, 29–30

Parents Television Council (PTC), 194

Parker, Tonia and David, 206–7

The Passion of the Christ, 184

Patrick, Tera, 171

patriotism: sacrifice and, 311; virtue and, 69

Peale, Norman Vincent, 299

Pei, Ieoh Ming, 205

Pelosi, Nancy, 1, 16, 96, 136, 316; Supreme Court, U.S. and, 108, 116

Pence, Mike, 248

Penthouse, 165

People for the Ethical Treatment of Animals (PETA), 11

People's Liberation Army (PLA), 87, 89

Perry, Rick, 274

PETA. *See* People for the Ethical Treatment of Animals

Peterson, Scott, 164

Petraeus, David, 96

Pew Global Attitudes Survey, 82

Pillco, Diego, 51

PLA. *See* People's Liberation Army

Plan B. *See* "morning after" pill

Planned Parenthood, 128, 206, 271

Plato, 32, 299

Playboy, 165, 168, 178

Playboy Enterprises, 172–73

"PlayStation parenting," 24, 185–86

Pledge of Allegiance, 109, 119, 121

Podesta, John, 248

political correctness: diversity and, 134; education and, 6; Left and, 3; national security and, 95; public schools and, 203–6, 221; religious displays and, 304; universities and, 197

popular culture: adult entertainment industry and, 169–74; battling, 181–88, 188–94; celebrity obsession and, 159–60, 174–78; family and, 5, 13–15, 15–19, 37; fashion industry and, 191–92; God, faith in and, 182; "just turn it off" defense and, 160–65; Left and, 3; liberals and, 160–61; meaning of, 159; media and, 9–10; parenting and, 16; pornography and, 9–10; power to the people and, 181–88; sex and, 160–65, 165–69, 192–93; television and, 179–81

population growth, 15

pornography: accessibility of, 174; Constitution, U.S. and, 302; culture and, 9–10; First Amendment and, 188, 189; government and, 188–90; Internet and, 187, 243; speech, freedom of and, 125; Supreme Court, U.S. and, 189; taxation and, 35. *See also* adult entertainment industry

poverty, welfare and, 33

Powerline, 238

The Power of Positive Thinking (Peale), 299

power to the people: education and, 6, 199, 216–29; family and, 5, 37–39; God, belief in and, 10–11; illegal immigration and, 5, 61–69; Left and, 2–3, 287–88; liberty and, 287–89; local control and, 8, 134, 153–56; meaning of, 2; media, new and, 7–8, 252–55; national security and, 6, 89–99; popular culture and, 181–88; science and, 8–9; Supreme Court, U.S. and, 109, 129–31. *See also* empowerment

prayer in schools, 104, 107, 108, 119, 121–22

Pregerson, Harry, 107

prescription medications, abuse of, 276–78

President's Commission on Bioethics, 265

Price, Kirsten, 171

Price, Michael, 189

Princeton University, 210

prisons: illegal immigration and, 52, 61; Islam, conversions to in, 95 property rights: eminent domain and, 127, 130–31; erosion of, 7; public use and, 127, 145; Supreme Court, U.S. and, 7, 127, 130–31, 144–45

Providence College, 226

PTC. *See* Parents Television Council

public schools: alternatives to, 221–23; children, indoctrination of and, 203–6; government and, 219–21; history curricula in, 203–5; illegal immigration and, 46, 59, 61, 64; local control and, 143–44, 153–54; parental involvement in, 217–19; political correctness and, 221; prayer in, 104, 107, 119, 121–22; school choice and, 146–47, 223–25; sex education in, 206–9; teachers' unions and, 199–203; textbooks and, 221. *See* universities

Publisher's Weekly, 293

Pure Fashion, 191–92

Putin, Vladimir, 84

Q

Quindlen, Anna, 22

R

Ramos, Ignacio, 53–54

rap music, 168–69, 235–38

Rather, Dan, 8, 234, 238, 242

Ravitch, Diane, 205, 221

Reagan, Ron, 268

Reagan, Ronald, 217; Cold War and, 98, 316–17; education and, 143; "Evil Empire" speech of, 99; Fairness Doctrine and, 247; God and, 317; national security and, 96; religion and, 303, 309; Supreme Court nominations of, 102, 129

The Real World, 182

RedState, 244

Reeve, Christopher, 267

Reid, Harry, 45, 80, 96, 97, 105

religion: in America, 10–11; church and state, separation of and, 301; Constitution, U.S. and, 301; faith substitutes and, 298–300; First Amendment and, 118–22; government and, 301; Hollywood assault on, 290–93; Left and, 10; liberal assault on, 293–98, 301–5; Supreme Court, U.S. and, 118–22; universities and, 303–4; virtue and practice of, 288–89.

religious displays: Constitution, U.S. and, 304; Supreme Court, U.S. and, 7, 108; universities and, 303–4. *See also* religion

Republican National Committee (RNC), 46, 253

Republican Party, Republicans: illegal immigration and, 45, 46, 65, 245–46; Iraq war and, 79–80; liberalism, decline of and, 3; national security and, 80, 97, 98

Rescue Me, 180

Retrovaille, 39

Reubens, Paul (Pee Wee Herman), 175

Reuters, 50, 239, 240

Rhodes College, 226

Rice, Condoleezza, 75–76, 78

Richie, Nicole, 10, 176, 177, 278

rights: Declaration of Independence and, 3–4; as God-given, 4; illegal immigration and, 48–49; property, 7, 127, 130–31, 144–45; unalienable, 3–4

Riley, Michael and Carolyn, 277
Ritalin, 260, 277
Ritter, Bill, 272
Ritter, John, 22
Rivera, Geraldo, 52, 291
Rivers, Joan, 180
RNC. *See* Republican National Committee
Roberts, John, 104, 107, 123, 126, 130
Robinson, Peter, 227
Rodgers, T. J., 226–27
Roe v. Wade, 111–13, 124, 139
Roosevelt, Franklin D., 203, 262
Roosevelt, Theodore, 43–44, 48, 278
Rose, Charlie, 231
Rove, Karl, 50–51, 53
Rumsfeld, Donald, 91
The Rush Limbaugh Show, 8
Russia, 91
Rutgers National Marriage Project, 24
Rwanda, 75, 251
Ryan, Abigail, 271
Ryan, Meg, 9

S
sacrifice: love and, 310–15; military and, 310–11; patriotism and, 311
sacrificial concern, 312–15
Sadr, Moqtada al-, 81
same-sex marriage, 109
San Diego, Cali., 42
San Francisco, Cali., 53
Sanger, Margaret, 271, 272
Sanneh, Kelefah, 237
Santa Fe v. Roe, 139
Sapient, Brian, 295–97
Saudi Arabia, 61, 94, 317

Scalia, Antonin, 117, 121, 124, 125, 130
Schlafly, Phyllis, 179
Schlussel, Debbie, 237
Schram, Matt, 240
Schumer, Chuck, 97, 128
science: abortion and, 257–58, 269–70, 282; abuse of, 257–62; child-rearing and, 260; cloning and, 259, 263; cosmetic surgery and, 9, 260, 274–76; "designer baby" craze and, 9, 260–61, 269–72; embryonic stem cell research and, 259, 262–63, 262–69, 281–83, 282–83; empowerment and, 261; ethics and, 9, 282; global warming and, 278–81; goals of, 9; as God, 258–59; government funding for, 261; human life, sanctity of and, 282–83; Internet and, 261; morality and, 9; over-medication and, 276–78; politicization of, 261; power to the people and, 8–9, 281–83; scientific consensus and, 261–62; sex, promoting and, 272–74; STDs and, 272, 273
SCNT (somatic cell nuclear transfer), 264–65
Sears, Leah Ward, 36
The Secret (Byrne), 299–300
Senate, U.S.: Kyoto Protocol and, 150; representation in, 135
Send-A-Brick.com, 62
Seper, Jerry, 42, 58
September 11, 80–81, 94, 213; alleged American-Israeli conspiracy and, 82; illegal immigration and, 46, 56, 59, 60; national security and, 71–73, 78; sacrifice and love and, 311–12

sex: in advertising, 161–64; celebrity obsession and, 174–78; education and, 163, 206–9; "hook-up" culture and, 192–93; in media, 160–65, 165–69; media and, 9, 165–68; popular culture and, 160–65, 165–69, 192–93; rap lyrics and, 168–69; science and, 272–74; on television, 179–81
sexually transmitted diseases (STDs), 272, 273
Shakespeare, William, 210
Sharman, Brenda, 191–92
Sharpton, Al, 190
Shaw, George Bernard, 21
Sheen, Charlie, 35–36, 37
SICs (Special Interest Countries), 57
Simpson, Jessica, 163, 177
Singer, Peter, 271, 282
60 Minutes, 238
Sklar, Orit, 228
Smith, Anna Nicole, 10, 164, 176
Smith, Bradley, 250
Smith, Stephen, 227
Snoop Dogg, 169, 202
Snow, Tony, 245–46
society: children and, 32; family and, 20; marriage and, 30–31
sodomy, 124
Solanki, Sami, 279–80
somatic cell nuclear transfer (SCNT), 264–65
"Some People Push Back: On the Justice of Roosting Chickens" (Churchill), 213
Soros, George, 245, 246, 248
Souter, David H., 102, 107, 120
South, University of, 226
Southern Methodist University, 104
Soviet Union, 91, 316–17

Spann, Johnny "Mike," 116
Spears, Britney, 10, 175–76, 177, 317
Specter, Arlen, 246, 262, 267
speech: freedom of, 125–27; hate, 161, 214–16; political, 189, 247
A Spiritual Journey, 297–98
Spitzer, Robert, 277
Stacy, Judith, 30
The Staircase Murders, 22
Stanford University, 211–12
State Department, U.S., 88
states: democracy and, 141, 146–47; local control and, 133–34. *See also* states' rights
states' rights: local control and, 139; marriage and, 155; term limits and, 115–16. *See also* states
Stenberg v. Carhart, 113
Stenzel, Pamela, 192
Stern, Howard, 171
Stevens, John Paul, 102, 125
Stevenson, Nancy, 312–13
Stewart, Lynne, 117
Stewart, Marvin, 214–15
Steyn, Mark, 51
Stickel, Sue, 205–6
St. James, Chanel, 171
St. John's College, 226
St. Joseph's Covenant Keepers, 39
St. Louis Post-Dispatch, 263
Stossel, John, 201
Stovall, Thomas, 276
Stowers Institute for Medical Research, 268
Stowers, James and Virginia, 268
St. Thomas, University of, 226
Stubbe, Ray, 312
Stuff, 167, 168
Sudan, 86, 87

suffering: God and, 310; military and, 310–11; redemptive power of, 310

suicide bombings, 73, 82, 83

Supreme Court, U.S.: abortion and, 7, 104–5, 107, 108, 111–14, 124, 139; affirmative action and, 124, 131; America's Judeo-Christian moral heritage and, 111, 118–22; Bush, George W. nominations to, 101–5; campaign finance reform and, 131; conservatives and, 101, 103, 104, 105; Constitution, U.S. and, 102–4, 106–9, 111, 122–25, 129, 137; criminal law and, 139; death penalty and, 123, 139; democracy and, 111–16; executive branch, undermining of and, 111, 116–18; federalism and, 114, 144–45; Founding Fathers and, 7, 108; Fourteenth Amendment and, 139; illegal immigration and, 109; international law and, 111, 122–25; judicial activism and, 110, 111, 118, 125, 130; judicial passivism and, 125–27, 130; judicial restraint and, 102, 103, 106, 115, 128, 129; judicial review and, 125; life tenure and, 7, 104, 108; Miers, Harriet Ellan nomination to, 101–5; national sovereignty and, 111, 122–25; people, will of and, 7, 116; Pledge of Allegiance and, 109, 119, 121; pornography and, 189; power to the people and, 109, 129–31; prayer in schools and, 104, 107, 108, 119, 121–22; property rights and, 7, 127, 130–31, 144–45; religion and, 118–22; religious displays and, 7, 108, 120–21; term limits and, 114–16; War on Terror and, 7, 111, 116–18

Survivor, 180

The Swan, 181

Swift Boat Veterans for Truth, 241

Syria, 83

T

tabloids, 158–59

Tabor, James, 297

Taiwan, Communist China and, 84–85

Talent, Jim, 91–92

Taliban, 116

talk radio: conservatives and, 8; Democrats and, 8, 247–49; Fairness Doctrine and, 247–49; immigration reform and, 243–46; impact of, 243–46; liberals and, 161; media, liberal monopoly of and, 234–35, 241; media, liberal monopoly on and, 7–8; regulation of, 247–49; Supreme Court nominations and, 105

Tancredo, Tom, 43, 55, 250

Tanzania embassy bombing (1998), 80

Task Force on the Sexualization of Girls (APA), 177

taxation: AMT, 34–35; children and, 16; Democrats and, 34–35; estate, 35; family and, 34–35; local control and, 152–53; in Massachusetts, 145–46; pornography and, 35

Taylor, Amillia, 282

teachers: firing bad, 202; merit pay for, 200–201; performance evaluation and, 202; tenure system for, 200–201 teachers' unions, 200; public schools, collapse of and, 199–203; quality standards and, 198–99; school choice and, 224

television: family on, 14–15, 21–22, 28; fathers, maligning of on, 23; men, maligning of on, 22–23; popular culture and, 179–81, 187–88; profanity on, 7; reality, 180–81; sex on, 179–81

Ten Commandments, religious displays and, 7, 120–21, 156

Tenth Amendment, 135, 137, 140, 154–55

Teresa, Mother, 294, 314

terrorism: counter-, 90–91, 118; illegal immigration and, 58–59; Islamic jihadists and, 80–83; Left and, 94; national security and, 71–74; popular culture, battling and, 194; "root causes" of, 94; state sponsors of, 83, 91

Thomas, Clarence, 102, 115–16, 125, 129, 130, 227

Thomas Aquinas, St., 294

Thomas More College, 226

Thompson, Tommy, 146

Thorn, Nautica, 171

Time magazine, 15, 178, 249, 282

To Catch a Predator, 179

Tocqueville, Alexis de, 140

Today show, 71, 158

Tolkien, J. R. R., 153

Tribe, Laurence, 112

True Love Revolution, 192

Truman, Harry, 304

U

UN. *See* United Nations

Unfit for Command (O'Neill and Corsi), 241

UNICEF. *See* United Nations Children's Fund

United Nations (UN), 147, 150; American foreign policy and, 76, 78; Iranian nuclear program and, 83; local control and, 140

United Nations Children's Fund (UNICEF), 32

UN Resolution 1441, 77

UN Security Council, 77

UN World Conference Against Racism, 214

United States. *See* America

U.S.-China Commission, 85

U.S. Court of Appeals for the Ninth Circuit, 121

U.S. News & World Report, 210

U.S. Term Limits v. Thornton, 115

Universal Motown, 169

Universal Music Group, 168

universities: anti-Americanism and, 6; conservatives and, 214–16; curricula in, 210–11; decline of, 209–11; diversity and, 210, 211–14; faculty in, 211–14; fixing, 225–29; ideological diversity in, 6; liberals and, 211; political correctness and, 197; religious displays and, 303–4; speech, freedom of and, 213. *See also* education; public schools

V

Vaghi, Peter, 307–8

Vagina Monologues, 228

Van Orden v. Perry, 120

Venezuela, 84, 251

Verizon Wireless, 236

Vermont, gay marriage in, 109

The View, 253

Virginia, illegal immigration and, 63, 65
Virginia Tech, 312–13
virtue: citizenship and, 288; education and, 198; liberty and, 4, 288; patriotism and, 69; religious practice and, 288–89

W
Wake Forest University, 282
Wallace, William Ross, 17
Wall Street Journal, 45, 65
The Waltons, 13, 21
Ward, Tommy, 57
Warner, Christopher A., 276
Warner, Judith, 26
War on Terror: Britain and, 82; Bush, George W. and, 117; Supreme Court, U.S. and, 7, 111, 116–18; winning, 95–99
Washington, D.C., sniper shootings, 73
Washington, George, 136, 204, 289, 316
Washington Post, 49, 50, 56, 57, 65, 86, 276
Washington Times, 42, 58, 219
Watson, James, 270
weapons of mass destruction (WMD), 78, 85
Webb, James, 97
Weeds, 21
Weekly Standard, 103
welfare: government and parenting and, 32–33; local control and, 154; poverty and, 33; reforming, 33, 146
Wellesley College, 210

What's Liberal About the Liberal Arts? (Berube), 212
Whitehead, Barbara Dafoe, 24
Wilberforce, William, 185
Will and Grace, 22
Williams, Tennessee, 21
Williams, Treat, 22
Williams College, 212
Willis, Ellen, 30
Willis, Kent, 63
Winfrey, Oprah, 110
Winter, Ralph K., Jr., 102
Wirthlin, Joseph and Robin, 206–7
Wisconsin Works, 146
Wolf, Frank, 115
Wolf, Mark, 207
women: family and, 21; marriage and, 21; as mothers, 26, 29–30; objectification of, 164, 166–67; oppression of, 21; sexualization of young, 25–26, 166–69, 176–77
Wood, Howard, 307
Woolf, Rebecca, 24–25
World Trade Center bombing (1993), 80, 117
World War II, 76

Y
Yale University, 210
Young, Donald, 51
Young America's Foundation, 211
YouTube, 8, 242–43, 249, 250

Z
Zahn, Paula, 232
Zhu Chengu, 84–85